A Complete Guide to Brass

A Complete Guide to Brass

Instruments and Pedagogy

SCOTT WHITENER

Rutgers University

Foreword by CHARLES SCHLUETER
Principal Trumpet, Boston Symphony Orchestra

Illustrations by CATHY L. WHITENER

SCHIRMER BOOKS
An Imprint of Simon & Schuster Macmillan
NEW YORK

Prentice Hall International
LONDON · MEXICO CITY · NEW DELHI · SINGAPORE · SYDNEY · TORONTO

Schirmer Books
An Imprint of Simon & Schuster Macmillan
1633 Broadway, New York, NY 10019-6785

Library of Congress Catalog Card Number: 89-4132

Printed in the United States of America

printing number
  8   9   10

Library of Congress Cataloging-in-Publication Data

Whitener, Scott.
  A complete guide to brass instruments and pedagogy / Scott Whitener ; foreword by Charles Schlueter ; illustrations by Cathy L. Whitener.
    p. cm.
  Bibliography: p.
  Includes index.
  ISBN 0-02-872861-0. — ISBN 0-02-873050-X (pbk.)
  1. Brass instruments. 2. Brass instruments—Instruction and study. I. Whitener, Cathy L. II. Title.
ML933.W52 1989   89-4132
788'.01—dc19   CIP
                                    MN

To Cathy, Richard, Alexandra, and Diana

Contents

Figures

Foreword

Charles Schlueter
Principal Trumpet, Boston Symphony Orchestra

For many years there has been a recognized need for an authoritative guide to brass instruments in a single, comprehensive volume. Now, with the appearance of *A Complete Guide to Brass: Instruments and Pedagogy* by Scott Whitener, this need has been admirably met. Not only is the author's extensive knowledge of the various brass instruments apparent throughout, but the clarity and manner of presentation transcend that usually associated with books of this kind.

The detailed discussions of instruments and brass playing include many aspects presented for the first time as well as topics which have hitherto received inadequate attention. For example: the use of C, D, E, E♭, F, G, and piccolo B♭/A trumpets; rotary valve trumpets; how the double horn works; historical instruments in use today; the movement of the air column in brass playing; common problems in tone production; the organization of the brass section; how the conductor can achieve a good brass sound.

The individual chapters for each instrument include lists of recommended study material and solo literature for beginning, intermediate, and advanced levels, as well as books pertaining to the instrument and brass playing generally.

While the text is directed to college courses designed to train instrumental music teachers, it also serves as an invaluable and up-to-date reference source for composers, conductors, music historians, as well as brass players.

The notable appendices include a selective discography for each instrument and ensembles, along with an extensive and useful listing of instrument and mouthpiece manufacturers, sources for historical instruments and brass music, and periodicals.

Aside from being a valuable text, this highly commendable survey will prove to be an indispensible guide to the technical and practical aspects of brass instruments and their pedagogy and represents a significant contribution to the field.

Preface and Acknowledgments

For some time I have felt the need for a book which, in a single volume, would present up-to-date and detailed information on brass instruments together with a practical approach to learning to play. The present work is intended to serve as a text in college brass methods courses to prepare teachers of instrumental music. It can also serve as a useful reference for composers, conductors, brass players, and anyone having an interest in the world of brass.

Significant changes have occurred in today's brass playing. New instruments are in use, and there have been changes in existing ones. Orchestral trumpeters now make use of an entire range of trumpets; it is of interest to know how and in what circumstances they are employed. The same is true of the various types of horn, particularly the descant and triple horn. There are also several new configurations of bass trombone. It is important to understand their advantages, along with the valve systems and keys in which tubas are built.

Aside from the more recent developments, there is renewed interest in traditional instruments such as the Vienna Horn, rotary valve trumpet, "shepherd's crook" cornet, alto and contrabass trombones—all virtually unchanged since the 19th century. Historical instruments, too, now have an established place in the performance of music from the Renaissance through the Classical era. The cornett and sackbut, natural trumpet and horn are now heard regularly in performances of a quality that could only be imagined two and a half decades ago.

Important changes are taking place, as well, in the pedagogy of brass instruments. The most significant developments are an approach to tone production that focuses on the movement of the air as wind (an approach that will surely become the leading mode of instruction in the future) and the TRU-VU transparent mouthpiece. The latter allows brass players to see for the first time how the embouchure vibrates within the mouthpiece while the instrument is being played. This book is the first to present a method based on these two important developments.

It is a sad fact that books on orchestration tend to be outdated and incomplete in their coverage of the brass. While a volume many times the size of the present one would be necessary to do full justice to every aspect of brass playing, this work should provide the reader with a reliable and informative overview of the field.

The book is divided into two parts. Chapters 1 through 9 contain discussions of the instruments in use today and an outline of their development. Chapters 10 through 13 are concerned with pedagogy. The final chapter provides information specifically directed to conductors.

Many people have contributed to this book, and without their assistance it could not have been written. I should particularly like to express my appreciation to Paul Hlebowitsh, Dr. Richard Plano, John Bewley, Scott Mendoker, Kenneth Kemmerer, Dr. Robert Grechesky, Jonathan Korzun, Ralph Acquaro, Matthew Paterno, and Dr. William H. Trusheim.

I am especially indebted to my friend, Steven De See, who generously undertook the arduous task of collecting most of the photographs that appear in this book. We are grateful to those organizations and individuals who were kind enough to contribute photographs, particularly Mrs. Margaret Fletcher, Prof. Roland Berger, and Philip and Ursula Jones. A highlight of the book is undoubtedly the superb photographs of Dale Clevenger, Jay Friedman, and Arnold Jacobs of the Chicago Symphony Orchestra in which they illustrate various playing positions. I hope that their generosity in posing for these pictures will in some way be recompensed by the inspiration they provide to young brass players.

Steven De See and Dr. William H. Trusheim also read and commented on the completed manuscript.

One of the great trumpeters of our time, Charles Schlueter, principal trumpet of the Boston Symphony Orchestra, graciously consented to provide a foreword to the book, and I very much appreciate his taking the time to do so.

I should also like to thank the following: Brooke McEldowney, for the kind gift of one of his inimitably witty musical cartoons; Prof. Roland Berger, for his unique insights on the Vienna horn; Joseph Hetman, for his help with original photography; and Prof. Roger Tarman, Maribeth Anderson Payne, Michael Sander, Prof. William Fielder, Joan Hetman, Prof. Daniel Tanner, and Dr. Bruce Roland.

Most of all, I am grateful to my wife Cathy, a gifted horn player, who painstakingly drew all of the illustrations and contributed in incalculable other ways to the completion of this book.

Scott Whitener
Middlebush, Somerset, N.J.

PART ONE

INSTRUMENTS

CHAPTER 1
How Brass Instruments Work

Brass instruments are among the oldest of all instruments. In antiquity, instruments such as the Scandinavian lur and the Roman buccina admirably fulfilled their ceremonial and musical functions. As each epoch unfolded, instruments were modified to serve the musical requirements of the new era. The line of development from ancient to modern is a process of refinement of a basic idea: the sounding of a flared tube through the vibration of the lips. While the outward appearance of the instruments has changed, their internal operation is unaltered from a millennium ago.

In years past brass players often conceived of the instrument as something like an old-fashioned phonograph horn or megaphone which amplified a buzzing sound made by the lips. Now, due to the research of acousticians such as Arthur H. Benade,[1] such conceptions are known to be false. Actually, the lips do not make an audible sound, nor does a horn function like an amplifier to radiate sound into the surrounding environment. The bell flare of a brass instrument is designed to contain acoustical energy within the instrument in order to set up standing waves at specific frequencies.

The player's embouchure may be seen as a flow-control valve acting on the steady air flow coming from the lungs. Puffs of air are emitted into the mouthpiece, setting in motion a sound wave which eventually reaches the instrument's expanding bell. As the bell flare widens, the wave encounters a drop in impedance (resistance) which, perhaps surprisingly, causes it to reflect back toward the mouthpiece (Fig. 1.1). It is then reflected at the mouthpiece where it is modified by the motion of the lips, encouraging a specific frequency. The vibratory motion of the lips is itself modified by the reflecting wave so that its pattern of vibration corresponds to the instrument's timbre and the desired pitch. As the wave bounces back and forth while interacting with the instrument and the vibrating lip, the standing wave characteristic of brass instrument sound is gradually formed. In reality, the process takes only a few hundredths of a second.

Although some acoustical energy leaks through the "barrier" in the expanding bell flare, most is reflected in middle and low frequencies. As frequencies rise, the reflective threshold moves ever closer to the mouth of the bell and less energy is reflected. This is the reason why high notes are more difficult to play than pitches in the middle register.

In the production of a sustained tone, the fluctuations in pressure within the mouthpiece brought about by the standing wave help the flow-control valve to open and close (the vibration of the embouchure).[2] The player adjusts his embouchure and its aperture so that vibration at a specific frequency is favored. The changes in pressure within the mouthpiece act upon the adjusted embouchure to produce a steady tone. The pressure variations have been measured inside the mouthpiece and the peaks that occur at specific frequencies (indicating greater input impedance) recorded on a graph.[3] The resonance peaks—points at which the

1. See Arthur H. Benade, *Fundamentals of Musical Acoustics* (New York: Oxford University Press, 1976), pp. 391–429. Also Benade's article, "the Physics of Brasses," *Scientific American*, July 1973, pp.. 24–35. I am grateful to Dr. Richard J. Plano, Professor of Physics at Rutgers University, for enlightening discussions on this subject.

2. In the author's view, the flow-control valve never completely closes.

3. See Benade, *Fundamentals*.

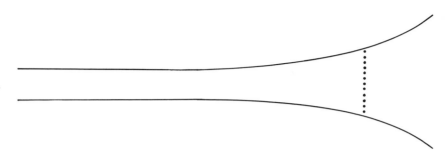

Figure 1.1. Approximate point of wave reflection in a horn bell.

standing wave's amplitude is greatest—conform to the harmonic series (notes that can be played without using the valves) in a well-designed brass instrument. The length and shape of the instrument govern the pitches produced at the resonance peaks, but in each brass instrument the peaks always appear in the same pattern.

THE HARMONIC SERIES

Notes of the harmonic series are familiar to all brass players since a certain amount of practice time is usually devoted to studies based on them. Prior to the invention of valves, these were the only notes available to the natural trumpet and horn, although a technique of handstopping (used after 1750) allowed hornists to fill in the gaps between partials. What is not often recognized is the importance of the bell flare in deriving a usable harmonic series. If one attempts to play the overtone series on an appropriate length of cylindrical pipe, such as a garden hose, the following series will result:[4]

If a well-designed flared bell is attached, the partials will be raised to form the familiar pattern below:[5]

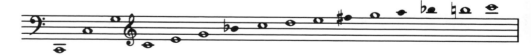

While different fundamental pitches occur depending on the length of the instrument, the structure of the harmonic series is always the same. For example, the series for the horn in F:

8va⏌

4. See Richard Merewether, *The Horn, The Horn* . . . (London: Paxman Musical Instruments, 1978), p. 36.

5. Pitches are approximate for the two series shown. Certain partials do not agree with the equal-tempered scale.

During the 17th and 18th centuries, trumpets were made of sufficient length to enable the player to utilize the area of the harmonic series that more or less resembles a diatonic scale. The shorter length of modern trumpets places the fundamental proportionally an octave higher, since the spaces between partials can be filled by notes played with the valves. The fundamental is positioned similarly in the other brass instruments with the exception of the horn, which retains the octave-lower fundamental of the natural horn.

Another important aspect of the harmonic series is that overtones of the series also sound in greater or lesser degree when a note is played. This is what defines the characteristic tone quality of an instrument. Also, notes with less sharply defined resonance peaks (making these notes more difficult to produce) are made more stable by the participation of other harmonically related peaks when the instrument is played at medium and loud dynamic levels.

VALVES

The valve is an ingenious device which opens an additional section of tubing for the air column to pass through, thus lengthening the instrument and making available notes of the harmonic series of a different fundamental. The segments of tubing that can be added by the valves lower the fundamental by a tone (1st valve), a semitone (2nd valve) and a tone-and-a-half (3[d] valve).[6] The valves can also be used in combination by depressing valves simultaneously. The air column is then directed in turn through the tubing of each valve that has been opened, making accessible up to three additional harmonic series (2–3, 1–3, 1–2–3).

Trumpet (fundamentals not shown)

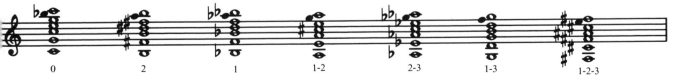

By utilizing the various partials of the seven harmonic series, the instrument is made fully chromatic.

6. In a descending valve system. In France, and parts of Belgium, a system is in use on the horn in which the third valve raises the pitch by one tone. The so-called *cor ascendant* is discussed in Chapter 4.

Trumpet

0	1-2-3	1-3	2-3	1-2	1	2	0	2-3	1-2	1	2	0	

Since the 7th, 11th, 13th, 14th, and 15th partials of the harmonic series are n[...] in tune within the equal temperament system in use today, they are substituted b[...] valve notes. In the interest of finger dexterity, the 1–2 combination, which als[...] lowers the fundamental a tone-and-a-half, is normally used in place of the thi[...] valve alone. A basic problem of the valve system is inadequate tube length whe[...] the valves are used in combination, causing sharpness. Various approaches ar[...] used to correct this deficiency.[7]

There are three types of valve in use today. All function similarly, but diff[...] in their method of opening and closing the ports between the main tube and th[...] tubing that can be added by the valve. In each, the vibrating air column runs dow[...] the valve section from one end or the other (depending on the construction of th[...] instrument) and, with the valves closed, continues directly into the bell. If a valv[...] is depressed, the air column is sent through the valve tubing before it proceed[...] toward the bell. The operation of the various valve types can be seen in Figure[...] 1.2, 1.3, and 1.4.

Piston valves offer a light, quick action but have slightly less direct and accurat[...] windways than the other two types. A shorter finger stroke may be used on rotar[...] valves, but their action is not quite as immediate as piston valves. An advantage [...] the rotary type is that the diameter of the windway is maintained with somewh[...] greater consistency, providing less resistance. Vienna valves (now found only o[...] Vienna horns) cause the least disturbance to the air column enabling the Vienn[...] horn to play and sound more like the natural instrument. With the valves closed, th[...] air column goes straight through the valve section, avoiding the sharper angles an[...] misshapen windways inherent in rotary and piston designs. Although their actio[...]

7. This problem is discussed in depth under *"Intonation"* in Chapter 6; related discussions appear under the sam[...] heading in Chapters 3 and 7.

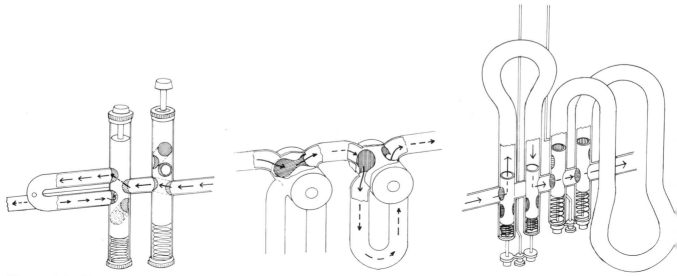

Figure 1.2. Piston valve.   Figure 1.3. Rotary valve.   Figure 1.4. Vienna valve.

not quite as fast as other valve types, Vienna valves contribute greater fluency and smoothness to slurred passages.[8]

In using any type of valve, it is important to recognize that there are only two positions, open and closed. Therefore, valves should always be depressed as quickly as possible to avoid an audible discontinuity between notes. In slow passages, students often have a tendency to move their valves sluggishly. This produces an unattractive sound, particularly on slurs. Sometimes placing the finger tips slightly above the valve caps or levers encourages a quicker motion.

DESIGN CONSIDERATIONS

Every brass instrument consists of four basic parts: the mouthpiece with its tapered backbore, a conical leadpipe, a section of cylindrical tubing containing the valves, and the gradually expanding flare of the bell. The diameter of the bore, the shape of the tapered sections, the thickness and type of material, and overall mass are variables that cause instruments of the same type to play and sound differently.

Bore size is determined by the diameter of the tubing of the instrument's cylindrical section, although the bell throat and leadpipe usually conform to the main bore. Instruments of smaller bore generally respond with less effort and have a lighter tone. While their timbre is exceptionally pure, they can be overblown at high dynamic levels. Large-bore instruments typically have a darker tone and retain a more even timbre from soft to loud.

How the bell is shaped is of primary importance in determining the quality of an instrument and the character of its timbre. The size of the bell, how sharply it is flared, and especially the diameter and taper of the bell throat strongly influence tone, intonation, and response. The rate of expansion of the bell section from the valves onward also has a significant effect on timbre. (Bell tapers are discussed in relation to the horn in Chapter 4). How the bell is made is a factor governing the overall quality of the instrument. The finest bells are formed from sheet brass which is beaten on a mandrel and spun on a lathe by hand. This requires the skill of an expert craftsman and is reflected in the instrument's price.

Brass instruments are made from yellow brass, gold (red) brass, and nickel silver. Each of these materials contributes certain qualities to the timbre, and players have definite opinions as to their respective merits. (The effect of different alloys is considered in Chapters 4 and 5.) The finish that is applied to the metal is another issue. Some feel that any type of finish degrades an instrument's tone and response, while others have a definite preference for either lacquer or silver plating. An instrument's mass also affects its playing and tonal qualities. A heavier instrument will have a darker timbre and require somewhat more exertion than one of lesser weight. Lighter instruments often feel more responsive and flexible to the player, but exhibit tonal differences from one of greater mass.

8. The Vienna valve is discussed further in Chapter 4.

CHAPTER 2

Anatomy of the Mouthpiece

As was discussed in Chapter 1, the mouthpiece forms a chamber in which the air coming from the lungs is converted to acoustical energy to make the instrument sound. This is why the mouthpiece is so crucial in influencing tone quality, response, and intonation. Mouthpieces must be chosen carefully; a good one will advance one's playing, while a poor one will hinder it.

There are five basic parts to a mouthpiece (Fig. 2.1). The main points to consider are:

1. Rim: width, contour, and edge (bite)
2. Cup: diameter, depth, and shape
3. Throat: diameter and shape of opening
4. Backbore: rate of taper
5. Shank: accuracy of fit into receiver

All of these factors affect how a mouthpiece will perform and the timbre it will produce. In order to clarify their functions, we will consider each item separately.

RIM

Cup Diameter

Although identified as the diameter of the mouthpiece cup, this measure is the distance between the inner edges of the rim and therefore should be considered with the other aspects of rim design. This distance defines the area in which the lips will vibrate and thus, is the primary factor governing the size of sound that will be produced, although the throat, backbore, and particularly the cup depth are also important. A cup of larger diameter allows a wider aperture to be used, which admits a greater flow of air into the instrument. A narrower diameter has the opposite effect.

In general, somewhat greater embouchure strength is necessary for large cup diameters. Smaller mouthpieces usually have a lighter tone and require a bit less effort. At one time, narrow cups were thought to facilitate the high range, but this idea is largely discredited today. In fact, overly narrow cups can restrict the free vibration of the embouchure, impeding airflow. Most professional players use a large-diameter cup for all of their playing, including the higher trumpets and descant horn, although cups of shallower depth are sometimes substituted on these instruments. (An exception might be the piccolo trumpet.)

It should be emphasized, however, that the choice of a mouthpiece is highly individual. Players with thicker lip tissue often require a large cup diameter, while players with thin lips may get equally fine results from a smaller mouthpiece.

Rim Width

While the thickness of the mouthpiece rim is of concern to brass players generally, it is of vital importance to the horn player. Wide rims provide more cushion to the lips but tend to deaden the resonance of the sound and inhibit flexibility. The latter is particularly noticeable in slurred intervals. A narrow rim is clearly better suited

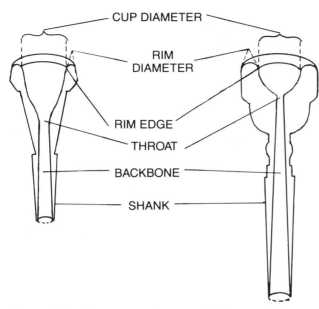

Figure 2.1. The parts of a mouthpiece.

the horn player who must make wide slurs with glissando-like smoothness. On the other brass instruments, a medium-wide rim offers the best compromise between good endurance, tone, and flexibility

Rim Contour

The shape of the uppermost part of the rim is known as the rim contour. It can be round, flat, or with the high point shifted toward the inside or outside. These variations affect individual players differently. The only generalization that can be made is that flat rims tend to have some of the negative characteristics of the wide rim—that is, to the movement of the lips, impairing flexibility. Balanced-contour rims (neither round nor flat) are most widely used today.

Rim Edge

Actually part of the rim contour, the presence of an inner edge can be clearly detected by the lip or reduced to imperceptibility. Some performers believe that a discernible edge improves response and attack, while others find this type of rim to be uncomfortable. There may be a relationship between rim width and the need for definition in its edge. Medium rims probably require a subtle edge to feel responsive. Narrower rims, with their more direct response, cause discomfort if the edge becomes noticeable. The edge factor has been taken into account in any well-designed mouthpiece, and the player only needs to be aware of it in trying different models. Rims can be altered to suit individual preferences and, if desired, the rim of one model can be substituted on another cup.

CUP

Cup Depth and Shape

Of all the elements of mouthpiece design, the shape and depth of the cup have the greatest influence over the quality of tone. Deeper cups lend fullness to the sound and a somewhat darker character. Shallow cups produce a timbre which is both lighter in weight and brighter in color. The instrument designer, Vince Bach, attributed these differences to the way in which overtones are present in the sound. With deep cups, the fundamental tends to predominate with fewer of the highest harmonics present. A tone more endowed with the upper overtones results when a shallow cup is used. The goal is to find the right balance of these qualities to achieve a full and characteristic timbre consistent with good intonation and response.

The two hypothetical cup shapes are the bowl and the cone; most brass mouthpieces are carefully derived combinations of the two. The horn mouthpiece is the most conical. In earlier periods, horn mouthpieces were totally conical, but today most incorporate a very slight cup while preserving the basic funnel shape. A few designs have attempted to create a more distinct cup, with negative results in tone quality. Cornet and euphonium mouthpieces are more conical than corresponding trumpet and trombone mouthpieces to give these instruments their soft, mellow tone. Although trumpet and trombone cups are the most bowl-like, the bottom of the cup has a slightly conical shape to gain a characteristically clear ringing sound. For much of their previous history, conical mouthpieces, similar to those used on the horn, were favored by trombonists. These produced a pure centered tone quality which was particularly effective on smaller bore trombones. This type of mouthpiece enhanced the expressive and melodic qualities of the instrument, and the idea is worth reviving today.

The depth of the cup also affects to some extent the high and low ranges. Deep cups are normally used, for example, by fourth horn players and bass trombonists to facilitate the low register. Conversely, trumpeters often substitute a shallow cup when performing on the piccolo trumpet. Jazz and studio players generally prefer shallow cup depths to cope with the formidable range demands of their field and to produce an appropriately brilliant timbre. At times, this has had a negative effect on students who adopt shallow mouthpieces hoping to gain range quickly. Shallow cups are not conducive to good development in the formative stages, and wreak havoc in school bands and orchestras. A shallow mouthpiece should be viewed as a specialized tool for a specific performance situation.

THROAT

The main consideration is the throat's diameter, although how the opening is shaped and its overall length are contributing factors. Large throats darken the tone and give it body. Smaller diameters have the opposite effect. The diameter can be measured by inserting numbered drill bits into the throat until the correct size is found. Drill bits are numbered so that the higher the number, the smaller the diameter. For example, the standard throat bore of Bach trumpet mouthpieces is 27 (3.67mm; .144″). Symphony players typically use larger throats in the 25 to 23 range. There is less consistency among horn mouthpieces, with throats varying from 1 to 17 (5.79–4.39mm; .227–.172″). Advanced trombone and euphonium throats usually run from 6.4 millimeters (.252″) to 7.4 millimeters (.291″), and tuba throats from 7.4 to 8.3 millimeters (.327″). Most professional brass players determine their preference in throat diameter through experimentation and have their mouthpiece drilled to that size.

How the opening of the throat is shaped also influences the sound and response. In the 18th century, trumpet mouthpieces were bowl-shaped with sharp-edged throats drilled directly into the bottom of the cup. In modern mouthpieces, the cup's lower portion is fairly conical and any edge is smoothed out to blend with this shape. In some designs, more of a shoulder is left at the throat opening, while in others, the opening itself takes on a conical shape. The latter lessens resistance and adds depth to the sound. The throat bore is cylindrical and its length must be refully worked out in relation to the backbore and cup depth to ensure good tonation.

BACKBORE

cause it is rather hidden from view, the backbore is the least understood aspect the mouthpiece. All judgments must be made by trial and error. Intonation, ne, and endurance are influenced by the backbore.

It might be assumed that backbores are drilled to a constant rate of taper but is is rarely the case. Large backbores expand at a steeper rate during the first third their length and thereafter very gradually until the final diameter is reached. e final diameter should match the leadpipe taper. These proportions are usually versed with smaller backbores. Standard backbores represent a compromise tween these extremes. The larger bores such as "symphony" or "Schmidt" models fer a fuller tone, but require more air and greater embouchure strength than andard models.

SHANK

e purpose of the mouthpiece shank and instrument receiver is to bring the ckbore into contact with the leadpipe without interruption so that a continuous per is formed. If it were not so inconvenient, mouthpieces and leadpipes would obably be made in one piece to ensure this acoustically important taper. Any exactness at this point will impair the instrument's performance, so it is essential at the shank fit the receiver accurately.

American shanks are normally made with a Morse 0 or number 1 taper. This es not automatically assure that the correct interface will be formed with the adpipe. Sometimes a gap will occur between the end of the mouthpiece and the adpipe. There is a difference of opinion among designers of trumpet mouthpieces to the negative or positive effect of such a gap. Horn mouthpieces sometimes too far, or not far enough, into the leadpipe, affecting the instrument's pitch nter on certain notes.

No consistent standard similar to the Morse taper is used among European akers. Since the instruments are usually handmade, each firm has their own ique receiver and mouthpiece shank. On German horns, for example, American-ade mouthpieces usually go too far into the mouthpipe. Similar complications ise with rotary valve trumpets and tubas. A mouthpiece maker can correct any oblems of this sort by copying the mouthpiece with a larger or smaller shank, by altering the cup, rim, and throat of a European mouthpiece to the player's quirements while leaving the original shank unchanged.

GENERAL MOUTHPIECE SUGGESTIONS

- Choose a mouthpiece of a recognized manufacturer.
- Remember that no single manufacturer produces the best mouthpieces for all brass instruments.
- Keep in mind that, while the upper range may suffer temporarily after a change to a larger mouthpiece, it should soon return.
- Avoid shallow mouthpieces.
- Test every mouthpiece individually—because of the way mouthpieces are made, different examples of the same mouthpiece may not be identical.
- Study the catalog descriptions and dimensions, if given. Since mouthpiece

makers do not use a consistent system of numbering, this is the only way determine the characteristics of a particular model.

- While searching for the "ideal" mouthpiece is unproductive, it is importa to try different models at various points in your development to see if the offer any improvements.
- Remember that ultimately it is the player who determines the results, not tl mouthpiece. Great brass players often use widely differing equipment, y achieve an equally high standard of performance.

MOUTHPIECE RECOMMENDATIONS

Trumpet and Cornet

Some clarification of how models are identified by various manufacturers mig be helpful.[1] Bach, Denis Wick, and Giardinelli indicate progressively larger c diameters as the numbers become smaller. Schilke uses an opposite system. Tl system used by other firms should be determined from their catalog. Cup dept on Bach mouthpieces are frequently misunderstood: A = deep; number witho letter = medium-deep; B = medium; C = medium; D and E = shallow.

The medium-deep cups identified by number only were intended by Vince Bach as a standard model for the Bb and C trumpets. In recent years, they hav tended to be overlooked in favor of the C cup. While both cups yield good resul unlettered models offer a fuller, more resonant tone.

Cornet mouthpieces must be made with the smaller cornet shank; this should l specified when ordering. The only cornet mouthpieces currently available havir an authentic cup depth and shape are the Denis Wick models.

TRUMPET

Beginner	Intermediate	Advanced
Bach 7 or 7C	Bach 6, 5, or 5C	Bach 2, 1, X1, or 1C
Schilke 9 or 11	Schilke 14 or 17	Schilke 18, 20, or 20D2d
Denis Wick 4	Denis Wick 3	Denis Wick 2 or 1
		Giardinelli HG1 or MB1

CORNET

Beginner	Intermediate	Advanced
Denis Wick 7 or 5B	Denis Wick 5B	Denis Wick 5 or 4
Bach 7	Bach 5A	Bach 5A
	Schilke 11E	Schilke 11E

Horn

There is greater variation among horn mouthpieces used today than any oth brass instrument. Some of the popular mouthpieces frequently recommended fc beginning students are simply too small to promote stable response and centerin of notes. It is important to make certain that the shank fits the receiver to th correct depth. It is also wise to check the throat diameter. Some mouthpieces ca be improved by enlarging the throat.

---

1. For additional information, see Gerald Endsley, *Comparative Mouthpiece Guide for Trumpet* (Denver, Col Tromba, 1980).

HORN

Beginner	Intermediate	Advanced
Giardinelli C12 or S15	Giardinelli S15 or C12	Giardinelli C12, C8, C4, or S15
Schilke 27 or 30	Schilke 27 or 30	Schilke 27 or 30
Holton MDC	Holton MDC	Denis Wick 7N, 5N, or 4N
Conn 1	Denis Wick 7N	Holton MDC, DC
Denis Wick 7N		

Trombone

Before a player purchases a trombone mouthpiece, it is necessary to know whether the instrument's receiver has been designed to accept a large or small shank. Large-bore tenor trombones such as the Conn 88H and Bach 42B require large shanks, while medium- and small-bore tenors normally accept the smaller size. Bass trombones invariably take the large shank. Most mouthpieces for tenor trombone (with the exception of the largest models) are available with either shank, so the correct size must be specified in ordering.

TENOR TROMBONE

Beginner	Intermediate	Advanced
Denis Wick 12CS or 9BS	Denis Wick 6BS or 6BL	Denis Wick 5BS, 5BL, 4BS, 4BL, or 4AL
Bach 12C, 12, or 11	Bach 9, 7C, 7, or 6-1/2AL	Bach 6-1/2AL, 5, or 4
Schilke 46	Schilke 47 or 50	Schilke 51B or 51
	Giardinelli 4D	Giardinelli 3D or Sym.T

BASS TROMBONE

Beginner	Intermediate	Advanced
—	Denis Wick 5AL, 4AL or 3AL	Denis Wick 2AL
—	Schilke 57	Schilke 58, 59, or 60
—	Bach 5G or 3G	Bach 2G, or 1G

Baritone and Euphonium

Again, the question of shank sizes arises. American instrument manufacturers and Yamaha use a standard size equivalent to the small trombone shank. In the Denis Wick catalog, these are identified by the letter Y (the last letter of the mouthpiece's number indicates shank size). Boosey and Hawkes/Besson euphoniums made since 1974 accept the normal large trombone shank (L), but earlier models required a special shank size which the Wick catalog designates as the letter M. When ordering Bach and Schilke mouthpieces, a player should specify the shank size or the instrument with which it is to be used.

Trombone and euphonium mouthpieces are not interchangeable because of the need for a deeper, more conical cup to achieve an authentic euphonium tone.

True baritones are used almost exclusively in brass bands. Since their bore is narrower, somewhat smaller mouthpieces such as the Denis Wick 6BS or 6BY are normally used.

EUPHONIUM[2]

Beginner	Intermediate	Advanced
Denis Wick 6BY, 6BM, 6BL	Denis Wick 6BY, 6BM, 6BL	Denis Wick 4AY, 4AM, 4AL or 4-1/2A, Y, or M
Schilke 46D	Schilke 46D	Schilke 51D
Bach 7	Bach 6-1/2A, 6-1/2AL	Bach 5G, 3G

Tuba

Considering the international range of tubas in use today, the safest procedure i ordering a mouthpiece is to indicate the manufacturer of the instrument it must fi since there is considerable variation in receivers. American tubas such as Conr King, and so forth, and some imported instruments (Mirafone, Yamaha) take standard shank.

TUBA

Beginner	Intermediate	Advanced
Schilke 62	Schilke 66	Schilke 66 or 67
Bach 25	Bach 22	Bach 18, 12, or 7
Denis Wick 5	Denis Wick 4 or 3	Denis Wick 2
Mirafone H2	Mirafone 22	Mirafone C4
Giardinelli 25	Giardinelli 24W	Giardinelli WD24

2. See David R. Werden, "Euphonium Mouthpieces—A Teacher's Guide," *The Instrumentalist*, May 1981, pp 23–26.

CHAPTER 3

Trumpet and Cornet

Trumpeters have an unprecedented array of instruments that enable them to meet today's exacting performance demands (see Fig. 3.1). In fact, trumpets are now found pitched in the keys of every scale note of a full octave above the traditional Bb instrument. These fall into two basic categories: Bb and C trumpets for general use, and higher trumpets pitched in D, Eb, E, F, G, piccolo Bb/A, and C for orchestral and solo literature demanding a high tessitura.

It is fair to ask why so many trumpets are necessary. The answer can best be illustrated through an example. While a strong player might possibly be able to sustain the high range called for in Bach's *B Minor Mass* on a Bb trumpet, that part of the harmonic series where the partials fall fairly close together would be used. By changing to a piccolo trumpet in A, the same notes may be played lower on the harmonic series where the partials are more widely separated. This facilitates the "picking out" of entrance notes and improves accuracy. Also, the undue effort required to maintain the high tessitura on the larger instrument would prove severely fatiguing. A smaller, lighter trumpet brings such parts more under the player's control.

Aside from the question of accuracy, the larger tone of the Bb, while well suited to the works of later composers, would be unsuitable for the light balances required in Bach's orchestration. The basic idea is to provide the trumpeter with a set of specialized instruments to enable him to adapt more readily to the diverse repertoire performed by today's orchestras.

Trumpets in higher keys are not a recent development. Teste, solo trumpeter of the Paris Opera, performed Bach's *Magnificat* on a G trumpet as early as 1885, and such instruments have been available since that time. During the last quarter-century, however, high trumpets have undergone extensive research in the quest for improved instruments to cope with the mounting demands placed on modern orchestral trumpeters.

Several factors have combined to create these pressures. The trend toward longer orchestral seasons, an oversupply of well-trained players, and the expectation by conductors and audiences of the note-perfect accuracy in live performances that they are accustomed to on recordings have all had their effect. Most important, however, is that principal trumpeters are now regularly expected to perform the demanding Baroque literature with the flawless skill that was previously reserved for exceptional players and Baroque specialists.

Another important influence is the emergence of the trumpet as a major solo instrument. Just as Jean-Pierre Rampal popularized the flute, and Dennis Brain the horn, Maurice André has brought the trumpet into a new era of solo recordings and international concert appearances. Since the greater part of the solo literature comes from the Baroque and Classical periods, the need for more responsive and in-tune high trumpets has grown significantly.

THE Bb AND C TRUMPET

By the end of the 19th century the modern Bb trumpet had replaced the longer F trumpet as the standard orchestral instrument. While the passing of the old F

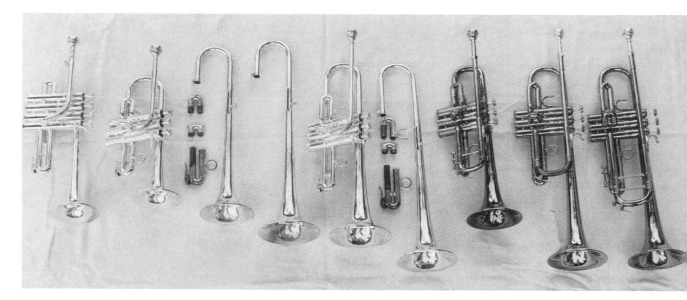

Figure 3.1. The trumpets in use (l–r): Piccolo B♭/A; G; F bell and slides; E bell E♭; D bell and slides (Schilke); E♭; C; and B♭ (Bach).   *(Photo: Joseph Hetman*

trumpet timbre was lamented by many,[1] trumpeters were confronted with parts of increasing difficulty from composers such as Strauss and Mahler, and the new instrument proved more tractable in meeting these demands. The popularity of the B♭ cornet also contributed to the change, since many orchestral players also played the cornet and were accustomed to the technical advantages of an instrument in B♭. Trumpets in C also made their appearance about this time and became particularly well established in France and Austria.

The present widespread acceptance of the C trumpet in orchestras can be traced to the appointment in 1920 of Georges Mager as principal trumpet of the Boston Symphony. A first prize winner at the Paris Conservatory and one of this century's greatest players, Mager used the C trumpet as his primary instrument during his 30-year tenure in Boston. He led a section of C trumpets (unknown in orchestras of the time) and established the pattern that has become standard in American orchestras today.

Among the first major figures beyond Boston to adopt the C trumpet was William Vacchiano, solo trumpet of the New York Philharmonic, 1934–1973. The worldwide influence of American brass playing, particularly that of Adolph Herseth, principal trumpet of the Chicago Symphony,[2] is responsible for the present trend toward the C trumpet. (The use of C trumpets in France and Austria has continued independent of this influence.)

The trend is not universal, however. British trumpeters following in the great tradition of Ernest Hall, George Eskdale, and Harold Jackson have maintained their allegiance to the B♭, preferring its rounder tone and blending qualities. The B♭ has to some extent retained its position in German and Eastern European orchestras as well.

In bands, the B♭ remains the primary instrument due to its fuller timbre and greater ability to blend within an ensemble of wind instruments. The literature

1. See, for example, the discussion of the horn and trumpet by Ralph Vaughan Williams in *The Making of Music* (Ithaca, N.Y.: Cornell University Press, 1955), p. 29.
2. Adolph Herseth is a former student of Georges Mager.

r band is almost entirely written for the Bb instrument and would have to be
ansposed if C trumpets were used.

Another area in which the C trumpet has failed to gain a foothold is in the
zz and studio fields. The C trumpet's timbre and playing characteristics do not
em to be particularly adaptable to the musical requirements of jazz performers.

Given the trend toward C trumpets in orchestral playing, it is important to
mphasize that trumpeters are in agreement that students should begin and play
rough their formative years on the Bb instrument. In this way a good tonal
ncept and tone production will be firmly established.

It would be well to consider what specific advantages the C trumpet has to
ffer the orchestral player. The primary factor underlying the trend to C trumpets
related to the nature of orchestral playing with its long periods of rest. The
sponse of the C seems to be better suited to making "cold" entrances than
e Bb, and it provides a greater feeling of security and control. This feeling is
ugmented by its being in the same key as the string section. The C also seems
 be more compatible with the range in which the first trumpet plays and the
xtreme dynamic contrasts required. The timbre of the C carries well, and this
llows the player to project the sound with slightly less effort than that required
y the Bb.

C trumpets are now available with a number of leadpipe and bell combinations
nd these have contributed to an improved instrument. American orchestral players
enerally prefer a large-bore C, and a medium-large Bb.

The parallel use of Bb and C trumpets is likely to continue indefinitely.
y having two primary instruments available, the player is afforded maximum
exibility in adapting to the requirements of the part to be performed. There has
een superb orchestral playing on the Bb trumpet as well as the C. How to utilize
ese instruments to best advantage ultimately remains a matter of individual
hoice.

THE D TRUMPET

he high trumpet in D was developed in the late 19th century in response to
e enthusiasm of the time for the choral works of Bach and Handel. It was
ften referred to as a "Bach trumpet," but this name is now discouraged to
void confusion with the natural trumpet, which has enjoyed a revival in recent
ears. (The fundamental of the natural trumpet in D is an octave below the valve
umpet.) The D trumpet offered an excellent solution to the problem of performing
e difficult parts in Bach's *B Minor Mass,* Handel's *Messiah,* and other Baroque
orks. Modern composers, such as Ravel and Stravinsky, have also utilized the
strument for colorful high-range effects in some of their compositions.

At present there are three types of D trumpet available: a medium-bore and
ell model suitable as a Baroque instrument; a large-bore which can be used in
lace of the Bb or C in regular orchestral passages; and the D–Eb combination
ctually an Eb trumpet provided with a set of longer D slides).

Students are sometimes under the impression that the higher trumpets provide
instant range," as in the flute-piccolo relationship. Actually, trumpeters usually
nly add a note or two above what can be played on their regular instrument.
Vhat can be gained is better control and consistency in performing high-register
assages.

In recent years, the D trumpet has largely been replaced by the piccolo Bb/A
rumpet. The smaller instrument has brought the Baroque literature within the
apabilities of a greater number of performers. While it offers additional security,
he inherent small bore and bell of the piccolo results in a timbre which is thin
n comparison to the D trumpet, and is far removed from the tone of the natural

trumpet of Bach's time. The D trumpet is a more effective substitute for the natural trumpet, combining the advantages of a valve instrument and a tone quality that is closer to the Baroque ideal.[3]

THE E♭ TRUMPET

E♭ trumpets are used today primarily in the performance of the Haydn and Hummel[4] concertos, and occasionally for orchestral passages. This raises an additional aspect of the use of high trumpets which is unrelated to playing register: some passages lie better on one instrument than another. For example, the above concertos can be played fluently on the B♭; however, they are more oriented to the E♭ which places the player in the key of C. Many trumpeters feel that this facilitates fingering (especially on trills) and accuracy. Others find that the use of an E♭ trumpet creates a new set of problems, particularly intonation and tone quality, and prefer to remain with the B♭. There have been equally fine performances using either instrument.

The principle of substituting one trumpet for another applies to the entire range of trumpets and affords the performer a choice in matching the instrument to the part:

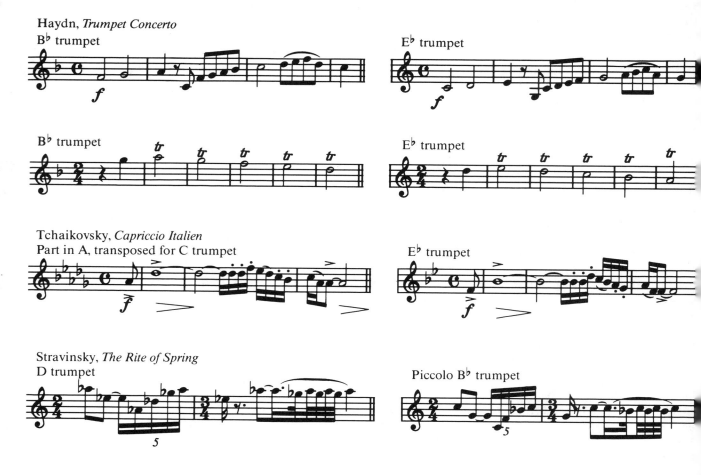

Haydn, *Trumpet Concerto*
B♭ trumpet

E♭ trumpet

B♭ trumpet

E♭ trumpet

Tchaikovsky, *Capriccio Italien*
Part in A, transposed for C trumpet

E♭ trumpet

Stravinsky, *The Rite of Spring*
D trumpet

Piccolo B♭ trumpet

3. The finest Baroque performance the author has heard was of Bach's *Christmas Oratorio* by Fritz Wesenigk, solo trumpet of the Berlin Philharmonic on a Monke rotary valve trumpet in D. He also recalls some superb D trumpet playing from his student days by Charles Schlueter, now principal trumpet of the Boston Symphony.

4. The Hummel concerto was composed for a keyed trumpet pitched in E. It is most often performed in editions transposed to E♭ so that it may be played comfortably on the B♭ or E♭ trumpet.

TRUMPETS IN E, F, AND G

The E trumpet was developed specially for players who wish to perform the Hummel trumpet concerto in its original key of E major. At present, few instruments are available. A custom model is made by Blackburn, and another is part of the Schilke well-tuned G–F–E combination, which consists of a G trumpet with interchangeable bells and valve slides for G, F, and E. Bell tuning is a recent development which allows different bells to be used on the same instrument. Many players feel this option offers improved playing qualities.

F trumpets were originally constructed for the difficult trumpet part in Bach's *Second Brandenburg Concerto*. They have now largely been superseded by the piccolo B♭.

The G trumpet is preferred as a baroque instrument by players who want the tone and feel of an instrument larger than the piccolo. The G combines a timbre more like the D trumpet with some of the playing advantages of the piccolo.

THE PICCOLO TRUMPET

Of all the high trumpets, the piccolo B♭/A is the most widely used today. This is due to the extensive development of these instruments over the past two decades. Trumpeters first used the piccolo B♭ more or less exclusively for the *Second Brandenburg Concerto* and for other Baroque parts that did not require the written low C of the D trumpet. Since this note is beyond the compass of the three-valve piccolo and figures in a number of scores, the piccolo's use was fairly limited. D or G trumpets were normally used for these parts. With the addition of a fourth valve, which extended the range of the piccolo downward a perfect fourth, works such as Bach's *Christmas Oratorio* and Handel's *Messiah* began to be performed on the piccolo. It was soon found that if the piccolo B♭ were lengthened to A (by extending the mouthpipe), parts written for the D trumpet could be played in the key signature of F, a more fluent and responsive key than the B♭ piccolo's E major:

Bach, *B Minor Mass*
Trumpet in D

Piccolo B♭ trumpet

Piccolo A trumpet

Orchestral players soon began to use the piccolo for non-Baroque passage such as Ravel's *Bolero* and Stravinsky's *Petrouchka* and *Rite of Spring*. At the sam time, the piccolo was brought into prominence by artists like Adolph Scherbau and Maurice André. Most recently, the piccolo is enjoying widespread popularit in the film and recording fields.

The fourth valve adds five notes to the player's range below the limit of th three-valve piccolo. A by-product is a number of alternate fingerings to improv intonation. The sharp 1–2–3 and 1–3 combinations can be improved by usin 2–4 and 4, respectively, a procedure normally used on four-valve euphoniums an tubas. There are other options throughout the piccolo's range.[5]

As stated earlier, the piccolo trumpet does not automatically bestow high rang What it does do is bring these notes down into the trumpet's most stable an accurate register by raising the fundamental. While comparable skill is require in performing in the upper register from one instrument to another, the piccol trumpet offers the player the acoustical advantage of producing these notes in th instrument's middle range, providing greater control and security.

The choice of a mouthpiece for the piccolo trumpet is highly individual. Som players use their standard mouthpiece for all the high trumpets, while othe change to a smaller cup depth and rim diameter. Screw-rim mouthpieces are ofte used, which allow the player to retain the same rim while altering cup, throat, o backbore.[6]

A variety of piccolo designs are available; the best way of selecting one trying a number of instruments. Certain instruments will work better for individua players than others. Schilke has recently introduced a new four-valve piccolo i C. Several advantages are claimed for this instrument, but it is too early to asses how widely it will be adopted.

ROTARY VALVE TRUMPETS

There is increased use of rotary valve trumpets in American orchestras (see Fig 3.2). This has come about in response to the desire for a more authentic an homogeneous sound in the 19th-century Germanic repertoire. While the rotar valve trumpet is less flexible in technical passages, it possesses a darker, mor resonant timbre which is ideal in the works of Beethoven, Brahms, Bruckner Strauss, and others. Also, these instruments have a greater capacity to blend wit woodwinds and strings and at the same time produce a larger volume of tone i forte passages.

The rotary valve trumpet followed a separate line of development and has bee used as the primary instrument in central European orchestras for over a century Piston valve instruments, on the other hand, were centered in France and England and from there came to the United States. Today, rotary valve trumpets can b heard with great distinction in the Vienna Philharmonic and Berlin Philharmonic as well as major orchestras in this country.

Although the cylindrical bore of the rotary valve trumpet is slightly smalle than its piston valve counterpart, the leadpipe and bell are decidedly larger. Th instrument is designed with a wider pattern to avoid sharp curves in the tubing

---

5. See Vincent Cichowicz, *The Piccolo Bb-A* Trumpet, available from the Selmer Co.; David Hickman, *The Piccolo Trumpet* (Denver, Colo.: Tromba, 1973); Roger Sherman, *The Trumpeter's Handbook* (Athens, Ohio Accura Music, 1979); Gerald Webster, *Piccolo Trumpet Method* (Nashville, Tenn., Brass Press, 1980).

6. Common piccolo mouthpieces are the Schilke 14A4a, 13A4a, 13A4c, 11A, or 11X; the Bach 7D or the wide-rim 7DW, 7E, 7EW, and 10-1/2C. Bach offers a 117 backbore for piccolo mouthpieces. The receiver of some piccolo trumpets are designed to accept a cornet shank while others take the normal trumpet shank. Cornet mouthpieces are often preferred and can be used with an adapter on models requiring a trumpet shank.

Figure 3.2. Rotary valve trumpets (l–r): Heckel models—B♭ (Ganter), C (Yamaha); Monke C and D.

(Photo: Joseph Hetman)

These factors, combined with the less resistant rotary valves, create the impression of a much larger instrument requiring greater air support.

There are two basic designs of rotary valve trumpet and although they appear similar, they have different proportions and tonal characteristics. One type is made by the Cologne firm of Josef Monke. Several others follow the style of instrument perfected by F.A. Heckel (and later, Windisch) of Dresden. Lechner (Bischofshofen), Ganter (Munich), and Yamaha (Hamamatsu) fall into this category. Instruments are built in all of the standard keys.

Leading American players who frequently use rotary valve trumpets are Adolph Herseth (Chicago Symphony) and Charles Schlueter (Boston Symphony). In Europe, Adolf Holler (Vienna Philharmonic), Konradin Groth and Martin Kretzer (Berlin Philharmonic) play the instrument exclusively.

THE CORNET

There has been a remarkable resurgence of interest in the cornet in recent years. Most of the major manufacturers have developed new lines of traditional short cornets as they are being revived in bands to lend authenticity to repertoire originally written for them (see Fig. 3.3). Conductors are interested in achieving an authentic sonority in such works as Gustav Holst's suites for military band and Ralph Vaughan Williams's *Toccata Marziale*. Brass bands are enjoying rising popularity in the United States, and this constitutes a developing market for high-quality cornets. In orchestras, cornets are being used more frequently when specified by the composer. In the past, these parts were usually played on trumpets, thus negating the effect of contrasting tone color between cornets and trumpets which was intended by Berlioz, Franck, and others.

Figure 3.3. Cornets in B♭ and E♭ (Besson).

(Photo courtesy of the Boosey & Hawkes Group)

There should be a significant difference in tone and style between trumpet and cornet. Genuine cornet tone is darker and mellower than the clear, ringing trumpet timbre and should be colored with an expressive vibrato. Such a timbre can only be achieved through the use of a mouthpiece with a distinctly deeper and more conical cup. Trumpet players often use the same mouthpiece with a smaller shank when performing on the cornet, thereby losing much of the contrast inherent in the two instruments. The only traditional cornet mouthpieces available in the United States are the Denis Wick models, which were designed in collaboration with leading British cornetists. In the Bach range, only the 5A approaches the requisite cup depth.

For a number of years, "long-model" cornets have been produced by most manufacturers. These are constructed in more of a trumpet pattern and omit the traditional "shepherd's crook" of the bell section. The changes unfortunately affect the timbre, which is closer to the trumpet than the cornet.

The cornet is at its best in melodic passages where its soft, voice-like tone can be uncommonly expressive. Another asset is its extraordinary agility, which surpasses that of the trumpet. The best way to form a concept of genuine cornet tone and style is to seek out recordings of the many superb British brass bands. These bands have an unbroken performance tradition reaching back to the 19th century and have maintained their style independent of the influence of the trumpet and modern orchestral brass playing. Another excellent source is Salvation Army brass bands where a premium is placed on melodic expression. Of particular interest is a recording produced by the International Trumpet Guild of performances of the legendary Herbert L. Clarke dating from 1904 to 1921 (Crystal S450).

Cornets are also made in E♭ and are used exclusively in brass bands. The E♭ cornet is the highest voice of the brass band and is an important solo part. Cornets are occasionally made in C, but are rare today.

THE TRUMPETS IN USE

With the wide range of trumpets available, it might be helpful to know which instruments are needed by players in various situations. Students should have little need for any instrument beyond the Bb trumpet or cornet unless they aspire to major in trumpet on the college or conservatory level. In such cases, four trumpets will be needed: Bb, C, Eb/D, and piccolo Bb/A. Professional symphonic players usually have several instruments of each type, with individual instruments offering different playing qualities. In addition, the professional might own several rotary valve trumpets, a G trumpet, Bb cornet, and a flugelhorn. Jazz and studio players generally prefer a Bb trumpet of lighter weight than the orchestral instrument, and also have available a flugelhorn and possibly a piccolo trumpet.

It is worthwhile for conductors of high school and college bands to make available a set of cornets for loan, when desired. Similarly, conductors of school and youth orchestras should have a few C trumpets available.

INTONATION

Before going into the specific problems of trumpet intonation, it would be useful to consider more generally the problem of playing brass instruments in tune. By far, the most common difficulty is that students tend to allow the instrument to determine intonation rather than controling it themselves. The majority of notes require subtle adjustments of embouchure, air pressure, tongue, and jaw to bring them into tune. Certain notes must be corrected by some mechanical means, such as extension of a valve slide or alternate fingering. (The acoustical problem of sharpness when valves are used in combination is discussed in Chapter 6.)

The aural-mental process which enables the brass player to pick out specific pitches and to play in tune involves an ability to pre-hear the note that is to be played. A pitch signal is sent from the "mental ear" to bring the embouchure and other elements of tone production into a specific adjustment for a note. Tone and style are guided in the same way. Any inaccuracy of note or intonation is caused by the elements not being in optimum adjustment, or an imprecise or hazy pitch signal.

The procedure is the same as in singing. The time-honored method of training brass players is through the study of solfège or sightsinging. This study serves to fix pitches definitely in the mind so that a clear signal will be sent to the voice. Any lack of clarity will be revealed in the intervallic structure of the melody being sung. By learning to reproduce exact vocal pitches, players will rapidly develop the ability to predetermine pitch and carry this over to the instrument. It is a good practice to have students sing as well as play the etudes and exercises being studied.

The study of sightsinging, however, is rather neglected in this country, and this accounts for a great deal of the intonation difficulties in school and college ensembles. More emphasis could be given to working on chorales and chords in school groups, since the practical experience of matching pitches with other players is the primary means of developing the skills necessary for good ensemble playing.

In examining intonation charts for the trumpet, one can become dismayed by the number of notes apparently needing correction. In practice, most of these are controlled by the adjustment of the embouchure, jaw, and so on. Technical demands limit the number of notes that can be altered by lengthening the first and third valve slides. There are, however, certain notes that require this type of correction to bring them into tune:

very sharp slightly
sharp   sharp

correction: extend 3rd valve slide

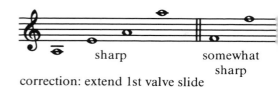

sharp   somewhat
                     sharp

correction: extend 1st valve slide

Obviously, valve slides cannot be moved in very rapid passages. What th
player looks for are notes that have sufficient duration to make correction prac
ticable. Another approach is to pre-set the slide for a prominent note within
moving passage. This focuses the passage on a corrected pitch center and make
the entire passage sound more in tune. While some players must make greate
use of the slides than others, because of variations in tone production, the genera
tendency is not to use them enough; this results in less-than-accurate intonatior
(There is an advantage to a trigger over a ring for the first valve slide in that onl
one motion is necessary, rather than the double action required by the ring.)

Specific notes needing correction can be identified through the use of an elec
tronic tuner (serious students should purchase one). After the degree of correctio
has been determined, general intonation can be improved by carefully playin,
scales, intervals, and arpeggios against a reference pitch sounded by the tuner.

The low F♯, G, and G♯ tend to vary in pitch from player to player. Some mus
use the third valve slide, while others can play these notes in tune with minima
or no adjustment.

A more complex problem involves the D, E♭, and E, particularly on the (
trumpet.[7]

These notes are minimally up to pitch and require an adjustment of embouchur(
and air stream to bring them into tune. On the C and higher trumpets, alternate
fingerings are often used to improve the intonation of these notes, but their us(
brings on technical (fingering) complications. The problem is aggravated by to(
high a placement on the third-space C, which has an unusually wide range o
possible placements, and by not using the trigger on the F above. These factor:
cause some players to have fairly severe intonation problems in the C to G range
The solution is to cultivate a lower placement on the C. This can be accomplished by centering the C between the G below, and E above. As a temporary
measure, the C might be fingered 2–3 until the feel of a lower C is established
(The 2–3 combination should only be used as an exercise since its pitch is to(
low for actual use. The player should return to the normal open C once a lowe
placement has been achieved.) When tuning, one should check the D, E♭, and E
against the tuning note. If they seem flat, the main tuning slide should be brough
inward until these notes form accurate intervals with the reference pitch. In resolv-
ing the problem, the player must use the first valve trigger on the top-line F and A
above, to bring them into a better pitch relationship with the D, E♭, and E. While
this problem is present on the B♭ trumpet, and most acute on the C and highe
trumpets, for some reason it causes fewer difficulties on rotary valve trumpets.

Playing in tune is, above all, a practical skill which requires careful listening
and experience in matching other players in ensembles. Too much analysis often
creates further problems. The best plan is to adopt a relaxed, natural approach to
intonation, as one would in singing. Playing in small ensembles provides invaluable

7. The author is indebted to Professor Clifford Lillya for clarifying this problem.

xperience, as do sectional rehearsals. A useful rehearsal procedure is to have two r three parts play alone. In this way, problems in intonation and balance can be learly heard and corrected.

TRANSPOSITION

'he question is often asked as to why transposition is necessary. Would it not be impler to provide parts already transposed for B♭ or C trumpet?

The origin of the problem goes back to the era of the natural trumpet when it vas customary for notes of the harmonic series to be read in C. A crook would e inserted to obtain the desired sounding pitch. For example, Mozart notated he trumpet parts to the *Prague Symphony* (No. 38 in D, K. 504) in the key of C with the instruction that the D crook be used. By keeping the notation of he harmonic series the same, irrespective of the key of the composition, the parts vere made easier for the players to read, and performance on a natural instrument vas facilitated. The tradition of writing the fundamental and its overtones in C :ontinued into the valve era and persists today. Trumpeters must be prepared to ranspose from parts originally written for trumpets in A, D, E♭, E, and F, to name ome of the common keys.

Transposed parts are not usually provided for several reasons. Orchestral rumpeters often substitute trumpets on various parts and it would be difficult or publishers to keep up with individual preferences. Also, switching instruments s made easier by the player having learned the part in its original notation. Above ill, there is a certain pride in craftsmanship in being able to play the part as the :omposer wrote it; therefore trumpeters tend to look down on the use of transposed parts. New compositions, however, should be notated at concert pitch, leaving the :hoice of which trumpet to use to the player. This applies to parts for the piccolo rumpet as well. Band parts are best written for the B♭ trumpet.

There are two methods used in transposition: interval and clef. In the interval iystem, the notes are mentally moved upward or downward the correct distance between the key of the trumpet specified in the part and the trumpet that will be used. The key signature must be altered in the same way. For example, in Strauss's *Ein Heldenleben,* the part for E♭ trumpet must be read up a perfect fourth when played on a B♭ trumpet, since the B♭ sounds a fourth below the E♭ instrument. If the part is to be played on a C trumpet, the notes must be moved upward a minor third:

Trumpet in E♭   Transposed for B♭ trumpet

Transposed for C trumpet

When the distance is only a half step, as in transposing A parts on the B trumpet, one of two procedures can be used, depending on the key signature. If the part is written without key signature or in a sharp key, the passage may be read in the parallel flat key by altering the key signature:

Tchaikovsky, *Capriccio Italien*
Cornet in A

Transposed for B♭ cornet/trumpet

If the passage is written with a flat key signature, the notes are visually moved downward to the next line or space and the key is lowered a half step:

Berlioz, *Benvenuto Cellini*
Cornet in A

Transposed for B♭ cornet/trumpet

In the clef method, the notes need not be moved on the staff. Only the appropriate clef and key signature are mentally inserted at the beginning of the line:

Strauss, *Don Juan*
Trumpet in E

Transposed for C trumpet

The common transpositions are shown in the following tables:

TRANSPOSITION TABLE—INTERVAL METHOD

Key of part	Played on B♭ trumpet	Played on C trumpet
A	Half-step lower	Minor 3rd lower
B♭	—	Major 2nd lower
C	Major 2nd higher	—
D	Major 3rd higher	Major 2nd higher
E♭	Perfect 4th higher	Minor 3rd higher
E	Augmented 4th higher	Major 3rd higher
F	Perfect 5th higher	Perfect 4th higher

Note: key signature must also be changed.

TRANSPOSITION TABLE—CLEF METHOD

Key of part	Played on B♭ trumpet	Played on C trumpet
A	Tenor clef	—
B♭	—	Tenor clef
C	Alto clef	—
D	Bass clef	Alto clef
E♭	Mezzo-soprano clef	Bass clef
E	Mezzo-soprano clef	Bass clef
F	—	Mezzo-soprano clef

Note: key signature must also be changed.

In performing Baroque works written for trumpet in D on the piccolo b trumpet, the player will find it easier to read a major third higher while fingering an octave lower than to read downward a minor sixth. If the piccolo is used in A, the part should be read a perfect fifth lower. C parts may be read on the A piccolo by using the bass clef.

Ultimately, it is the time that can be given to the study of transposition that is important, rather than the method used. Not all of the study time must be with the instrument. Although some daily instrumental work is necessary to orient the ear to different pitch levels, eye and finger coordination may be developed by reading silently and pretending to operate the valves. In this way, non-practice hours can be used to further transposition skills. Simple materials, such as familiar etudes and melodies, should be used at first, gradually progressing to studies specifically designed for transposition.[8]

MUTES

In scores where no specific indication is provided other than that a passage be muted, it is assumed that the straight mute is intended. To achieve a blend in muted sound, it is best if mutes of different materials or makers are not mixed within the same section since they tend to vary in intonation and timbre. The conventional straight mute is usually made from aluminum (although sometimes plastic and other metals are used) and produces a resonantly pungent timbre. Straight mutes are also constructed from fiber; these have a softer, less cutting sound. It is customary for a composer to specify when a fiber mute is to be used in place of the customary metal type.

Because the bell throats of various trumpets vary in size, it may be necessary to sandpaper a mute's corks to obtain good intonation. A properly adjusted mute will still play slightly sharp; the best method of correcting this is to place a pencil mark on the trumpet's main tuning slide at the beginning of rehearsal. The slide can be extended for muted passages and returned to the mark for open playing. The amount of correction necessary can be determined by playing open and muted pitches into an electronic tuner. A specially sized mute must be used on the piccolo trumpet due to its small bell.

There is an entire range of specialized mutes, each producing its own specific timbre. Of these, the cup mute and harmon or wa-wa mute are the most common. The latter incorporates an extendable tube which may be covered and uncovered to create the wa-wa effect. The tube can be adjusted to different lengths for distance effects, or omitted entirely for yet another color. The notation used for the wa-wa effect, and also with hats and plungers, is + (closed), and o (open). Occasionally,

TRUMPET MUTES

Straight mutes: metal	Fiber derby
fiber	Felt hat
plastic	Cloth bag
piccolo trumpet mute	Clear or solo tone mute
Cup mute	Rubber plunger
Felt-lined cup mute	Fiber plunger
Harmon or wa-wa mute	Plunger straight mute
(also version for piccolo trumpet)	bucket mute
Whisper mute	Buzz-wow mute

8. See Ernst Sachse, *100 Etudes* (International Music Co.); Bordogni-Porret, *24 Vocalises* (Alphonse Leduc); Mel Broiles, *Have Trumpet . . . Will Transpose* (Charles Colin).

a cloth bag is placed over the bell to dull and soften the sound. A useful mute is the whisper mute, which allows the performer to play comfortably, yet produces an extremely soft sound. It is sometimes used as a substitute for the straight mute in very quiet passages. Mutes designed for practicing have appeared recently and are helpful on tours and in other difficult situations.

RECOMMENDED LITERATURE[9]

Complete Methods

*Arban: *Complete Conservatory Method,* ed. Goldman and Smith (C. Fischer)
Arban: *Méthode complète,* ed. Maire, 3 vols. (A. Leduc)
Clodomir: *Méthode complète,* ed. Job (A. Leduc)
*Saint-Jacome: *Grand Method* (C. Fischer)

Elementary Methods

Clarke: *Elementary Studies* (C. Fischer)
Gordon: *Physical Approach to Elementary Brass Playing* (C. Fischer)
Longinotti: *l'Etude de la trompette* (Editions Henn)
Ridgeon: *Brass for Beginners* (Boosey & Hawkes)
Robinson: *Rubank Elementary Method* (Rubank)
Wiggins: *First Tunes & Studies* (Oxford)

Studies

Medium to Medium-Difficult

*Bordogni: *24 Vocalises,* trans. Porret (transposition) (A. Leduc)
*Bousquet: *36 Celebrated Studies,* ed. Goldman (C. Fischer)
Brandt: *34 Studies and 24 Last Studies,* ed. Vacchiano (Belwin-Mills)
Broiles: *Have Trumpet . . . Will Transpose* (transposition) (C. Colin)
*Chavanne: *25 Characteristic Studies,* ed. Voisin (International)
*Clarke: *Technical Studies* (C. Fischer)
*Clarke: *Setting Up Drills* (C. Fischer)
*Colin: *Advanced Lip Flexibilities* (C. Colin)
*Endresen: *Supplementary Studies* (Rubank)
*Gallay: *22 Exercises,* ed. Maire (A. Leduc)
*Glantz: *The Complete Harry Glantz* (C. Colin)
*Goldman: *Practical Studies* (C. Fischer)
Gower and Voxman (ed.): *Rubank Advanced Method* (Rubank)
Hering: *32 Etudes* (C. Fischer)
Hovaldt: *Lip Flexibility* (R. King)
Kopprasch: *60 Studies,* ed. Gumbert and Herbst, 2 vols. (C. Fischer)
*Laurent: *Etudes pratiques,* 3 vols. (A. Leduc)
*Parès: *Scales* (Rubank)
Salvation Army: *101 Technical Exercises* (Salvation Army)
*Schlossberg: *Daily Drills and Technical Studies* (M. Baron)
Skornicka: *Rubank Intermediate Method* (Rubank)
Smith: *Lip Flexibility* (C. Fischer)
Staigers: *Flexibility Studies,* 2 vols. (C. Fischer)
Stamp: *Warm-ups plus Studies* (Editions Bim)

9. Essential material is indicated by an asterisk. For additional literature, the reader is referred to the *Brass Player's Guide,* available from Robert King Music Sales, Inc., 28 Main St., Bldg. 15, North Easton, Mass. 02356. Repertoire lists appear in the texts by Dale and Sherman.

Vacchiano: *Trumpet Routines* (C. Colin)
Zauder: *Embouchure & Technique Studies* (C. Colin)

Difficult

André: *12 Etudes caprices dans le style baroque* (piccolo trumpet) (Editions Billaudot)
Balasanyan: *20 Studies*, ed. Foveau (International)
Balay: *15 Etudes* (A. Leduc)
*N. Bizet: *12 Grandes études de perfectionnement* (A. Leduc)
Bodet: *16 Etudes de virtuosité d'après* J.S. Bach (A. Leduc)
Broiles: *Trumpet Baroque*, 2 vols. (piccolo trpt.) (Queen City)
*Charlier: *Etudes transcendantes* (A. Leduc)
*Clarke: *Characteristic Studies* (C. Fischer)
Duhem: *24 Etudes* (C. Fischer)
*Gallay: *12 Grand caprices*, ed. Maire (A. Leduc)
*Gallay: *39 Preludes*, ed. Maire (A. Leduc)
Harris: *Advanced Studies* (C. Colin)
Hickman: *The Piccolo Trumpet* (Tromba Publications)
Longinotti: *Studies in Classical and Modern Style* (International)
*Petit: *15 Etudes techniques et melodiques* (A. Leduc)
*Petit: *Grandes etudes* (A. Leduc)
*Sachse: *100 Etudes* (transposition) (International)
*Smith: *Top Tones* (C. Fischer)
Webster: *Method for Piccolo Trumpet* (Brass Press)

Unaccompanied Trumpet (Cornet)

Difficult

Adler: *Canto I* (Oxford)
*Arnold: *Fantasy* (Faber)
Bozza: *Graphismes* (A. Leduc)
Burrell: *5 Concert Studies* (Oxford)
Cheetham: *Concoctions* (Presser)
Henze: *Sonatina* (Dunster Music)
*Persichetti: *Parable* (Presser)
Presser: *Suite* (Ensemble Publications)
Renwick: *Encore Piece* (Tromba Publications)
Sampson: *Litany of Breath* (Brass Press)
Schuman: *25 Opera Snatches* (Presser)

Trumpet and Cornet with Piano

Easy

Adams: *The Holy City* (Boosey & Hawkes)
Bach: *Aria: Bist Du Bei Mir*, arr. Fitzgerald (Belwin-Mills)
Bakaleinikoff: *Serenade* (Belwin-Mills)
Barsham (ed.): *10 Trumpet Tunes* (Oxford)
Barsham (ed.): *12 Trumpet Tunes* (Oxford)
Borst and Bogar (eds.): *Trumpet Music for Beginners* (Editio Musica)
Dearnley (ed.): *8 Easy Pieces* (Chester)
Dexter and de Smet: *First Year Trumpeter*, 2 vols. (E. Ashdown)
Haydn: *Andante*, arr. Voxman (Rubank)
Haydn: *A Haydn Solo Album*, arr. Lawrence (Oxford)
Handel: *A Handel Solo Album*, arr. Lethbridge (Oxford)

Hering (ed.): *Easy Pieces for the Young Trumpeter* (C. Fischer)
Lawton (ed.): *The Young Trumpet Player*, 3 vols. (Oxford)
Lawton (ed.): *Old English Trumpet Tunes*, 2 vols. (Oxford)
Lowden: *Easy Play-Along Solos* (recording incl.) (Kendor)
Mozart: *Concert Aria*, arr. Voxman (Rubank)
Mozart: *A Mozart Solo Album*, arr. Lethbridge (Oxford)
Philips (ed.): *Classical & Romantic Album*, vol. 1 (Oxford)
Tenaglia: *Aria*, arr. Fitzgerald (Presser)
VanderCook: *Marigold* (C. Fischer)
VanderCook: *Morning Glory* (C. Fischer)
Willner (ed.): *Classical Album* (Boosey and Hawkes)

Medium to Medium-Difficult[10]

Anderson: *Trumpeter's Lullaby* (Belwin-Mills)
Bakaleinikov: *Polonaise* (Belwin-Mills)
Balay: *Petite Piece Concertante* (Belwin-Mills)
Barat: *Andante et Scherzo* (A. Leduc)
*Bozza: *Badinage* (A. Leduc)
Chance: *Credo* (Boosey & Hawkes)
*+J. Clarke: *Trumpet Voluntary*, arr. Voisin (International)
Corelli: *Prelude & Minuet*, arr. Powell (Southern)
*Delmas: *Choral et variations* (Billaudot)
Forbes (ed.): *Classical & Romantic Album*, vols. 2 & 3 (Oxford)
Getchell (ed.): *Master Solos* (H. Leonard)
Fiocco: *Arioso* (Presser)
Fitzgerald: *English Suite* (Presser)
Gaubert: *Cantabile et Scherzetto* (C. Fischer)
*Goedicke: *Concert Etude* (Belwin-Mills)
Handel: *Aria con Variazioni*, arr. Fitzgerald (Belwin-Mills)
Handel: *Sonata No. 3*, arr. Powell (Southern)
Hovhaness: *Prayer of Saint Gregory* (Southern)
James: *Windmills* (B. Ramsey)
Ledger (ed.): *Warlike Music 1760* (Oxford)
Mortimer (ed.): *Souvenir Album* (Boosey & Hawkes)
Persichetti: *The Hollow Men* (Presser)
*Purcell: *Sonata*, ed. Voisin (transposed) (International)
Richardson (ed.): *6 Trumpet Tunes* (Boosey & Hawkes)
Ropartz: *Andante et Allegro* (Southern)
Simon: *Willow Echoes* (C. Fischer)
Telemann: *Heroic Music*, arr. Lawton (Oxford)
Wastall (ed.): *First Repertoire Pieces for Trumpet* (Boosey & Hawkes)
Voxman (ed.): *Concert & Contest Collection* (Rubank)

Difficult

+Albinoni: *Concerto in D Major*, arr. Thilde (Billaudot)
+Albrechtsberger: *Concertino* (Brass Press)
*Arban: *Carnival of Venice* (C. Fischer)
*Arban: *Piano Accompaniments to 12 Celebrated Fantasies* (C. Fischer)
Arnold: *Concerto* (Faber)
Arutunian: *Concerto* (International)
Bellstedt: *Napoli* (Southern)
Bellstedt: *La Mandolinata* (Southern)

---

10. Works requiring the use of high trumpets are noted with a plus sign (+).

Bitsch: *Quatre Variations sur un thème de Domenico Scarlatti* (A. Leduc)
*Bloch: *Proclamation* (Broude Bros.)
Bozza: *Rustiques* (A. Leduc)
Charlier: *Solo de concours* (Schott Frères)
*H. Clarke: Music of Herbert L. Clarke, 2 vols. (Warner Bros.)
*Enesco: *Legend* (International)
+Fasch: *Concerto* (Sikorski)
+D. Gabrieli: *Sonata No. 2 in D,* ed. Tarr (Musica Rara)
*Haydn: *Concerto in E♭,* ed. Robbins-Landon and Tarr (Universal Edition)
+M. Haydn: *Concerto in D* (A. Benjamin)
+M. Haydn: *Concerto No. 2,* ed. Tarr (Musica Rara)
+Hertel: *Concerto No. 2,* ed. Tarr (Musica Rara)
*Hindemith: *Sonate* (Schott)
*Honegger: *Intrada* (Salabert)
*Hummel: *Concerto,* ed. Stein (Musica Rara)
+Ibert: *Impromptu* (A. Leduc)
+Jacchini: *Sonata in D* (Musica Rara)
Jolivet: *Concerto No. 2* (A. Leduc)
*Kennan: *Sonata* (Warner Bros.)
Koetsier: *Sonatina* (Donemus)
Longinotti: *Scherzo Iberico* (Editions Henn)
Luening: *Introduction and Allegro* (Peters)
Mager (ed.): *9 Grand Solos de Concert* (Southern)
Mendez: *La Virgen de la Macarena* (Koff Music)
+Molter: *Concerto No. 1 in D* (Musica Rara)
*+L. Mozart: *Concerto in D,* ed. Thilde (Billaudot)
+Neruda: *Concerto in E♭ ,* ed. Hickman (Musica Rara)
Pilss: *Concerto* (King)
*+Purcell: *Sonata* (orig. key) (Schott)
Riisager: *Concertino* (W. Hansen)
Staigers: *Carnival of Venice* (C. Fischer)
*+Stanley: *Trumpet Tune,* arr. Coleman (Oxford)
+Stradella: *Sinfonia,* 2 vols. (Musica Rara)
*+Telemann: *Concerto in D* (Musica Rara)
Telemann: *Heroic Music,* arr. Lawton (Oxford)
Tisné: *Heraldiques* (Billaudot)
*Tomasi: *Concerto* (A. Leduc)
*+Torelli: *Concerto in D,* ed. Tarr (Musica Rara)
*+Torelli: *Sinfonia,* ed. Tarr (Musica Rara)
+Vejvanovsky: *Sonata* (Edition Ka We)

Recommended Books on the Trumpet and Cornet[11]

Altenburg, Johann Ernst. *Trumpeters' and Kettledrummers' Art.* Trans. by
  Edward H. Tarr. Nashville: Brass Press, 1974.
*Bach, Vincent. *The Art of Trumpet Playing.* Elkhart Ind.: Vincent Bach Corp.,
  1969.
*Bate, Philip. *The Trumpet and Trombone:* An Outline of Their History, Develop-
  ment, and Construction. 2nd ed. London: Ernest Benn, 1978. New York:
  Norton, 1978.
Bush, Irving. *Artistic Trumpet Technique and Study.* Hollywood: Highland Music,
  1962.
*Dale, Delbert A. *Trumpet Technique.* London: Oxford University Press, 1967.

11. Many interesting articles appear in the *International Trumpet Guild Journal* and other periodicals listed in
Appendix C.

*D'Ath, Norman W. *Cornet Playing.* London: Boosey & Hawkes, 1960.

Davidson, Louis. *Trumpet Techniques.* Rochester: Wind Music, 1970.

Foster, Robert E. *Practical Hints on Playing the Trumpet/Cornet.* Melville, N.Y.: Belwin-Mills, 1983.

Hanson, Fay. *Brass Playing.* New York: Carl Fischer, 1975.

Hyatt, Jack H. "The Soprano and Piccolo Trumpets: Their History, Literature, and a Tutor." D.M.A. thesis, Boston University, 1974. UM 74-20, 473.

Johnson, Keith. *The Art of Trumpet Playing.* Ames, Iowa: Iowa State University Press, 1981.

Lowrey, Alvin. *Trumpet Discography.* Denver: National Trumpet Symposium, n.d.

Mathie, Gordon. *The Trumpet Teacher's Guide.* Cincinatti, Ohio: Queen City Brass Publications, 1984.

Musique pour trompette. 2nd ed. Paris: Alphonse Leduc, n.d.

*Sherman, Roger. *The Trumpeter's Handbook.* Athens, Ohio: Accura Music, 1979.

*Smithers, Don. *The Music and History of the Baroque Trumpet Before 1721.* London: J.M. Dent, 1973.

Webster, Gerald. *Method for Piccolo Trumpet.* Nashville, Tenn.: Brass Press, 1980.

Other Books of Interest to Brass Players[12]

*Anderson, Paul G. *Brass Solo and Study Material Music Guide.* Evanston, Ill.: Instrumentalist Co., 1976.

*Baines, Anthony. *Brass Instruments: Their History and Development.* London: Faber & Faber, 1976.

Barbour, J. Murray. *Trumpets, Horns, and Music.* East Lansing, Mich.: Michigan State University Press, 1964.

Bellamah, Joseph L. *Brass Facts.* San Antonio, Tex.: Southern Music, 1961.

**Brass Anthology.* Evanston, Ill.: Instrumentalist Co., 1984.

Brown, Merrill E. *Teaching the Successful High School Brass Section.* West Nyack, N.Y.: Parker, 1981.

Carse, Adam. *Musical Wind Instruments.* London: Macmillan, 1940. Reprint: New York: Da Capo Press, 1965.

Devol, John. *Brass Music for the Church.* Plainview, N.Y.: Harold Branch, 1974.

Eliason, Robert E. *Early American Brass Makers.* Nashville, Tenn.: Brass Press, 1981.

*Farkas, Philip. *The Art of Brass Playing.* Rochester, N.Y.: Wind Music, 1962.

Farkas, Philip. *The Art of Musicianship.* Bloomington, Ind.: Musical Publications, 1976.

Lawrence, Ian. *Brass in Your School.* London: Oxford University Press, 1975.

Macdonald, Donna. *The Odyssey of the Philip Jones Brass Ensemble.* Moudon, Switzerland: Editions BIM, 1986.

Mende, Emilie. *Pictorial Family Tree of Brass Instruments in Europe.* Moudon, Switzerland: Editions BIM, 1978.

Rasmussen, Mary. *A Teacher's Guide to the Literature for Brass Instruments.* Durham, N.H.: Brass Quarterly, 1968.

Severson, Paul, and McDunn, Mark. *Brass Wind Artistry.* Athens, Ohio: Accura Music, 1983.

*Stewart, Dee. *Arnold Jacobs: The Legacy of a Master.* Northfield, Ill.: Instrumentalist Publishing Co., 1987.

*Taylor, Arthur R. *Brass Bands.* London: Granada Publishing, 1979.

---

12. A very useful guide to articles, books, and dissertations on brass instruments is Allen B. Skei's *Woodwind, Brass, and Percussion Instruments of the Orchestra: A Bibliographic Guide* (New York: Garland, 1985).

Trusheim, William H. "Mental Imagery and Musical Performance: An Inquiry into Imagery Use by Eminent Orchestral Brass Players." Ed.D. dissertation, Rutgers University, 1987.

Watson, J. Perry. *The Care and Feeding of a Community British Brass Band.* Farmingdale, N.Y.: Boosey & Hawkes, n.d.

Watson, J. Perry. *Starting a British Brass Band.* Grand Rapids, Mich.: Yamaha International, 1984.

Weast, Robert. *Keys to Natural Performance for Brass Players.* Des Moines, Iowa: Brass World, 1979.

CHAPTER 4

The Horn

Of the 43 or so varieties of horn available today,[1] some may be categorized as student instruments, others as general-purpose horns (see Fig. 4.1), and some a specialized high-register models, known as descant horns. There are difference in key: single F or B♭, F/B♭ full or compensating double, descant B♭/F-alt B♭/B♭-soprano, and triple F/B♭/F-alto. Horns are made with rotary, piston, an Vienna valves, and the third valve can be descending or ascending. There are als variations in bore and bell-throat taper, as well as the material from which th instrument is made (yellow brass, gold brass, and nickel silver).

THE SINGLE F HORN

Since horn players are more diverse in their approach to playing than other bras players, it is surprising that there is such unanimity of opinion as to the importanc of beginning on the F horn. Only in this way can the student develop a prope tonal ideal. Professional horn players strive for an F horn tone regardless of th instrument used. Thus, one integrated tone is sought on the double horn, an players of single B♭ and descant horns try to maintain a characteristic F timbr as far as possible.

Aside from tonal concept, by starting with an F horn the student will gai control over the basic processes necessary to play the horn, such as flexibility accuracy, register shifts, and the low range. Beginning with the B♭ horn woul impair normal development in these areas. If a single F horn is unavailable, the I section of a double horn will serve equally well.

THE DOUBLE HORN

There is a point in each student's development when it is time to change to th double horn. It is unwise to make this transition too early: the greater smoothnes of the double horn requires somewhat less control of embouchure and breath, an the student will be at a disadvantage if the basic elements of horn playing have not first been mastered on the F horn.

The principal horn in use today is the full double. Single B♭ horns wer frequently used on the first and third (high) parts and full doubles on second an fourth (low), but today entire sections of full doubles are found in most orchestra and bands. There are some notable exceptions, however.

The first double horn was developed by hornist Edmund Gumpert, and in strument maker Eduard Kruspe, whose firm introduced it at Erfurt, Germany, ir 1897. At that time, horn players were increasingly using the B♭ crook in orde to cope with the difficult parts being written by Strauss, Mahler, and other late

---

1. Paxman's catalog lists no fewer than 39 models; Alexander lists 29. The option of added stopping valves F extensions for single B♭ horns, ascending 3rd valve systems, differing bells, and the like accounts for the availability of so many models. The output of most other firms is considerably smaller.

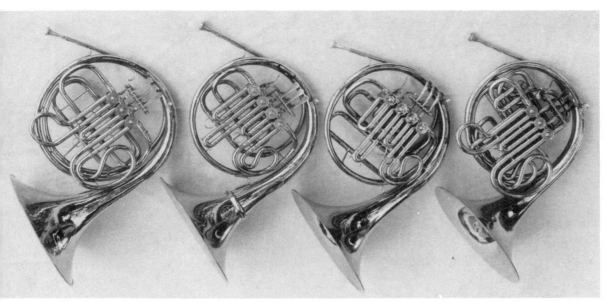

Figure 4.1. Single and double horns (l–r): single F, single B♭ with stopping valve, compensating F/B♭ double, full F/B♭ double (Alexander).

(Photo: Joseph Hetman)

9th-century composers. While this made performing such parts easier, the timbre was viewed somewhat unfavorably.

Gumpert and Kruspe had the idea of building a B♭ horn with double rotors and a change-valve which, when in the F position, directed the air column through both sides of the instrument—the normal B♭ tubing plus additional lengths to convert the horn's pitch to F. With the valve in the B♭ position, the F section was bypassed and the instrument functioned as an ordinary B♭ horn. This was the original type of double horn. Today it is known as the compensating double to distinguish it from the full double horn which appeared a short time later. The full double constitutes a more direct system and provides a better F section, but it is heavier due to the extra tubing required. The change valve routes the air column through either a complete F or B♭ section before it re-enters the bell tubing. The double rotors connect with valve loops of normal F and B♭ length (see Figs. 4.2 and 4.3).

While the double horn consists of two complete horns in one, it is not treated in that way by the player. A crossover point is established (usually written G♯ above middle C, or C♯ a 4th higher) and the instrument is approached as one horn, with the appropriate fingerings above and below the crossover point. Every effort is made to minimize differences in timbre between the two sides, and few can detect when a skilled player passes from one side to the other. The double horn combines the tone and intonation of the F horn in the low and middle ranges with the B♭ horn's security in the high register.

Both types of double horn are in use today. Compensating doubles are often preferred by hornists who play primarily on the B♭ horn, but want the availability of an F section. In such cases, the F side is used only for the low range and one or two other notes (particularly the middle G). Played in this manner, the compensating double is a superb solo instrument, being lighter in weight than a full double, yet incorporating a complete F section. Compensating doubles are also preferred by some orchestral players, particularly in Scandinavia and other parts of Europe.

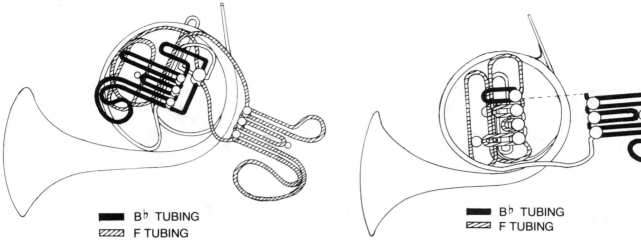

■ Bb TUBING	
▨ F TUBING	

Figure 4.2. Windways of a full double horn.

■ Bb TUBING	
▨ F TUBING	

Figure 4.3. Windways of a compensating double horn.

THE SINGLE Bb HORN

In the period following the introduction of the double horn, the changeover to the new instrument was not universal. Many players preferred the lighter Bb horn and felt that it offered better response and aided endurance. Use of the single Bb became widespread, particularly in Germany. It was found that a particularly good blend could be achieved with a mixture of single Bbs and full doubles—the Berlin Philharmonic used this format well into the 1950s. The same layout was popular in England. The Bb horn was less common in the United States due to a preference for the double horn, but one of the greatest players, Willem Valkenier, solo horn of the Boston Symphony during the Koussevitzsky era, played a single Bb throughout his long career with that orchestra.

The single Bb has always been a favorite solo instrument for its ease of response, technical agility, and accuracy. The great soloist Dennis Brain used it exclusively after switching from the French-type single F horn. The single Bb is preferred by several of today's leading soloists, including Alan Civil and Ifor James. Hermann Baumann also makes use of it in certain literature. Bb horns are also found in orchestras, and several principal players use it as their primary instrument. It also offers definite advantages in chamber music where its light response is an asset in achieving delicate balances.

Single Bb horns must be fitted with a stopping valve which routes the vibrating air column through an additional length of tubing to lower the pitch three-quarters of a tone to produce an in-tune stopped note (this can be accomplished on the F horn by transposing down a half step). An F extension is often added to enable the player to reach notes below the ordinary Bb range. The extension can either be attached to the stopping valve, or built into the instrument through an added fifth valve. With the slide of the stopping valve pushed in, the horn can be played in A which is useful for high-register parts such as Beethoven's 7th Symphony. A recent innovation is the addition of a C valve which provides some further high-range advantages.

THE ASCENDING THIRD VALVE HORN

The final two instruments that might be termed general-purpose horns are not in general use, but are standardized in specific geographical areas. The first of ese, known in France as the *cor ascendant,* is constructed with an ascending ird valve. This type of instrument dates from 1848, when Jules Halary invented horn in which the air column was normally directed through the tubing of the ird valve (without the valve being depressed). With a G crook, the extra length ne tone) of the third valve loop allowed the instrument to be played in F so long s only the first two valves were used. By depressing the third valve, the extra bing was bypassed and the instrument's pitch rose one tone to G. This proved be of advantage in avoiding certain problem notes in the upper register of the horn. Around 1930, Louis Vuillermoz developed a compensating horn based n this principle, and this has been the standard valve system used in France and elgium since that time.

Aside from the ascending third-valve feature, French-type horns have tradi-onally been made with piston valves and a slightly narrower bore and bell. Such struments are currently made by Selmer, Courtois, and Couesnon. Recently, the scending third-valve system has been receiving wider attention and normal bore tary valve models are now available from Alexander (Germany) and Paxman England). These, along with rotary valve instruments from French firms, are now ore often seen in French orchestras than piston valve instruments.[2]

THE VIENNA HORN

he most distinctive horn in use today is actually a survivor from an earlier poch. The principal instrument of the Vienna Philharmonic, the Vienna horn unchanged from the instrument introduced by Leopold Uhlmann in 1830. Of milar bore and bell to the natural horns of that era and incorporating a removable crook, the Vienna horn retains an authentic 19th-century tone quality and quires the skill of the great hornists of that period. It would have been easier r the Viennese players to adopt the Bb or double horn, but, to their credit, they ave remained steadfast in their commitment to maintain the special timbre of the ienna horn.

At low- and medium-volume levels, the Vienna horn has the pure, deep tone f the F horn and, as the volume increases, it condenses to a bright heroic quality t a lower dynamic level than the Bb and double horn. The lower threshold of the righter timbre is used to good effect by the Vienna players in works by Bruckner, trauss, and other 19th-century composers.

An important stylistic feature of Viennese horn playing is the glissando-like ur which adds expressive character to romantic compositions. The double-piston ienna valve[3] is thought to improve slurring by providing a better continuity of e air column through valve changes than the rotary valve.

Perhaps due to a combination of bore, bell, and its more direct airways, the igh register of the Vienna horn is usually better than other types of single F horn. his is a reason for its survival as a viable professional instrument. For unusually igh passages, a small F alto descant horn or the Paxman double F/F-alto is used.

Given today's exacting standards for accuracy and the difficulty of the single F orn, it is notable that Viennese hornists achieve a standard comparable to sections omposed of modern full double horns, while retaining their special sound. The reatest performers, such as the late Gottfried von Freiberg and Roland Berger, re revered by all hornists, and many consider their playing to be the summit of rchestral hornplaying (Fig. 4.4).

About a decade ago, the Vienna horn was threatened with extinction due to the aucity of instruments being made. A remarkable recovery has taken place with

---

The use of the ascending third valve is presented in Lucien Thevet's *Méthode Complète de Cor* (Paris: Alphonse educ, 1960).

The Vienna valve is discussed in Chapter 1.

Figure 4.4. Vienna horn with F crook (Lechner), played by Professor Rolan℞ Berger of the Vienna Philharmonic.

(Photo courtesy of R. Berge℞

renewed interest in these instruments throughout the world. Its future now seem℞ assured with new models being offered by Lechner (Bischofshofen [Austria]℞ Ganter (Munich), Engel (Vienna), Yamaha (Hamamatsu), Paxman (London) an℞ Ankerl (Vienna).

DESCANT HORNS

In the years following 1900, small horns pitched an octave above the F hor℞ appeared in Germany to aid the performance of Baroque horn parts, which ar℞ notorious for their high-register demands. The small bore and bell of these instru℞ ments were far from ideal, but in the absence of an alternative such horns wer℞ widely used until the late 1950s. At that time, the ingenious horn player-designe℞ Richard Merewether, joined Robert Paxman, a London instrument maker, in a℞ effort to develop an improved descant horn using a standard bell.

The idea of a double descant horn had been tried in Germany, but the in℞ strument embodied compromises because of the considerable differences betwee℞

s two sides. From their work with the single descant, Merewether and Paxman
eveloped a successful dual-bore double descant in F/F-alto. A B♭/F-alto soon
llowed, which allowed most of the range to be played on the B♭ side and the
-alto side to be used for the high register. In this form the instrument is widely
sed for the Baroque literature, some Haydn symphonies, and other works requir-
g a high tessitura. Double descant horns are now made by several manufacturers
ig. 4.5).

The descant horn is comparable to the higher trumpets in that it does not
rovide automatic high range, but places these notes lower on the harmonic series
here there is greater distance between partials, aiding accuracy. For unusually
gh parts, as are found in a few of Bach's cantatas, a B♭/B♭-soprano and an
-alto/B♭-soprano have recently been introduced.

Not really a descant horn in the usual sense, but more of a general-purpose
strument, the triple horn was developed by Richard Merewether from his work
ith descant horns. The full triple is constructed with three independent sections
 F, B♭, and F alto (Fig. 4.6). There is also a compensating model consisting of
 independent F-alto side combined with the B♭ and F sections of the normal
mpensating double. The difficulty in designing a triple horn was the problem of
e extra tubing's weight. Merewether was able to bring the instrument's weight
 an acceptable level through the use of hollow valve rotors. Double descant and
iple instruments are now also available with the French ascending third-valve
stem, and an F/B♭/B♭-soprano is forthcoming.

OTHER DESIGN FACTORS

side from the various types of instruments available, there are other important
onstructional factors which must be considered by the horn player. Chief among

igure 4.5. B♭/F-alto descant horn (Alexander).
(Photo courtesy of Gebr. Alexander, Mainz)

Figure 4.6. F/B♭/F-alto triple horn (Alexander).
(Photo courtesy of Gebr. Alexander, Mainz)

these are the size of the instrument's bell throat and the metal alloy from which it is made.

Small bells, such as those found on natural and earlier French valve horns, are no longer made, with the single exception of the Vienna horn. The bell throats of modern horns may be classified as medium, large, and extra-large. The variation is in the bell's inner profile, not the overall diameter, which averages between 12-1/8 inches (309.2mm) and 12-3/8 inches (314.6mm).

The profile of the bell throat has a profound influence on the horn's timbre. Large and extra-large profiles often give the impression of a fuller sound at close range, but fail to project well into the hall in comparison with medium bell throats, which produce a more focused tone with greater carrying power. Because the sound radiates away from the audience and undergoes a complex interaction with the acoustics of the hall, horn timbre must be evaluated from a distance. The bell throat also influences the color of the timbre. In the author's opinion, the warmth and character of the medium bell is lost on large-belled instruments.

Of equal importance to the bell profile is the alloy used in the construction of the horn. The three materials—yellow brass, gold (red) brass, and nickel silver—impart different qualities to the tone. Yellow brass consists of 70 percent copper/30 percent zinc; gold brass, 85 percent copper/15 percent zinc; nickel silver, 63 percent copper/27 percent zinc/10 to 12 percent nickel.[4] Yellow brass is the most widely used material and is, along with gold brass, preferred by a majority of professional players worldwide. Gold brass endows the timbre with a slightly darker and more veiled quality. Nickel silver was once believed to darken the tone but this has now been attributed to the large bell throats of the horns usually made with this material. In the view of the author, nickel silver imbues the timbre with a drab quality when compared with the rich color and tonal "bloom" of yellow or gold brass.

Confusion often surrounds the subject of horn bores. Part of this is caused by manufacturers who refer to the profile of the bell throat as the "bore." In actuality, the main bore is determined by the diameter of the cylindrical tubing found in the middle of the horn (around the valves), between the conical tubing of the leadpipe and bell. Thus it is not uncommon for horns identified as large bore to incorporate a smaller main bore, but larger bell throat. Outward appearances can be deceptive as well. Some horns are wound more compactly than others but this gives no indication of their internal bore dimensions. Most manufacturers offer two or three bell profiles, but only one main bore.

Most horns are available with either a fixed or detachable bell. With the latter, the horn may be carried in a flat case rather than the usual form-fitting type. Some players find no important difference in the playing qualities of detachable-bell models, while others have a negative view of this option.

HAND POSITION

Hand position has long been a subject of concern to horn players, but, until recently, most discussion centered on individual preferences and custom. The use of the right hand is now being recognized for its acoustical function, actually forming part of the instrument itself. As described in Chapter 1, when the instrument is sounded a standing wave is set up between the mouthpiece and a reflective threshold in the bell section. As the pitch rises, the threshold moves increasingly toward the bell opening; at G above the staff, it has reached the player's hand. From this point

---

4. Richard Merewether, *The Horn, the Horn . . .* (London: Paxman Musical Instruments, 1979), p. 14. Walter A. Lawson gives the percentages for nickel silver as 65 percent copper, 17 percent zinc, and 18 percent nickel. Walter A. Lawson, *Development of New Mouthpipes for the French Horn* (Boonsboro, Md.: Lawson, n.d.), p. 14.

pward, the hand essentially lengthens the bell throat by reducing its diameter o that the reflective function can continue to operate optimally.[5] This can be onfirmed by trying to play the range above G without the hand in the bell.

The need to form an acoustically effective duct dictates how the hand should e formed in the bell. The position described in Chapter 11 will insure good results. the hand position is incorrect, the instrument's intonation will be affected. The and F♯ at the top of the staff will tend to be low and uncentered, and notes nmediately below the staff will be sharp. The right hand also refines the timbre y absorbing some of the higher overtones and deflecting the sound toward the ody. The player can control these effects still further by covering the bell to a reater or lesser degree to create a more mellow or brighter timbre. Intonation is ontrolled in the same way—opening to raise the pitch, and closing to lower it.

HANDSTOPPING AND MUTING

he pungent, metallic timbre that is produced when the hand completely seals 1e bell is an effect unique to the horn. During the late 18th and early 19th enturies, this was the primary means of playing chromatic notes on the horn. It s important to distinguish between handstopping and the use of a mute. The horn 1ute functions the same as other mutes and causes no acoustical change within 1e instrument, as is caused by handstopping.

There has been a long-term controversy as to whether the pitch rises or escends when the bell is stopped. The rising-pitch hypothesis appears logical ince the instrument is shortened by this process. It would seem to be verified by 1e observation that, if the player transposes downward a half step and stops the ell, the same pitch as the open tone will be derived.

In fact, this is incorrect. It has been demonstrated that, as the hand is gradually losed, the pitch descends until, at full seal, it settles exactly one-half step above 1e next *lower* partial. This phenomenon can be seen in the chart below.[6]

Harmonic series—F horn

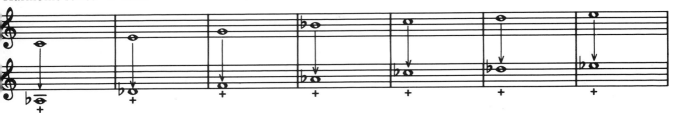

As the notes become higher, the distance between open and stopped notes decreases.)

To take a practical example, if the player wishes to play a stopped G, he ranposes downward a half step, using the second valve of the F horn. Although his appears to be an F♯, in reality it is the 7th partial of the harmonic series of the econd valve. If the bell were open, this note would sound as an A, but through 1e process of sealing the bell, it has descended to G.

. See Merewether, *The Horn*, pp. 28–32; Arthur Benade, "The Physics of Brasses," *Scientific American*, July 973, pp. 24–35; and B. Lee Roberts, "Some Comments on the Physics of the Horn and Right Hand Technique," *he Horn Call*, VL, no. 2 (May 1976), pp. 41–45.
. Adapted from Merewether, *The Horn*, p. 40.

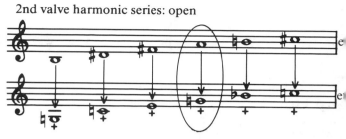

2nd valve harmonic series: open

2nd valve harmonic series: stopped

On the double horn, the player usually stops on the F side, although some notes in the upper register can be played with the half-step transposition using the Bb section. Normally, three-quarters of a tone are necessary on the Bb horn, requiring the use of a stopping valve. These valves are sometimes fitted to double horns as well as single Bbs, but the added weight is often seen as offsetting the convenience of not having to transpose when stopping. For the low register, a special (transposing) mute is used for stopping.

The standard horn mute (nontransposing) is basically a straight mute, but its timbre is less incisive than those used on the trumpet and trombone. Mutes must be selected with care, since good intonation is only possible if the mute fits the bell profile exactly. The best mutes are made to fit specific bells. Also, there is some variation of timbre between different brands of mute.[7]

USING THE F AND Bb SECTIONS OF THE DOUBLE HORN

The main concern in combining the sides of the double horn is to match the timbres of the F and Bb sections so that one "F horn" tone is produced throughout the range. The usual crossover is at written G#, although some players prefer C#, a fourth higher. The Bb side is sometimes used for a few low notes, particularly the low C#, to improve intonation but, in general, the Bb section tends to sound rather hollow and is less reliable in pitch below the crossover point. The F side is almost always preferred in this register.

When good tonal matching has been achieved, the changeover is almost imperceptible. An effective way of developing this ability is to play notes in the Bb range on the F side, and then change to the Bb side while concentrating on retaining the timbre of the F horn. It is helpful to occasionally practice solely on the F horn as this improves one's basic ability to play the horn. Similarly, it is advisable to be fluent with the Bb fingerings in all ranges for there will be tricky passages which can be facilitated through the use of the Bb horn. The following chart indicates the usual procedure for combining the F and Bb sections:

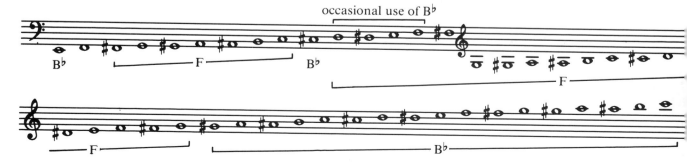

7. For detailed information on horn mutes, see Nicholas E. Smith, "The Horn Mute: An Acoustical and Historical Study" (D.M.A. thesis, University of Rochester, 1980) UM 80-19, 070.

TRANSPOSITION AND NOTATION

As was discussed in Chapter 3, the practice surviving from the pre-valve era of notating parts in the key of C and using crooks to obtain the desired sounding pitch has left trumpet and horn players with a legacy of parts in a variety of keys. Therefore, transposition skills must be developed as a normal part of the horn player's training. The table below presents the common transpositions.

TRANSPOSITION TABLE

Key of part	Interval method	Clef method
B♭	5th lower	Mezzo-soprano
C	4th lower	—
D	Minor 3rd lower	—
E♭	Major 2nd lower	Tenor clef
E	Half-step lower	Tenor clef
G	Major 2nd higher	Alto clef
A	Major 3rd higher	Bass clef

Note: key signature must also be changed.

The current practice of notation for the horn consists of writing for the F horn (a 5th above concert pitch) regardless of whether a double horn, single B♭, or one of the descant horns will be used. It is helpful to the player if the bass clef is used below G:

As in treble clef notation, the notes are written a fifth above where they are to sound. This manner of using the bass clef is known as "new notation." This is to distinguish the present system from a 19th-century tradition of writing bass clef notes an octave lower ("old notation").

concert   old   new
pitch   notation   notation

HORN CHORDS

A curious phenomenon associated with the horn is that a haunting three- or four-note chord can be made to sound by simultaneously singing a fifth or sixth above or below a played note in the lower register. Soloists in the natural horn era probably occasionally inserted the effect into cadenzas. Eugene Vivier caused a great stir in Paris with the device in 1843. Baffled as to how it could be produced, the composer Adolphe Adam compared it to the impossibilities of aerial navigation. In fact, most horn players can develop the technique, but it requires practice. Carl Maria von Weber included horn chords in the cadenza of his *Concertino in E Minor,* and it has been revived here and there by contemporary composers and a few soloists.

INTONATION AND TUNING

Since the pitch of any note may be raised or lowered by opening or closing the hand position in the bell, the horn player has a definite advantage in controlling intonation; this is used as a normal aspect of playing procedure. The horn exhibits the same deficiencies when the valves are used in combination as do other brass instruments. Unlike them, however, the outer tubing of the valve slides are shortened somewhat to allow the slide to be set in the best position to yield good intonation when the valve is used alone and in combination. Students sometimes mistakenly assume that the valve slides of the horn are similar to those of the trumpet or euphonium and try to play the horn with the slides fully in, with ruinous results to the instrument's intonation.

Among the first tasks to attend to in taking up a new horn is finding the correct settings for the valve slides. If a double horn is to be used, the tuning of the F and B♭ sections must also be adjusted so that they are in agreement. To do this, intervals should be played against a reference pitch and each slide moved as necessary. An electronic tuner or piano is useful in this process.

After adjusting the main tuning slide to a reference pitch of written G (concert C), the slurred interval G–C should be played to see if a good fourth results. The slide should be readjusted, if necessary. By playing intervals rather than matching single notes, one achieves a more consistent and accurate tone placement and the pitch of the second note will be more clearly revealed. The procedure below may be followed to find the slide positions for the F horn. The reference pitch should be set to sound the note circled. This note is played first, followed by either slurring to, or tonguing, the second note. The slide should be moved to whatever position produces the most exact interval.

discrepancies are found between the positions needed for single valve notes and
lve combinations, a compromise setting should be used.

A similar approach may be used with the double horn. The instrument's F
des should be set first with the procedure just given. Next, the B♭ section must
brought into agreement with the F section through the use of a common open
ne. This can be accomplished by playing the third-space C on one side of the
rn and then changing to the other side. The separate F and B♭ tuning slides
ould then be adjusted so that the two sides are in agreement.

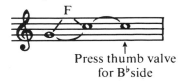

Press thumb valve
for B♭ side

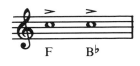

Once the correct settings for the F and B♭ tuning slides have been determined,
e player should move only the main tuning slide when tuning with the orchestra
band. The B♭ valve slides can be set using the following procedure:

ne D and A should be checked for possible sharpness, and the E and E♭ for
atness.

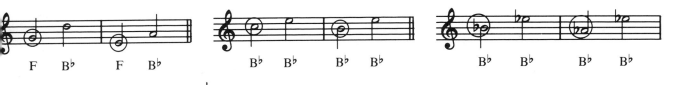

A few books attempt to give measurements for the slide settings, but these
ually prove problematic due to the variability of instruments and players. In a
ood horn section, some differences in slide settings will be noted, yet accurate
tonation will be achieved.

The 1-2 valve combination can often be played better in tune in the low
gister by using the third valve on the F horn. The sharp 1-2-3 combination on
e low C♯ can be avoided by playing this note 2-3 on the B♭ side.

For good intonation in school and college horn sections, it is essential that the
ide settings be checked and brought into agreement with each other. This can be
ne by tuning to a reliable open tone, such as middle G, and then playing single

notes, intervals, and chords together while making the necessary adjustments.
is useful to play a diatonic or chromatic scale slowly in unison from middle
to fourth-space E, stopping when necessary to change the slide settings.[8] Aft
the slide settings have been established, some careful work on trios, quartets, a
quintets should be undertaken. A progressive program of quartet playing can c
a great deal to improve a horn section in a relatively short time.

In the final analysis, good intonation is achieved by careful listening a
adjusting to other players. It is the right hand that plays the primary role
controlling intonation on the horn, and it is important that a flexible hand positic
be stressed as part of the student's normal training.

THE WAGNER TUBA

The Wagner tuba should be considered with the horn since the instrument, a
though a member of the tuba family, was intended to be played by hornists.
1853, during the composition of *Das Rheingold,* the idea occurred to Wagner
expand the brass at certain parts of the opera. The composer had become a
quainted with the saxhorns during a visit with Adolphe Sax in Paris. The Berl
firm of Moritz is believed to have supplied the original set of Wagner tubas f
the first complete performance of *Der Ring des Nibelungen* in 1875. These we
made in the traditional oval shape of the German military *tenorhorn* and *barit*
but with the valves on the left. Eight horns were called for in the score, four
which doubled on the new instruments. The quartet included two tenors in B♭ (
similar length to the B♭ horn), and two basses in F (which correspond to the
horn).

Both Bruckner and Strauss wrote for the Wagner tuba. The solo in *Do
Quixote,* which is now usually played on the euphonium, was originally intende
for this instrument. In an effort to improve intonation, the bell tapers of mo
modern Wagner tubas have been enlarged, thereby losing some of the cragg
timbre envisioned by the composer. An authentic set can be heard in the Vienr
Philharmonic. The latest development is an F-B♭ double tuba based on tl
compensating principle.[9]

RECOMMENDED LITERATURE[10]

Complete Methods

*Franz: *Complete Method* (C. Fischer)
 Pottag and Hovey: *Pottag-Hovey Method,* 2 vols. (Belwin-Mills)

Elementary Methods

 Burden: *Horn Playing—A New Approach* (Paterson's Publ.)
 Hauser: *Foundation to Horn Playing* (C. Fischer)
*Horner: *Primary Studies* (Elkan-Vogel)
 Skornicka: *Rubank Elementary Method* (Rubank)
 Clevenger, McDunn and Rusch: *Dale Clevenger Method,* 2 vols. (Kjos)
 Howe: *Method* (Marvin C. Howe)
*Tuckwell: *50 First Exercises* (Oxford)

8. A useful book for establishing some of these fundamentals is Robert W. Getchall and Nilo Hovey, *Sectic
Studies for French Horns* (Melville, N.Y.: Belwin-Mills, 1967).
9. For additional information on the historical background of the Wagner tuba, see James Harvey Keays, "A
Investigation into the Origins of the Wagner Tuba" (D.M.A. thesis, University of Illinois, 1977) UM 78-4044
10. Essential literature is noted with an asterisk. For additional material, see the *Brass Players' Guide* (Rob
King). Repertoire lists appear in the texts by Brüchle, Gregory, and Schuller.

Studies

Medium to Medium-Difficult

Brophy: *Technical Studies for Solving Special Problems on the Horn* (C. Fischer)
DeGrave: *Etudes for Modern Valve Horn* (Wind Music) (med. to diff.)
Gallay: *22 Studies* (International)
Gallay: *24 Studies* (International)
Gounod: *Dix études* (Billaudot)
Gower and Voxman: *Rubank Advanced Method,* 2 vols. (Rubank)
Kopprasch: *60 Selected Studies,* 2 vols. (C. Fischer) (med. to diff.)
Maxime-Alphonse: *Deux cents études nouvelles,* vols. 1–3 (A. Leduc)
Miersch: *Melodious Studies for French Horn* (C. Fischer)
Moore & Ettore: *Master Warm-up & Flexibility Studies* (Mel Bay)
Mueller: *34 Studies,* 2 vols. (International) (med. to diff.)
Parès: *Parès Scales* (Rubank)
Pottag: *Daily Exercises* (Belwin-Mills)
Pottag (ed.): *Preparatory Melodies to Solo Work* (Belwin Mills)
Pottag and Andraud (ed.): *Selected Melodious, Progressive, & Technical Studies,* vol. 1 (Southern)
Schantl: *Grand Theoretical & Practical Method* (Wind Music) (med. to diff.)
Singer: *Embouchure Building* (Belwin-Mills) (med. to diff.)

Difficult

Artôt: *19 Progressive Etudes* (Belwin-Mills)
Belloli: *8 Studies* (International)
Bergonzi: *Capricci,* 2 vols. (Doblinger)
Brahms: *10 Horn Studies* (Belwin-Mills)
Cugnot: *30 Etudes* (Wind Music)
Gallay: *12 Studies for Second Horn* (International)
Gallay: *12 Grand Caprices* (International)
Gallay: *12 Etudes brillantes* (International)
Gallay: *40 Preludes* (International)
Gugel: *12 Studies* (International)
Kling: *40 Studies* (International)
Maxime-Alphonse: *Deux cents études nouvelles,* vols. 4–6 (A. Leduc)
Neuling: *30 Special Studies for Low Horn,* 2 vols. (Pro Musica)
Pottag and Andraud: *Selected Melodious, Progressive, & Technical Studies,* vol. 2 (Southern)
F. Strauss: *17 Concert Studies* (Eulenburg)

Unaccompanied Solos

Difficult

Arnold: *Fantasy* (Faber)
Bach: *Cello Suites,* transcribed Hoss (Southern)
Bozza: *Graphismes* (A. Leduc)
Persichetti: *Parable* (Presser)

Horn and Piano

Easy

Anderson: *Prelude & March in Canon* (Boosey & Hawkes)
Kakaleinikoff: *Canzona* (Belwin)
Kakaleinikoff: *Cavatina* (Belwin)

Carse: *2 Easy Pieces* (Galaxy)
Franck: *Panis Angelicus* (Warner Bros.)
Handel and Haydn: *8 Solos from "Messiah" and "The Creation,"* arr. Lethbridge (Oxford).
Jones (ed.): *First Solos for the Hornplayer* (Schirmer)
Langrish (ed.): *8 Easy Pieces* (Oxford)
Lawton (ed.): *The Young Horn-player,* 3 vols. (Oxford)
Marshall (ed.): *An Album for the Horn* (Oxford)
Onozo and Kovacs (ed.): *Horn Music for Beginners* (Editio Musica)
Phillips (ed.): *Classical & Romantic Album,* vol. 1 (Oxford)

Medium to Medium-Difficult

Beethoven: *Little Rondo* (Schirmer)
Butterworth: *Romanza* (Hinrichsen)
*Chabrier: *Larghetto* (Salabert)
Dunhill: *Cornucopia* (Boosey & Hawkes)
Forbes (ed.): *Classical & Romantic Album,* vols. 2 & 3 (Oxford)
Françaix: *Canon in Octave* (International)
Glazounov: *Reverie* (Belwin-Mills)
James: *Windmills* (B. Ramsey)
James and DeHaan (ed.): *Horn Solos* (Chester)
Johnson (ed.): *Intermediate Horn Book* (Oxford)
Jones (ed.): *Solos for the Hornplayer* (Schirmer)
Marshall (ed.): *An Album for the Horn* (Oxford)
*Mozart: *Concerto No. 1 in D* (Breitkopf & Härtel)
*Mozart: *Concerto No. 3 in E♭* (Breitkopf & Härtel)
*Mozart: *Concert Rondo in E♭* (Breitkopf & Härtel)
Ployhar (ed.): *Horn Solos,* 2 vols. (Belwin-Mills)
Read: *Poem* (C. Fischer)
Richardson (ed.): *6 Horn Tunes* (Boosey & Hawkes)
*Saint-Saens: *Romance* (Belwin-Mills)
Stout (ed.): *Master Solos* (H. Leonard)
Voxman (ed.): *Concert & Contest Collection* (Rubank)

Difficult

Albrechtsberger: *Concerto* (International)
Balay: *Chanson du Forestier* (A. Leduc)
*Beethoven: *Sonata,* ed. Tuckwell (Schirmer)
Bitsch: *Variations* (A. Leduc)
Bozza: *Chant lointain* (A. Leduc)
Bozza: *En Foret* (A. Leduc)
*Cherubini: *2 Sonatas,* ed. Tuckwell (Schirmer)
Czerny: *Andante e Polacca* (Doblinger)
Danzi: *Concerto* (Heinrichshofen)
Danzi: *Sonata* (International)
Delmas: *Ballade Feerique* (Billaudot)
*Dukas: *Villanelle* (International)
Duvernoy: *Concerto No. 3* (Ka We)
Eccles: *Sonata in G Minor,* transcribed Eger (International)
Foerster: *Concerto* (Schirmer)
Gallay: *Concerto* (Ka We)
Gliere: *Concerto* (International)
Goedicke: *Concerto* (International)

Haydn: *Concerto No. 1* (Boosey & Hawkes)
Haydn: *Concerto No. 2* (Boosey & Hawkes)
M. Haydn: *Concertino,* ed. Tuckwell (Schirmer)
Hindemith: *Concerto* (Schott)
Hindemith: *Sonate* (Schott)
Hindemith: *Sonata for Alto Horn* (Schott)
Hoddinott: *Sonata* (Oxford)
Jacob: *Concerto* (Galaxy)
Kling: *Concerto* (H. Pizka)
Lewy: *Concerto* (H. Pizka)
Marais: *Le Basque* (Paxman)
L. Mozart: *Concerto in D,* ed. Tuckwell (Schirmer)
Mozart: *Concerto No. 2 in E♭* (Breitkopf & Härtel)
Mozart: *Concerto No. 4 in E♭* (Breitkopf & Härtel)
Musgrave: *Music* (Chester)
Nielsen: *Canto Serioso* (Skandinavisk Musikforlag)
Pilss: *Concerto* (R. King)
Pilss: *Tre Pezzi* (Doblinger)
Punto: *Concerto No. 11* (Medici Music)
Rosetti: *Concerto No. 2* (International)
Rossini: *Prelude, Thème et Variations* (Schirmer)
Saint-Saëns: *Concertpiece* (International)
Schuman: *3 Colloquies* (Presser)
F. Strauss: *Concerto,* ed. Tuckwell (Schirmer)
R. Strauss: *Concerto No. 1* (Schirmer)
R. Strauss: *Concerto No. 2* (Boosey & Hawkes)
Telemann: *Concerto in D,* ed. Tuckwell (Schirmer)
Tisné: *Lied* (A. Leduc)
Vinter: *Hunter's Moon* (Boosey & Hawkes)
Weber: *Concertino,* ed. Tuckwell (Schirmer)

Recommended Books on the Horn[11]

Bushouse, David. *Practical Hints on Playing the Horn.* Melville, N.Y.: Belwin-Mills, 1983.
Brüchle, Bernhard. *Horn Bibliographie.* 3 vols. Wilhelmshaven: Heinrichshofen's Verlag, 1970.
Coar, Birchard. *The French Horn.* DeKalb, Ill.: Coar, 1947.
Coar, Birchard. *A Critical Study of the Nineteenth-Century Horn Virtuosi in France.* DeKalb, Ill.: Coar, 1952.
Cousins, Farquharson. *On Playing the Horn.* London: Samski Press (distributed by Paxman Musical Instruments), 1983.
Farkas, Philip. *The Art of Horn Playing.* Evanston, Ill.: Summy-Birchard, 1956.
Farkas, Philip. *A Photographic Study of 40 Virtuoso Horn Players' Embouchures.* Rochester, N.Y.: Wind Music, 1970.
Fitzpatrick, Horace. *The Horn and Horn-Playing and the Austro-Bohemian Tradition, 1680–1830.* London: Oxford University Press, 1970.
Gregory, Robin. *The Horn.* London: Faber and Faber, 1969.
Hill, Douglas. *Extended Techniques for the Horn.* (Hialeah, Fla.: Columbia Pictures Publications, 1983.
Merewether, Richard. *The Horn, the Horn . . . .*London: Paxman Musical Instruments, 1979.
Morley-Pegge, Reginald. *The French Horn.* London: Ernest Benn, 1973.

1. Many interesting articles appear in *The Horn Call* (published by the International Horn Society) and other periodicals listed in Appendix C.

Pettitt, Stephen. *Dennis Brain.* London: Robert Hale, 1976.

*Pizka, Hans. *Hornisten-Lexikon/Dictionary for Hornists 1986.* Kirchheim b München: Hans Pizka Edition, 1986.

Schuller, Gunther. *Horn Technique.* London: Oxford University Press, 1971.

*Tuckwell, Barry. *Horn.* New York: Schirmer Books, 1983.

*Tuckwell, Barry. *Playing the Horn.* London: Oxford University Press, 1978.

Whaley, David R. "The Microtonal Capability of the Horn." D.M.A. thesis University of Illinois, 1975. UM 76-7010.

Yancich, Milan. *A Practical Guide to French Horn Playing.* Rochester, N.Y.: Win Music, 1971.

CHAPTER 5

The Trombone

The trend in trombone playing since the end of the second world war has been toward larger—and in the case of the bass trombone more complex and specialized—instruments. In earlier years, small-bore trombones, following the pattern established by the French instrument maker Antoine Courtois in the middle of the 19th century, enjoyed great popularity. When used with a conical mouthpiece, the instrument offered the pure tone and agile technique demanded by famous soloists of the era, such as Arthur Pryor (1870–1942).

Although trombones of this type were the mainstay of American bands and theatre orchestras, players in symphony orchestras of that era used instruments of considerably larger bore and bell dimensions. This was probably a result of the strong German influence in American orchestras during the late 19th and early 20th centuries. Large-bore German trombones served as the prototypes from which the modern symphonic trombone was developed.

Today, there are four general categories of trombone, based on their bore and bell dimensions (Fig. 5.1):

Type	Bore	Bell
small-bore tenor	Up to .500″ (12.7mm)	7–8″ (177.8–203.2mm)
medium-bore tenor*	.510–.525″ (12.9–13.3mm)	8″ (203.2mm)
large-bore tenor	.547″ (13.8mm)	8.5″ (216mm)
bass	.562″ (14.2mm)	9.5–10.5″ (241–267mm)

*The presence of an F attachment is not a factor in instruments being designated as medium-bore, large-bore, or bass trombones. Some models of tenor trombone are made with removable F attachment so that the instrument may be played in either format.

In the trombone sections of symphony orchestras, a typical layout would include two large-bore tenors and a bass, all pitched in Bb. The presence of an F attachment on the principal player's instrument is a matter of preference, but it is likely that one would be included on that used by the second. Possibly the bass trombonist would be using one of the new in-line double-rotor instruments or an earlier double- or single-trigger model. The same pattern would be followed in concert bands and wind ensembles. In jazz and studio work, small and medium-bore trombones are usually preferred for their more responsive upper register and brighter tone. Beginners generally start on the small- or medium-bore and later move to an instrument more specifically suited to their performance interests.

The situation is similar in Europe, where American-type symphonic trombones displaced small-bore instruments in England during the 1950s and in France slightly later. In Germany and Austria, however, traditional German trombones have developed along somewhat independent lines (Fig. 5.2). Aside from their wider construction and large bells, these instruments incorporate a more conical bore that includes a dual-bore slide (the lower slide is of larger diameter than the upper slide).[1]

. Leading examples are made by the firm of Herbert Lätzsch of Bremen, Germany.

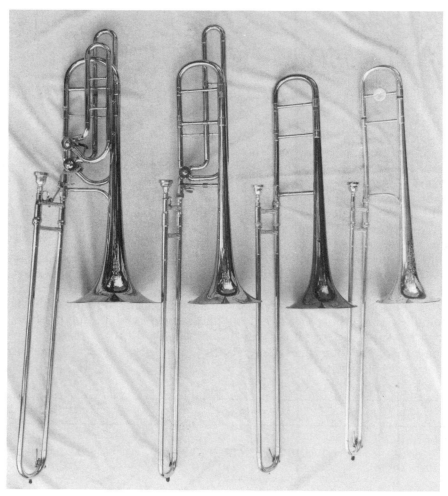

Figure 5.1. Bass and tenor trombones (l–r): bass with dual in-line independent valves (G & D) (King), large-bore tenor with F attachment (Conn), medium-bore tenor (Conn), small-bore tenor (King).

(Photo: Joseph Hetman)

Although American trombones are also used in these countries, orchestras such as the Berlin Philharmonic and Vienna Philharmonic maintain their commitment to the traditional instrument. The use of German trombones is important in achieving a blend of sound and matching the projection of rotary valve trumpets which are characteristic of these orchestras.

German trombones produce a dark, almost somber tone quality at softer dynamic levels and assume a resonant brightness at *fortissimo*. This contrasts with American trombones, which tend to hold a more consistent timbre throughout the dynamic range. (A similar change of timbre occurs in rotary valve trumpets and the horns used in the above orchestras—particularly the unique Vienna horn.) The distinctive qualities of the German trombone contribute a great deal to the overall effect the Vienna and Berlin brass sections achieve in Wagner, Mahler and Strauss.

Aside from the trend in modern trombone playing to larger bore and bell diameters, another direction taken has been toward more highly developed and efficient bass trombones. The inadequacy of the F attachment in completely filling

2. The Vienna horn is discussed in Chapter 4.

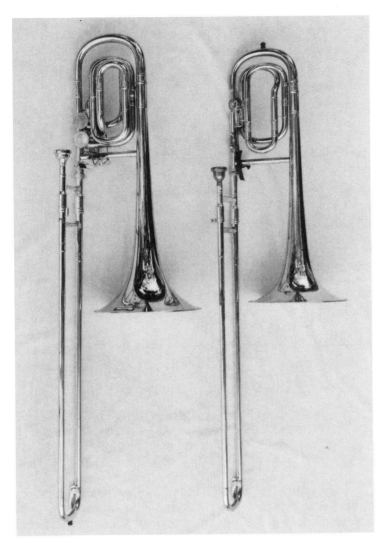

Figure 5.2. German trombones (l–r): bass with dual in-line independent valves, large-bore tenor with removable F attachment [Lätzsch]. *(Photo: Joseph Hetman)*

the gaps between the lowest overtone and the fundamental (pedal) range has led to the development of the double-rotor bass trombone.

THE ALTO TROMBONE

At the opposite end of the scale from the bass is the E♭ alto trombone, which, during the late 18th and early 19th centuries, led the orchestral trio of alto, tenor, and bass (Fig. 5.3). It is used today for parts requiring a high tessitura and lightness of tone. The alto trombone allows the player to achieve delicate balances without strain, and it makes high entrances a bit more secure. Its timbre blends well with woodwinds and strings and is particularly effective with voices.

In Germany, the alto trombone is regularly employed on parts that were originally written for it, but the instrument is used less frequently in the United States and Britain. Since the alto is pitched in E♭ or F, the player must learn a different set of positions, and many prefer to play such parts on their regular

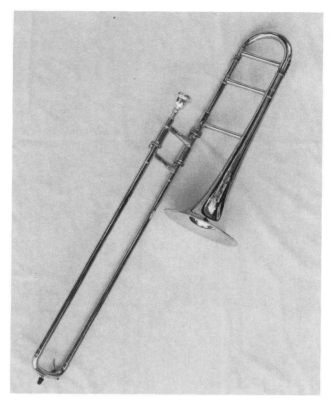

Figure 5.3 Alto trombone (Bach).
(Photo courtesy of the Selmar Company, Elkhart, Indiana)

instrument or on a small-bore tenor. Recently there has been renewed interest in the alto trombone in America, both for the solo literature available,[3] and in response to increased concern for authentic performance practice. As high-quality instruments become more widely available, it is likely that there will be greater use of the alto trombone in the future.

A soprano trombone pitched in B♭ appeared in Germany in the late 17th century. It was used principally in trombone choirs to play chorale melodies and continues in this function today. In America, the instrument is played in trombone choirs associated with the Moravian Church.

THE F ATTACHMENT

The origin of the F attachment can be traced to the bass trombone in F, which was used throughout the 19th and early 20th centuries. The idea of fitting additional F tubing to a B♭ trombone emerged in 1839 when the first instruments of this type were produced by C.F. Sattler in Leipzig. The purpose of the F attachment is to extend the compass of the B♭ trombone downward to the pedal range, and to provide some alternate positions to improve technical fluency in the low register. It consists of a rotary valve which diverts the air column through a secondary section of tubing to lower the instrument's pitch a perfect fourth. Unfortunately, the F attachment is unable to completely bridge the gap between the normal and

3. A list of literature and a discography for the alto trombone are provided in Stephen C. Anderson, "The Alto Trombone, Then and Now," *The Instrumentalist,* November 1985, pp. 54–62.

pedal ranges. The low C is at the very end of the slide, and a longer slide would be needed to reach the low B immediately above the first pedal tone (B♭).

The reason for this is that the distance between positions increases as the slide is extended. With the extra tubing for lowering the trombone's pitch a perfect fourth, a slide of greater length would be necessary to obtain the full seven positions (the F bass trombone had such a slide). As it is, the trombonist must play the more widely spaced F positions on the shorter B♭ slide, where there is room for only six positions. In practice, finding the F positions is not as difficult as it may appear since the player thinks of them as altered B♭ positions: 1, ♭2, ♭3, ♯5, 6, ♭7.

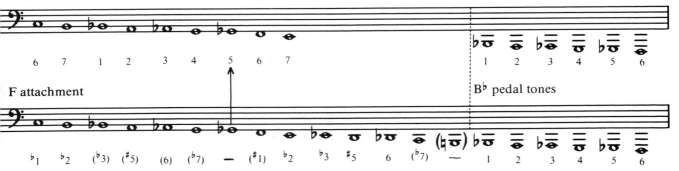

(The low F on the the F attachment can only be played in tune with instruments fitted with spring barrels since the 1st position must be brought inward.)

The problem of the absent low B and overextended C is not serious for the tenor player, but it presents a formidable obstacle to the bass trombonist since the literature calls for chromatic tones down and into the pedal range. This has led to the development of the double-rotor bass trombone, discussed below. Both C and B can be played on the F attachment provided that sufficient time is allowed to pull out the attachment's tuning slide (in effect making it an E attachment). Some bass trombonists are able to lip the low C down to B.

Another problem with the F attachment is that there is a difference in tone quality between normal B♭ notes and those played with the attachment. For this reason trombonists generally restrict its use to the lower register and invest a great deal of practice in attempting to equalize the sound.

One of the chief advantages of the F attachment is that alternate positions are provided so that awkward movements can be avoided:

The most effective way to learn to use the F attachment is to work through one of the books of studies designed for this purpose.[4]

A common method of tuning the F attachment is to play the middle F alternately in B♭ and F and adjust the attachment's tuning slide as necessary. However, in this tuning procedure, the low F on the F attachment tends to be flat and the main slide must be brought inward to bring it into tune (this is only possible on instruments with spring barrels). Also the second-space C is usually

4. A. Ostrander, *The F Attachment and Bass Trombone* (C. Colin); O. Blume, R. Fink (ed.), *36 Studies for Trombone with F Attachment* (C. Fischer); R. Fote, *Selected Kopprasch Studies for Trombone with F Attachment* (Kendor Music).

sharp, and the first position must be lowered accordingly. An alternative method of tuning the F attachment that is favored by many players is to tune the low F against the Bb a perfect fourth above. This ensures that the low F will be in tune when needed. This tuning, however, causes the low C to be sharp and more difficult to reach in the flat seventh position. Therefore, a decision must be made as to which is more important, an in-tune F, or an easily attainable low C. Tenor trombonists usually favor the F, and bass trombonists the C. (Bass trombonists normally use a sharper F attachment tuning on the double-valve bass trombone.) On some trombones, the low Db is a bit sharp when played in sixth position on the F attachment. In such cases the Db should be considered a flat sixth.

BASS TROMBONES

Bass trombonists must be able to play chromatically into the pedal range. Prior to the development of the double-rotor bass trombone, the player had to extend the tuning slide of the F attachment to produce an acceptable low C, and, even with this measure, the low B was generally unsatisfactory in pitch and tone quality.[5]

With a second rotary valve and added tubing in the F attachment, the pitch could be lowered a further half-step to E.[6] The two problem notes could be played on the E attachment without pulling out the tuning slide.

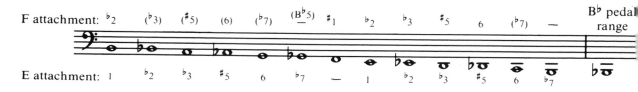

It was soon found that lengthening the tubing of the second valve to Eb or D resulted in low notes that could be played with less extension of the main slide and therefore better tone, response, and improved slide motion.

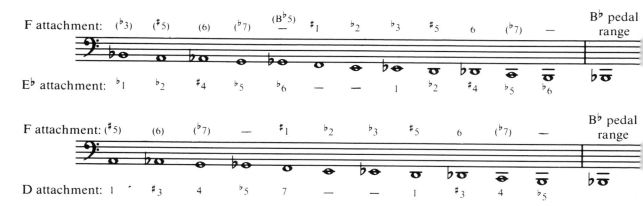

The latest development is the in-line double-rotor bass trombone in which both valves are located in the main tubing of the bell section. This allows the valves to be used independently. The instrument is currently available in two forms, depending on whether G or Gb is chosen as the pitch of the second rotor. (Some models

5. The low C and B were easily accessible on the 19th-century bass trombone in F which had a longer slide fitted with a handle. As a result, these notes are found in the literature.

6. The second valve cannot be used independently since the added tubing is an extension built into the F attachment. Both triggers must be depressed to use the E (Eb or D) valve.

come with both a G and a longer G♭ tuning slide for the second rotor tubing so that either format is available to the player.)

When the first rotor is activated, the normal F attachment positions may be played. If the lever of the second rotor is depressed, an alternative set of G or G♭ positions are made available. Using both rotors together lowers the trombone's pitch to either E♭ (G format) or D (G♭ format). It is essentially four trombones in one: B♭, F, G♭ (G), D(E♭).

G attachment:

<table>
<tr><td>1</td><td>♭2</td><td>♭3</td><td>#5</td><td>#6</td><td>(7)</td><td>—</td><td>1</td><td>♭2</td><td>♭3</td><td>#5</td><td>#6</td><td>(7)</td></tr>
</table>

G♭ attachment:

<table>
<tr><td>1</td><td>♭2</td><td>#4</td><td>5</td><td>♭6</td><td>(♭♭7)</td><td>—</td><td>1</td><td>♭2</td><td>#4</td><td>5</td><td>♭6</td><td>(♭♭7)</td></tr>
</table>

Attention has been given in the design of bass trombones to shaping the tubing from the rotors in a more open pattern. This is to provide better response and less resistance. Recent experiments have lengthened the second rotor's tubing so that C is in first position when the rotors are used together. Other developments[7] are the axial-flow valve,[8] improved activating levers, and oversized rotary valves.

SLIDE MOVEMENT

How effectively the trombonist moves his slide is the basis of both technique and intonation. Obviously the slide must be in good condition and free of any tendency to bind. The instrument's weight should be supported by the left arm so that the right hand is free to control the slide.

To achieve a clean technique, the player must have the slide reach a precise position before each note begins without shortening the duration of the previous note. Due to the distances involved, it takes a great deal of practice to develop the necessary coordination to place the slide in position accurately. Through practice, the player develops an automatic feel for the location of each position and aims for the quickest possible movement between positions. In legato, quickness of slide motion is essential. Students sometimes interrupt the air flow to compensate for slow slide motion. Although this eliminates obvious glissandos, the legato suffers. The player must develop good intonation through careful listening and should refuse to accept notes that reflect any imperfection of slide movement.

ALTERNATE POSITIONS

Alternate positions play a more important role in trombone technique than do alternate fingerings in the playing of valve instruments. Through their use, a

7. See Douglas Yeo, "The Bass Trombone: Innovations on a Misunderstood Instrument," *The Instrumentalist,* November 1985, pp. 22–28.

8. The axial-flow valve would appear to be a significant development. The design features more direct windways than the rotary valve. This is said to provide improved response especially between the valve section and the open instrument. It is available from its inventor, O. Edward Thayer, 173 Queen Avenue, S.E., Albany, Oregon 97321.

number of changes of slide direction and long shifts between positions can be avoided. For example, in a moving passage, if sixth-position C is followed by the F above, it is preferable to play the F also in sixth rather than return the slide to first position. Unlike most alternate fingerings, differences in intonation between the regular and altered position can be corrected by the trombone slide.

By selecting alternate positions, the trombonist tries to maintain the direction of slide motion where possible. These patterns become established through the practice of scales and arpeggios. Having an alternate position available does not automatically mean that it should be used. If there is any deficiency of tone, the normal position should be chosen even if it entails a somewhat awkward shift of the slide. In rapid passages, small differences in timbre may not be noticed, but in notes of longer duration, tone must be the primary consideration. Positions that involve long extensions of the slide tend to be less resonant and more difficult to control physically, due to the imbalance of the instrument. A more consistent tone will be achieved by minimizing the intermixing of notes taken in Bb or F on trombones with F attachments. Usually, the F attachment is rarely used above second-space C. Practice must be directed toward matching the timbre and intonation of regular and alternate positions. By playing a note in each position, the trombonist can equalize tone, stability, and intonation to an acceptable level on most notes.

Students often resist using alternate positions and cling to familiar positions no matter how awkward the slide motion. It is important that the use of alternate positions be included within their normal technical development to avoid problems when more difficult literature is encountered. Most method books incorporate this skill progressively within their studies.

The following are the most commonly used alternate positions:

INTONATION

The trombone is unique among wind instruments in being capable of completely variable pitch. This is both an advantage and a challenge to players. Having a greater capacity to adjust intonation than other brass players, trombonists must rely more on their ear in locating exact pitch centers. In this sense, trombone playing is similar to string playing, where it takes considerable time and effort to learn to play in tune. Apart from the general suggestions presented in the discussion of the trumpet, the following notes will most often need correction:

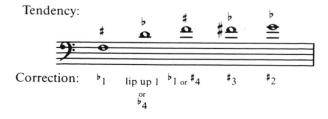

The highest octave will vary with individual players and instruments, and will require fine adjustment. It is common for students to exhibit sharpness in the upper register because of too much embouchure tension and insufficient air pressure.

Within a brass section, the first trombone must concentrate carefully on the pitches played by the first trumpet. It is helpful if these players can sit next to each other in order to hear as clearly as possible. The bass trombone should be seated next to the tuba since the parts often double and a good blend is important. Specific guidelines for seating the brass section for optimum balance and intonation are presented in Chapter 14.

The trombone section must work outside of full rehearsals if good intonation is to be achieved. Only through sectional rehearsals is adequate time available for meticulous tuning and balancing of chords. It is useful if the tubist occasionally joins these sessions since the low brass must work as a team. In bands, both euphoniums and tubas should be included.

TRILLS ON THE TROMBONE

Trills are not often called for in the literature for the trombone, but when they are, the player must be able to produce a smooth and reliable lip trill. Fortunately, the upper register of the trombone lends itself to whole-tone lip slurs and these, with work, can be refined into usable trills.

Lip trills are difficult for everyone at first. By working slowly and gradually increasing the speed, the player will develop a trill. Hornist Barry Tuckwell has suggested that if the usual way of practicing lip trills is reversed, the trill can be developed more easily:[9]

THE GLISSANDO

The special capability of the trombone's moving slide to produce a glissando has not been lost on composers, who like to make use of this effect. There are, however, some glissandos that have been written without an adequate awareness of what the instrument can do. Continuous glissandos can only take place within the seven positions of the slide:

Occasionally, problematic glissandos are found which cross over the first (ascending) or seventh (descending) positions. Experienced trombonists have found

9. Barry Tuckwell, *Playing the Horn* (London: Oxford University Press, 1978), pp. 17–18.

their way around such "broken glissandos"[10] but it would be better if composers considered the length of slide available above or below the starting note before writing this effect.

Another problem is, for example, the glissando from low B to F in Bartók's *Concerto for Orchestra* which was written for the longer slide of the obsolete F bass trombone. While this poses a difficulty for the B♭-F bass, it is manageable on the double-rotor instrument. In fact, the various configurations of double-rotor bass trombone have created new possibilities for glissandos.

THE F, C, AND G CLEFS

Although the trombonist is free of the burden of transposition that challenges horn and trumpet players, he will encounter parts in tenor, alto, and occasionally treble clef in addition to the usual bass clef. His training should prepare him to function comfortably in these clefs. (Such parts were originally intended for alto, tenor, and bass trombone.) In writing for the trombone today, the use of clefs is extremely helpful as a means of avoiding excessive ledger lines:

More use could be made of the nontransposed treble clef, particularly in the jazz and studio fields, as an alternative to the ledger lines required in bass clef by the high tessitura of the trombone writing. An anomaly is the transposed treble clef in which the trombone sounds down a ninth from where it is written. Trombone parts in brass bands (other than the bass trombone) are written in this manner. Players who are familiar with tenor clef can perform such parts by replacing the treble clef with a tenor clef and subtracting two sharps (or adding two flats).

Students of orchestration are often confused when they are told that the trombone is a nontransposing instrument sounding an octave below the B♭ trumpet. The trombone (with its movable slide) predates the horn and trumpet as a chromatic instrument and did not go through a "natural" era during which notes were limited to the harmonic series. To facilitate accuracy in performing on the harmonic series, natural trumpet and horn parts were notated in C regardless of their actual sound. The practice of writing the fundamentals of the horn and trumpet as C continues today. Consequently, when the trumpeter plays open (written) C on the B♭ trumpet, concert B♭ sounds. Open position on the trombone (first position) has always been read as concert B♭, the fundamental pitch.

MUTES

Trombone mutes follow the same pattern as those for the trumpet, but are constructed in appropriately larger dimensions. With the variety of bell sizes in use, it is important to use a mute that has been designed for a specific bell. Even with a well-designed mute, it may be necessary to make further adjustments by sanding the corks. The low register, particularly F attachment notes, should be checked when selecting a mute.

10. Some solutions, as well as a table of glissandos, may be found in Denis Wick, *Trombone Technique* (London: Oxford University Press, 1971), pp. 62–66. See also Edward Kleinhammer, *The Art of Trombone Playing* (Evanston, Ill.: Summy-Birchard, 1963), pp. 58–61.

Where possible, the same brand of straight mute should be used between trumpets and trombones to ensure evenness of tone color. Cup mutes, harmon mutes, and so forth, may not blend as well between the two sections. One irritating problem that seems to occur with regularity is that the composer has failed to allow adequate time to insert or withdraw the mute. Composers should check their muting instructions carefully and mentally go through the motions they are asking of the performer. Generally, more time is needed for mute changes by trombonists in comparison with trumpeters.

MISCELLANEOUS

Although some trombones are produced with a silver-plated finish, most professional performers prefer lacquered brass. The latter is considered to offer better response and a warmer tone. Some players favor bells made of gold (red) brass. This material includes a greater percentage of copper and produces a darker timbre.

Another matter of preference is whether the F attachment rotor is operated by string, as is common with horns, or by a ball and socket connection. Many feel that string action delivers a quicker valve change. The ball and socket is easy to maintain but tends to be noisy, although improved rotor-actuating levers and linkages are now available.

Among the latest experiments is the addition of a band around the expanding bell taper, behind the large flare (not a bell garland). This is believed to help the timbre to remain centered and round in louder dynamics. Leadpipes are also the subject of experimentation, and some instruments are made with removable leadpipes to allow performers to select one that more precisely matches their specific requirements. Existing instruments can be modified to accept different leadpipes.

THE TROMBONE IN NEW MUSIC

Within the last two decades composers have shown special interest in the trombone's unlimited capacity to vary pitch and produce exceptional sounds. Microtonal effects, singing or speaking through the instrument, and passing air through the tubing are a few of the devices that have been employed. A number of solo compositions have appeared and have been received with interest at new music concerts. Works such as Luciano Berio's *Sequenza V*, Adler's *Canto II*, Erickson's *General Speech*, and others have brought the trombone into a new era as a viable solo instrument admirably suited to today's compositional techniques.

RECOMMENDED LITERATURE[11]

Complete Methods

Arban: *First and Second Year*, ed. Prescott (C. Fischer)
*Arban: *Famous Method*, ed. Randall and Mantia (C. Fischer)
Josel: *Posaunenschule*, 3 vols. (L. Krenn)
Lafosse: *Méthode complète*, 3 vols. (A. Leduc)

11. Essential literature is noted with an asterisk. For additional material, see the *Brass Players' Guide* (Robert King). Repetoire lists may be found in the texts by Fink, Gregory, Griffiths, Kleinhammer, and Wick.

Elementary Methods

Beeler: *Method*, 2 vols. (Warner Bros.)
Cimera: *Method* (Belwin-Mills)
E. Clarke: *Method* (C. Fischer)
Long: *Rubank Elementary Method* (Rubank)
Ridgeon: *Brass for Beginners* (Boosey & Hawkes)

Studies

Medium to Medium-Difficult

Blume: *36 Studies*, vols. 1 & 2 (C. Fischer)
Bordogni: *43 Bel Canto Studies*, transcribed Roberts (bass trom.) (R. King)
*Bordogni: *Melodious Etudes*, transcribed Rochut, vol. 1 (C. Fischer)
Colin: *Advanced Lip Flexibilities* (C. Colin) (med. to diff.)
Endresen: *Supplementary Studies* (Rubank)
*Fink: *Introducing the Tenor Clef* (Accura Music)
Fink: *Studies in Legato* (C. Fischer)
*Gower and Voxman: *Rubank Advanced Method*, 2 vols. (Rubank)
LaFosse: *School of Sightreading and Style*, 5 vols. (A. Leduc) (easy to diff.)
*Little: *Embouchure Builder* (Pro Art Publ.)
Mueller: *Technical Studies*, vols. 1 & 2 (C. Fischer)
*Ostrander: *F Attachment and Bass Trombone* (C. Colin)
*Parés: *Scales* (Rubank)
*Remington: *Warm-up Studies* (Accura Music) (easy to diff.)
*Remington: *Warm-up Exercises* (Accura Music) (bass trom.) (easy to diff.)
*Schlossberg: *Daily Drills and Technical Studies* (M. Baron) (med. to diff.)
Slama: *66 Etudes in All Keys* (C. Fischer)
Skornicka and Boltz: *Rubank Intermediate Method* (Rubank)
*Tyrrell: *40 Progressive Studies* (Boosey & Hawkes)
Voxman (ed.): *Selected Studies for Trombone* (Rubank)
Wiggins: *First Tunes & Studies* (Oxford) (easy to med.)

Difficult

Aharoni: *New Method for the Modern Bass Trombone* (Noga Music)
Anderson: *Complete Method for Alto Trombone* (Modern Editions)
*Blazevich: *Sequences* (International)
*Blazevich: *Clef Studies* (International)
Blume: *36 Studies*, vol. 3 (C. Fischer)
*Bordogni: *Melodious Etudes*, transcribed Rochut, vols. 2 & 3 (C. Fischer)
*Dufresne and Voisin: *Sightreading Studies* (C. Colin)
Fink: *Introducing the Alto Clef* (Accura Music)
Fink: *Studies in Legato for Bass Trombone & Tuba* (C. Fischer)
*Kopprasch: *60 Selected Studies*, 2 vols. (C. Fischer)
Kopprasch: *Selected Studies*, ed. Fote (bass trom.) (Kendor)
Maxted: *20 Studies for Tenor Trombone* (Boosey & Hawkes)
Mantia: *Trombone Virtuoso* (C. Fischer)
Mueller: *Technical Studies*, vol. 3 (C. Fischer)
*Ostrander: *Double-Valve Bass Trombone Low Tone Studies* (C. Colin)
*Raph: *Double-Valve Bass Trombone* (C. Fischer)

Unaccompanied Solos

Difficult

*Adler: *Canto II* (bass trom.) (Oxford)
*Arnold: *Fantasy* (Faber)

Bach: *6 Cello Suites,* transcribed Brown (Tenor Trom.) (International)
Bach: *6 Cello Suites,* transcribed Marsteller, 2 vols. (bass trom.) (Southern)
Berio: *Sequenza V* (Universal Ed.)
Bernstein: *Elegy for Mippy II* (Schirmer)
Childs: *Sonata* (Presser)
Erickson: *General Speech* (Seesaw Music)
Hartley: *Sonata Breve* (bass trom.) (Presser)
Ross: *Prelude, Fugue, and Big Apple* (with tape) (bass trom.) (Boosey & Hawkes)
Telemann: *12 Fantasies* (C. Fischer)

Trombone and Piano

Easy

Adams: *The Holy City* (Boosey & Hawkes)
Bach: *Aria, Bist du bei mir,* tr. Fitzgerald (Belwin-Mills)
Bakaleinikoff: *Meditation* (Belwin-Mills)
Bakaleinikoff: *Andantino Cantabile* (Belwin-Mills)
Barnes: *The Clifford Barnes Trombone Album* (Boosey & Hawkes)
Dearnley (ed.): *More Easy Pieces* (Chester)
Lawton (ed.): *The Young Trombonist,* 3 vols. (Oxford)
Mendelssohn: *On Wings of Song* (Boosey & Hawkes)
Mozart: *A Mozart Solo Album,* arr. Lethbridge (Oxford)
Perry (ed.): *Classical Album* (Boosey & Hawkes)
Phillips (eds.): *Classical & Romantic Album* (Oxford)
Smith (ed.): *First Solos for the Trombone Player* (Schirmer)
Strauss: *Allerseelen* (Rubank)
Verdi: *A Verdi Solo Album,* arr. Lethbridge (Oxford)

Medium to Medium-Difficult

Bach: *Sinfonia,* transcribed Fote (bass trom.) (Kendor)
Baker (ed.): *Master Solos* (H. Leonard)
Barat: *Andante & Allegro* (C. Fischer)
Berlioz: *Recitative & Prayer* (Presser)
Galliard: *6 Sonatas,* 2 vols., transcribed Brown (International)
Gaubert: *Cantabile et Scherzetto* (C. Fischer)
Handel: *Sonata 3,* arr. Powell (Southern)
Marcello: *Sonata in C* (International)
Marcello: *Sonata in E Minor* (International)
Ostrander (ed.): *Concert Album* (Editions Musicus)
Pryor: *Annie Laurie* (Ludwig)
Richardson (ed.): *6 Classical Solos* (Boosey & Hawkes)
Smith (ed.): *Solos for the Trombone Player* (Schirmer)
Tcherepnine: *Andante* (Belaieff)
Telemann: *Sonata in F Minor* (International)
Voxman (ed.): *Concert & Contest Collection* (Rubank)

Difficult

Bloch: *Symphony* (Broude Bros.)
Corelli: *Sonata in F,* transcribed Brown (International)
*Creston: *Fantasy* (Schirmer)
*David: *Concertino* (C. Fischer)
Defaye: *2 danses* (also for bass trom.) (A. Leduc)
*Gaubert: *Morçeau symphonique* (International)
Gregson: *Concerto* (Novello)
*Guilmant: *Morçeau symphonique* (Warner Bros.)

Hartley: *Arioso* (bass trom.) (Fema Music)
*Hindemith: *Sonate* (Schott)
Hoddinott: *Ritornelli* (Oxford)
Jacob: *Cameos* (bass trom.) (Emerson Ed.)
Jacob: *Concertino* (Emerson Ed.)
Jacob: *Sonata* (Emerson Ed.)
*Jacob: *Concerto* (Galaxy)
*Koetsier: *Sonatina* (Donemus)
Larsson: *Concertino* (Gehrmans Musikforlag)
*Martin: *Ballade* (Universal)
*Milhaud: *Concertino d'hiver* (Associated)
L. Mozart: *Concerto* (Ludwig)
Pilss: *Concerto* (bass trom.) (R. King)
*Pryor: *Thoughts of Love* (C. Fischer)
*Pryor: *Blue Bells of Scotland* (C. Fischer)
*Rimsky-Korsakoff: *Concerto* (Boosey & Hawkes)
Ropartz: *Piece in Eb Minor* (International)
*Saint-Saëns: *Cavatine* (Durand)
Salzedo: *Piece Concertante* (A. Leduc)
Stevens: *Sonata* (Southern)
Wagenseil: *Concerto* (Boosey & Hawkes)
White: *Sonata* (Southern)
White: *Tetra Ergon* (Brass Press)
Wilder: *Sonata* (bass trom.) (Margun Music)

Books on the Trombone[12]

Arling, Harry J. *Trombone Chamber Music*. Nashville, Tenn.: Brass Press, 1983.
Baker, David. *Contemporary Techniques for the Trombone*. 2 vols. New York: Charles Colin, 1974.
*Bate, Philip. *The Trumpet and Trombone:* An Outline of Their History, Development, and Construction. 2nd ed. London: Ernest Benn, 1978. New York: Norton, 1978.
*Dempster, Stuart. *The Modern Trombone*. Berkeley, Calif.: University of California Press, 1979.
*Fink, Reginald H. *The Trombonist's Handbook*. Athens, Ohio: Accura Music, 1977.
Everett, Thomas G. *Annotated Guide to Bass Trombone Literature*. Nashville, Tenn.: Brass Press, 1978.
*Gregory, Robin: *The Trombone*. New York: Faber and Faber, 1973.
Griffiths, John R. *The Low Brass Guide*. Hackensack, N.J.: Jerona Music, 1980.
Kagarice, Vern L., *Solos for the Student Trombonist: An Annotated Bibliography*. Nashville, Tenn.: Brass Press, 1979.
*Kleinhammer, Edward. *The Art of Trombone Playing*. Evanston, Ill.: Summy-Birchard Company, 1963.
Knaub, Donald: *Trombone Teaching Techniques*. 2nd ed. Athens, Ohio: Accura Music, 1977.
Naylor, Tom L. *The Trumpet and Trombone in Graphic Arts, 1500–1800*. Nashville, Tenn.: Brass Press, 1979.
Senff, Thomas E. "An Annotated Bibliography of the Unaccompanied Solo Repertoire for Trombone." D.M.A. thesis, University of Illinois, 1976. UM 76-16, 919.
*Wick, Denis. *Trombone Technique*. London: Oxford University Press, 1975.
*Wigness, C. Robert. *The Soloistic Use of the Trombone in Eighteenth Century Vienna*. Nashville, Tenn.: Brass Press, 1978.

12. Many interesting articles appear in the *International Trombone Association Journal* and other periodicals listed in Appendix C.

CHAPTER 6
Baritone and Euphonium

The origin of the euphonium and baritone (Figs. 6.1 and 6.2) is more obscure than the tuba, which has a definite starting point and clear lines of development.[1] Tenor-range brass instruments built in Bb with three valves were part of German military bands during the late 1820s. The next clue is an instrument known as the euphonion, which was developed in 1843 or 1844 by Sommer of Weimar. This may be the same Sommer (his first name is unknown) who caused a stir with a similar instrument at the 1851 Crystal Palace Exhibition in London.

About this time, Adolph Sax patented his complete family of saxhorns which included two low Bb instruments: the *saxhorn baryton*, which was of similar dimensions to the modern baritone, and the *saxhorn basse,* a larger instrument originally of greater bore than the euphonium. The originality of Sax's instruments was disputed at the time, and it is clear that the German instruments both preceded them and developed independently. Sax should, however, be credited with developing a complete group of instruments of this type, and he is largely responsible for their acceptance in countries beyond the Rhine.

Today, the baritone and euphonium (both are in the key of Bb) are constructed similarly, but differ in their bore and bell dimensions. There are important differences in timbre and playing characteristics between the two instruments. Baritones from British and European manufacturers (including Yamaha) are made with a distinctly narrower bore than euphoniums. For example, the Boosey & Hawkes and Besson baritones are built with a 13.11-millimeter (.516″) main bore, as opposed to 14.72 millimeters (.579″) for their euphoniums.

In the United States, the difference is less defined. This is due to a lack of clarity in identifying the instruments and a tendency for American firms to produce larger bore baritones and smaller euphoniums than those used in England. (This trend is changing, however, in response to the almost total domination of British-type instruments.) Further confusion is generated by the habit among conductors and players of referring to both instruments as "baritone."

The picture is blurred still further by the names applied to these instruments in other countries. In Germany, the baritone is known as the *tenorhorn* and the euphonium as the *baryton.* In England, the Eb alto horn is the tenor horn. Sax's designation of *baryton* (baritone) and *basse* (euphonium) is still used in France.

Greater clarity would prevail if the name euphonium were used only for instruments with a bore larger than 14 millimeters (.551″). The differences between the baritone and euphonium can be readily observed by comparing the cylindrical tubing of the valve section. If tubing from the baritone is inserted into the euphonium, the difference in main bore will be quite apparent. Even more obvious is the taper of the bell sections. On the baritone, this profile is more slender and the bell throat is significantly smaller. These factors give the baritone its light, clear tone in comparison to the darker timbre and more tuba-like appearance of the euphonium (in particular, the size of the bottom bow should be noted). The brass band is the only ensemble where a clear distinction between the instruments

1. The development of the euphonium is sketched as clearly as it probably can be in Clifford Bevan's *The Tuba Family* (New York: Scribner's, 1978), pp. 90–94.

Figure 6.1. Baritone (Besson).
(Photo courtesy of the Boosey & Hawkes Group)

Figure 6.2. Euphonium (Besson).
(Photo courtesy of the Boosey & Hawkes Group)

is made. Brass band scores include separate baritone and euphonium parts, and players specialize on one instrument or the other.

INTONATION

The ability of a player to correct intonation by lipping a faulty note into tune (in reality, forcing the air column to vibrate at a different frequency from that which should be produced by the tube's length) decreases as the vibrating air columns become longer, and greater quantities of air are used. Hence, the trumpet is more under the player's control than the lower brass. Hornists make the necessary corrections by altering their hand position; this is accomplished on the trombone by varying the positions of the slide. With the euphonium and tuba, the problem becomes especially acute.

Aside from problems with the overtone series itself (which should be minimal in a well-designed instrument), errors occur when the valves are used in combination. For example, the total length for a euphonium in B♭ is 115.325 inches (2929.25mm). When the first valve is depressed, 14.175 inches (360.4mm) of tubing are added to lower the pitch one tone to A♭. By activating the third valve, the instrument's pitch is lowered one and one-half tones to G, adding 21.825 inches (554.35mm). The difficulty arises when the first and third valves are used together to lower the instrument to F.

Just as progressively more tubing is required between each trombone position to arrive at the correct measurement for a given pitch, so the valve tubing would need some means of extending itself for the lower pitch. The length of vibrating air column necessary for the low F is 153.960 inches (3910.58mm). If 14.175 inches (360.4mm) of the first valve, and the third valve's 21.825 inches (554.35mm) are added to the euphonium's fundamental length of 115.325 inches (2929.25mm), the total tubing available for the F is 151.325 inches (3843.65mm)—that is, 2.635

nches (66.93mm) too short, producing a sharp pitch. When all three valves are used to play a low E, the discrepancy is even greater.[2]

The usual way around this problem is for the manufacturer to increase the length of the third valve tubing to more than the one-and-one-half-tone extension it was originally intended to provide. This introduces a compromise that is workable in the high brass instruments due to their greater responsiveness to embouchure control. Of course, in this process the third valve is diverted from its original purpose and is almost never used alone. In its place, the first and second valves are used in combination for the one-and-one-half-tone extension, but their combined length is slightly short. This is why trumpeters must use the first valve trigger on notes played in this combination. (the 1st valve is usually constructed slightly long to reduce the amount of correction necessary).

There have been various approaches to finding a practical solution to this difficulty. In the case of the trumpet, the compromises work well enough, provided that the instrument is fitted with both a first- and third-valve trigger or ring. A similar approach is taken by some euphonium manufacturers by adding rings to the third- and/or first-valve slides or a trigger to the main tuning slide. While these offer some measure of correction, they are awkward to use in an instrument of this size and do not offer a very viable solution. Most commonly, a fourth valve is incorporated into the design; this affords definite improvement by providing alternate fingerings for the 1–3 and 1–2–3 combinations. There are serious limitations, however, of the four-valve system in the range above the pedal tone, and this has led tubists to consider the further addition of a fifth valve to be absolutely essential.

The most effective solution of all for the euphonium is the system of automatic compensation designed by David J. Blaikley for the Boosey company in 1874. In this system, each valve contains a second loop of tubing which is the necessary length to correct intonation when the valve is used in combination with the master valve. There are both three- and four-valve compensating systems. In the preferable four-valve system, the fourth valve acts as the master valve and has its normal loop routed through the other valves. The valves perform normally when used independently of the fourth valve. In combination, however, the vibrating air column is directed through the compensating loop as it passes along the fourth valve's tubing (Fig. 6.3).

The advantage of the compensating system may be seen in Chart 6.1 which compares the intonation of compensated and uncompensated four-valve systems.

An additional advantage of the compensating system is that on instruments of this type, the third valve is constructed in the exact length for the one-and-one-half-tone extension (not longer, as in uncompensated instruments) and may be used in place of the sharp 1–2 combination, whenever the fingering pattern or the duration of the note permits. (The 1–2 combination may still be preferred for rapid passages since it follows the first valve more naturally in rapid fingering sequences.) This gives the player of a compensated instrument an advantage in intonation control. It is a pity that many players are unaware of this feature and still cling to the 1–2 combination rather than using the third valve as it was originally intended.

While the four-valve compensating system does improve intonation to a certain degree, it falls short of a complete solution to the problem and alternate fingerings play an important role in technique. Beyond the beginning level, a four-valve instrument is a necessity. (Even the three-valve compensating system offers little improvement). Ultimately, good intonation depends on players getting to know the idiosyncracies of their own instrument.

2. F.C. Draper, *Notes on the Besson System of Automatic Compensation of Valved Brass Wind Instruments* (Edgware, England: Besson, 1953).

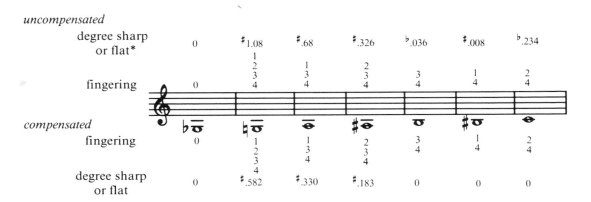

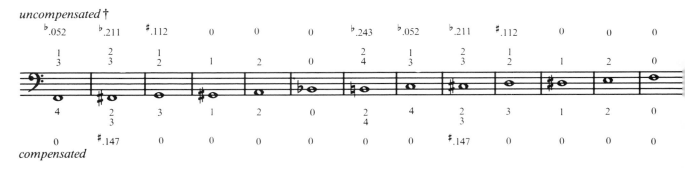

* Of a semitone.

† The fourth valve would normally be used in place of the 1–3 combination on uncompensated instruments, providing improved intonation.

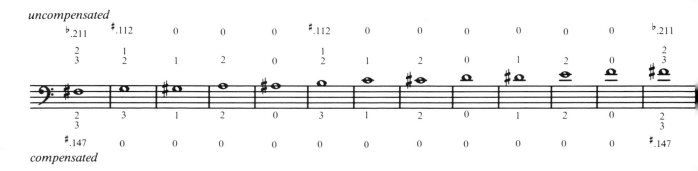

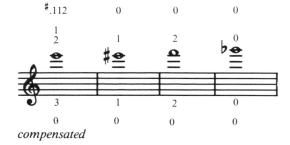

Chart 6.1. Comparison of intonation of compensated and uncompensated four-value systems.

(Adapted from Draper, Notes on the Besson System)

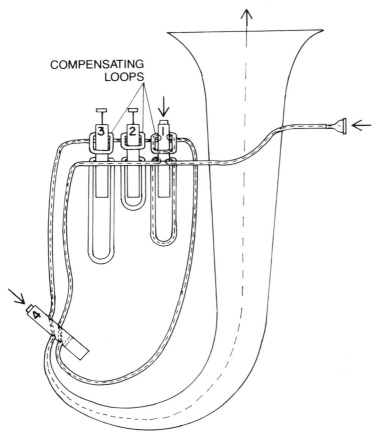

Figure 6.3. Blaikley's four-valve compensating system.
(Adapted from Draper, Notes on the Besson System)

TONE AND PLAYING STYLE

Perhaps a word should be said about euphonium tone and style of playing. Euphonium playing bears a relationship to cornet playing in that the main emphasis should be melodic and expressive. While both instruments lend themselves to technical display—and this is exploited in the literature—their very essence is a subtle capacity to emulate the human voice. This quality can be heard by listening to British brass bands, where all 25 players (regardless of instrument) strive for this single concept. The use of a natural, voice-like vibrato is fundamental to this style and lends expressiveness and sensitivity to the tone.

The euphonium was originally designed to blend with the other conical-bore instruments of the brass band, therefore it should have a deep, mellow tone quality without any trace of edge or hardness. If the trombone tone needs a certain "ring" in the timbre, the euphonium and baritone timbre should have richness and softness. The difference in tone quality between euphonium and baritone is one of degree: the concept is similar, but the baritone timbre is somewhat lighter in both color and weight.

To achieve an authentic tone quality, it is essential to use a mouthpiece of adequate depth and throat bore. It is quite common to find students using trombone mouthpieces that are too small to yield a satisfactory tone. (In orchestras, a trombonist is usually appointed to perform the euphonium parts, and this often results in a hollow, rather hard timbre.) By examining the expanding tubing along the bell section, a player can see the need for a large-capacity mouthpiece. In order to fill tubing of this diameter, a great quantity of air is necessary and small mouthpiece places a restriction on the air column. A large backbore (as o the Denis Wick 4AL) is helpful in achieving the characteristic dark timbre.

In orchestral circles, the euphonium is known as the tenor tuba and is general played without vibrato. The *Bydlo* solo in *Pictures at an Exhibition* (Mussorgsk Ravel), however, gains character from the addition of some vibrato. In othe passages, such as those found in the Janáček *Sinfonietta* and Holst's *Mars* (*Tf Planets*), a pure, straight tone is more effective. In Strauss's *Don Quixote,* th vibrato question is less clear and some experimentation is in order. Sometimes German rotary valve euphonium (known as *Baryton* in Germany) is employee This instrument has an unusually sturdy tone but lacks an effective system o compensation. For this reason, it is important that a four-valve model be use and the fit of the mouthpiece into the receiver must be carefully checked. (Th problem is discussed in Chapter 2.)

The euphonium is in its natural element in bands, where it is treated a an important solo voice. Composers have taken advantage of the instrument technical agility, and the player is provided with many interesting and challengin parts. This is even more true of euphonium writing in the brass band. Th instrument is employed in truly virtuosic fashion in the leading British bands suc as Black Dyke Mills, Besses O'the Barn and Grimethorpe Colliery, to name onl a few.

The euphonium is a superb solo instrument with a long tradition, althoug today's audiences are rather ignorant of this fact. What is needed is more exposur and, perhaps, a more broad-minded attitude on the part of audiences and conce organizers. Programs could be enriched by occasional different offerings from th long line of violinists, pianists, and cellists playing the same repertoire over an over.

MISCELLANEOUS

The first use of a mute for the euphonium can be found in Strauss's *Don Quixot* Mutes are infrequently called for in the literature, and it is probably incumber upon the band or orchestra to make one available when required. An exampl of muted writing can also be found in Karel Husa's *Music for Prague 1968* (fc band).

The baritone and euphonium are obviously bass clef instruments; this shoul be the normal practice of notation. There is, however, a longstanding custom o writing for euphonium and baritone as transposing B♭ instruments in the trebl clef (like the cornet), sounding a ninth lower. This is the case in brass bands, an it is common for wind-band parts to be furnished in both treble and bass clef. Thi practice probably came about in order to make it easier for cornet players to switc to other instruments. It is important, therefore, for euphonium players to be equall comfortable in bass or treble clef. An important reason for learning the treble cle is that a great quantity of vital study and solo literature for cornet and trumpe will be made accessible. The tenor clef is useful as well for trombone and bassoo literature. Orchestral players will occasionally have to deal with transposed bas clef parts and other oddities.

Passing mention might be made of double-bell euphoniums although they ar now considered to be valuable antiques. These were popular as solo instrument during the Sousa-Pryor era. The normal tone could be modified by being route through a second smallish bell to produce echo and trombone-like effects. Superio instruments in their time, double-bell euphoniums are sought today as much fo their playing qualities as for the novelty of their design.

RECOMMENDED LITERATURE[3]

Complete Methods

Arban: *Method,* ed. Mantia and Randall (trom.) (C. Fischer)
Saint-Jacome: *Grand Method* (cornet) (C. Fischer)

Elementary Methods

Beeler: *Method* (Warner Bros.)
Ridgeon: *Brass for Beginners* (Boosey & Hawkes)
Wiggins: *First Tunes & Studies* (Oxford)

Studies

Medium to Medium-Difficult

Blume: *36 Studies,* vol. 1 (trom.) (C. Fischer)
Bordogni: *Melodious Etudes,* ed. Rochut, vols. 1 & 2 (trom.) (C. Fischer)
Clarke: *Technical Studies,* ed. Gordon (C. Fischer)
Fink: *From Treble to Bass Clef* (Accura)
Kopprasch: *60 Selected Studies* (trom.) (C. Fischer) (med. to diff.)
Miller: *60 Studies* (R. King)
Mueller: *30 Leichte Etuden* (F. Hofmeister)
Mueller: *Technical Studies,* vols. 1 & 2 (trom.) (C. Fischer)
Parés: *Scales* (Rubank)
Tyrrell: *40 Progressive Studies* (trom.) (Boosey & Hawkes)
Voxman (ed.): *Selected Studies* (Rubank)

Difficult

Blume: *36 Studies,* vol. 2 (trom.) (C. Fischer)
Bordogni: *Melodious Etudes,* ed. Rochut, vol. 3 (trom.) (C. Fischer)
Charlier: *32 Etudes de perfectionnement* (H. Lemoine)
Gordon: *30 Velocity Studies* (trom.) (C. Fischer)
Harris: *Advanced Daily Studies* (C. Colin)
Mueller: *Technical Studies,* vol. 3 (trom.) (C. Fischer)

Unaccompanied Solos

Difficult

Bach: *Dance Movements from the Cello Suites,* transcribed Torchinsky (Schirmer)
Croley: *Sonata* (Philharmusica Corp.)
Paganini: *Caprice 24* (Whaling)

Baritone-Euphonium and Piano[4]

Easy

Adams: *The Holy City* (trom.) (Boosey & Hawkes)
Fearnley (ed.) *More Easy Pieces* (trom.) (Chester)
Gluck: *2 Classic Airs* (trom.) (Editions Musicus)

Essential material is noted with an asterisk. For additional literature, see the *Brass Music Guide* (Robert King) and texts by Bevan, Griffiths, Louder, and Winter.

See Earle L. Louder, "Original Solo Literature and Study Books for Euphonium," *The Instrumentalist,* May 1981, pp. 29–30; also "Begged, Borrowed, and Stolen Solo Euphonium Literature," by Paul Droste in the same issue (pp. 30–32).

Haydn: *Aria & Allegro* (Rubank)
Johnson (ed.): *Sacred Solos* (trom.) (Rubank)
Laycock: *The Dove* (trom.) (Boosey & Hawkes)
Mendelssohn: *On Wings of Song* (trom.) (Boosey & Hawkes)
Mozart: *Arietta & Allegro* (Southern)
Perry (ed.): *Classical Album* (trom.) (Boosey & Hawkes)
Strauss: *Allerseelen* (Rubank)
Wagner: *Song to the Evening Star* (Kendor)

Medium to Medium-Difficult

*Barat: *Andante & Allegro* (trom.) (C. Fischer)
*Capuzzi: *Andante & Rondo* (Hinrichsen)
 Corelli: *Prelude & Minuet* (Southern)
*Cowell: *Tom Binkley's Tune* (Presser)
 Ewald: *Romance* (Editions Musicus)
 Galliard: *6 Sonatas,* transcribed Brown, 2 vols. (trom.) (International)
 Gliere: *Russian Sailors' Dance* (C. Fischer)
 Handel: *Andante & Allegro* (Southern)
 Handel: *Sonata 3* (Southern)
 Marcello: *Adagio* (Whaling)
*Pryor: *Annie Laurie* (trom.) (Ludwig)
*Pryor: *Starlight* (trom.) (C. Fischer)
*Pryor: *Blue Bells of Scotland* (trom.) (C. Fischer)
 Rossini: *Largo al Factotum* (Boosey & Hawkes)
 Senaille: *Allegro Spiritoso* (Southern)
*Simon: *Willow Echoes* (C. Fischer)
 Voxman (ed.): *Concert & Contest Collection* (Rubank)

Difficult

Alary: *Morçeau de Concours* (C. Fischer)
Bach: *Sonatas 1, 2, 3,* arr. Marsteller (Southern)
Barat: *Introduction et serenade* (A. Leduc)
Barat: *Morçeau de concours* (A. Leduc)
*Bellstedt: *Napoli* (Southern)
 Boda: *Sonatina* (tape) (Whaling)
 Brasch: *Fantasy on Weber's Last Waltz* (H. Brasch)
*Clarke: *Sounds from the Hudson* (cornet) (C. Fischer)
*Clarke: *Music of Herbert L. Clarke* (cornet) (Warner Bros.)
 Guilmant: *Morçeau symphonique* (trom.) (Warner Bros.)
 Hartley: *2 Pieces* (Presser)
*Hartley: *Sonata Euphonica* (Presser)
*Horovitz: *Concerto* (Novello)
*Jacob: *Fantasia* (Boosey & Hawkes)
*Mantia: *All Those Endearing Young Charms* (Whaling)
*Pryor: *Thoughts of Love* (trom.) (C. Fischer)
 Saint-Saëns: *Morçeau de concert* (Shawnee)

Baritone-Euphonium Books[5]

*Bevan, Clifford. *The Tuba Family.* New York: Scribner's, 1978.
*Bowman, Brian L. *Practical Hints on Playing the Baritone (Euphonium).* Melville
    N.Y.: Belwin-Mills, 1983.

---

5. Articles of interest to euphonium players appear in *The Instrumentalist,* the *T.U.B.A. Journal,* and other
periodicals listed in Appendix C.

Griffiths, John R. *The Low Brass Guide.* Hackensack, N.J.: Jerona Music, 1980.

Lehman, Arthur. *The Art of Euphonium Playing.* Poughkeepsie, N.Y.: Robert Hoe.

Louder, Earle L. *Euphonium Music Guide.* Evanston, Ill.: Instrumentalist Co., 1978.

Rose, W.H. *Studio Class Manual for Tuba and Euphonium.* Houston, Tex.: Iola Publ., 1980.

Winter, Denis. *Euphonium Music Guide.* New London, Conn.: Whaling Music, 1983.

CHAPTER 7

The Tuba

To the non-tubist, today's tuba world is a confusing jumble of differing keys, valves, compensating systems, and the like. Actually, there is greater order than might at first appear. As with other brass instruments, the variety of available tubas reflects the need for more specialized and improved instruments to fit different performance situations.

There are two broad categories of tuba: bass tubas in F and E♭, and contrabass tubas in C and B♭ (the latter are usually identified as CC and BB♭ tubas—large-bore E♭ tubas are sometimes designated EE♭). Orchestral tubists generally prefer a five-valve CC as a standard instrument (Fig. 7.1), but also use a five-valve or four-valve E♭ for high passages and some solo work. In the United States, the BB♭ is usually considered a band instrument, but it is widely used in orchestras in Germany and Eastern Europe. The E♭ tuba, once familiar in American bands, is now rarely seen as a principal instrument outside England, where it is extensively used in orchestras, brass, and military bands. The E♭ is currently enjoying a revival among American orchestral players as an alternative to the F tuba.

VALVE TYPES

Among the most obvious differences in tubas is that some are built with rotary valves and others with piston valves. In most symphony orchestras one will find a rotary valve instrument in use, yet this does not really represent a preference for one valve type over another. In fact, most professional tubists would prefer to have a piston valve tuba if one could be obtained with sufficiently large bore and bell dimensions. Piston valves offer a cleaner articulation and are generally better in technical passages. Rotary valves, on the other hand, encourage a smooth legato and fluent slurs.

The current predominance of rotary valve tubas came about as a result of the previous unavailability of large-bore piston valve CC tubas suitable for orchestral use. A few such instruments were once made by American manufacturers, but today's output consists almost entirely of medium-bore concert band instruments. To fill this void, orchestral tubists turned to large-bore German tubas which are traditionally made with rotary valves. As these became standardized in American orchestras, they were also adopted by bands and wind ensembles.

Over the past decade, there have been persistent rumors of the reemergence of large piston valve CC tubas. Several models have now made their appearance, such as the Hirsbrunner copy of a half-century-old American York tuba owned by Arnold Jacobs, Principal tuba of the Chicago Symphony. B&S-Perantucci also now offers both rotary and piston valve models, and it is likely that more manufacturers will make new instruments available in the future. In the meantime, considerable attention has been given to improving the action of rotary valves and the overall design of these instruments.

The placement of the valves is an important consideration for the player. On rotary valve tubas, the valve levers are arranged vertically at the center of the instrument. This allows the right arm and hand to be in a relaxed position, which assists finger dexterity. An additional benefit of this layout is that the valve slides

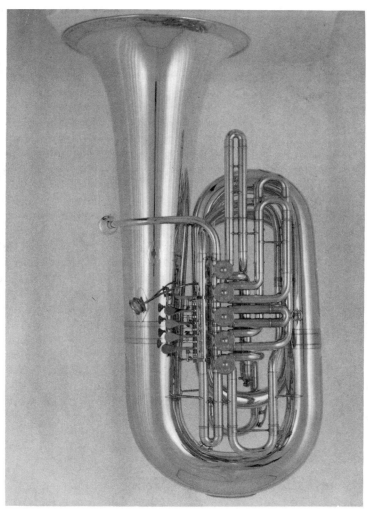

Figure 7.1. Five-valve CC tuba (Alexander).
(Photo courtesy of Gebr. Alexander, Mainz)

directed upward so that they can be moved by the left hand in controlling
onation. The opposite of this is the top-action piston valve tuba in which the
lves are placed horizontally beneath the top bow. Many tubists feel that this
ces the right hand in an uncomfortable position, causing tension. Side-action
ont-action) piston valves, which are located in a position similar to rotary valve
as, offer the same advantages.

DIMENSIONS AND BORE

ere is substantial variation in the size of tubas, not only in bore and bell diameter,
in overall dimensions and weight. For example, BB♭ tubas are made with main
re diameters of .610 inches (15.5mm) to .920 inches (23.4mm). Bell diameters
y vary from 14 3/8 inches (365.55mm) to 24 inches (609.6mm). Weights range
m 6.132 kilograms to 14.512 kilograms.[1]

lifford Bevan, *The Tuba Family* (New York: Scribner's, 1978), p. 126.

Among rotary valve tubas, three general sizes can be distinguished: a small bore of approximately .740 inches (17.8mm), a standard bore of .778 inch (19.7mm), and an extra-large bore of .835 inches (21.2mm). These are sometim identified as 3/4, 4/4, and 5/4 models. There is, however, considerable variatic between manufacturers as to the actual bore used under each label. The large bore sizes are descendants of Václav Cerveny's *kaiserbass*, introduced in the 188((Cerveny produced the first contrabass tubas in CC and BB♭ in 1845).

CC tubas are built in the same large-bore sizes as BB♭s. This gives the CC ﹤ equal volume of tone, while preserving its advantages in fingering and projectic The bores of orchestral (5-valve CC) tubas are usually in the range of .778 .835 inches, but even larger bores are sometimes used. Thus far, the largest pist(valve CC is .750″ (Hirsbrunner-York). Typical F tuba bore sizes are .681 inch (17.3mm) to .770 inches (19.5mm). E♭ tuba bores usually average around .7: inches (18.5mm). (In comparison, 3-valve student models in BB♭ generally r(from .610 inches [15.5mm] to .670 inches [17mm].)

Tubas may be wrapped in a compact or more open pattern, with heights varyil from 33 inches (838.2mm) to 48 inches (1219.2mm). Some players feel that tl more compact instruments are rather stuffy in response because of sharp bends the tubing (the latter are sometimes referred to by tubists as "piggies"). The heig of the largest instruments sometimes presents problems to individual players wl must alter their playing position to reach the mouthpiece.

The variables of key, bore, and so forth, allow tubists to adapt more ful to the needs of differing repertoire. For example, an orchestral tubist might u a large-bore CC in performances of Bruckner and Wagner, but change to smaller instrument for less massive compositions. Similarly, an F or E♭ tul would probably be chosen for the high register solos in *Bydlo* from *Pictures an Exhibition* (Mussorgsky-Ravel) and *Petrushka* (Stravinsky).

VALVE SYSTEMS

If the valve systems fitted to modern tubas appear complex, it should be not(that the first tuba (in 1835) by Wieprecht and Moritz was a five-valve model F. Today, tubists generally agree that three valves are inadequate, while six valv(are excessive. On standard four- and five-valve models, the purpose of the add(valves should be kept in mind.

Unlike the trumpet, the fundamental of the tuba's harmonic series is a ful usable note. A fourth valve is added to extend the range downward from the low(valve combination (1–2–3) to the fundamental, since notes of the chromatic octa from the fundamental to the 2nd partial are often called for by composers. Tl sharpness caused when valves are used in combination is severe in this octav although intonation can be corrected to some extent by pulling valve slides (individual notes. The best solution is a fifth valve, which affords a greater selecti(of fingerings and yields the most accurate intonation in this range. Six-valve tub(were developed for players who wish to use the F tuba as their principal instrumei The sixth valve enables these instruments to cover the same range as the CC. M(tubists (outside France) find the six-valve arrangement overly complex and pref a five-valve system.

USING THE FOURTH AND FIFTH VALVE

Greater mechanical correction is necessary on the tuba than on other bra instruments due to the length of the vibrating air columns. The most effecti method of controlling intonation is moving valve slides while playing. In order move, the valve slides must go upward, as on rotary valve and side-action tub; On instruments of this type, all but the second valve slide are accessible to the l(

hand, with the first slide being used most often. The fourth and fifth valves come into play in the lowest octave and are used in combination with the adjustment of valve slides to center pitches in this range.

The fourth valve not only extends the range down to the fundamental, but offers an alternative to the sharp 1–3 and 1–2–3 fingerings:

To correct intonation, the valve slide should be pulled out for all fingerings circled (○).
When an arrow is added to the circle (↻), the valve slide should be pushed inward.

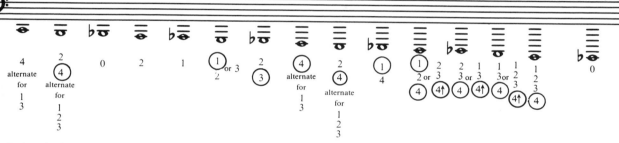

It is obvious that all tubas, except perhaps for inexpensive models intended for beginners, should be made with at least four valves. The four-valve system does have its limitations, however. The semitone above the fundamental is almost unusable, and it is only through the addition of a fifth valve that truly accurate intonation and a centered sound can be achieved.

In a five-valve system, the first four valves function as in the four-valve system. The fifth valve lowers the fundamental either five-quarters of a tone or two whole tones, depending on the length of the valve slide. The former is sometimes known as a "flat whole step" system and the latter as a "2/3" system (the 2/3 refers to the 5th valve's intervallic similarity to the normal 2–3 fingering which also lowers the fundamental by two tones). Either system is effective and the choice of one over the other is a matter of individual preference.

In the "flat whole step" mode, the fifth valve is used as follows:

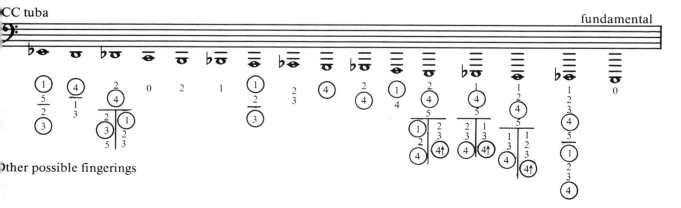

Other possible fingerings

The fingering pattern for the "two-tone lower" system is:

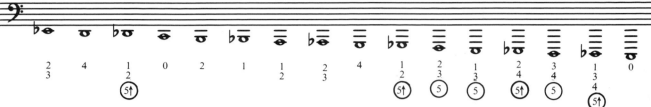

CC tuba

The same four–valve fingering possibilities as with the "flat whole step" system are available.

The well-known tubist Roger Bobo has recommended that a trigger mechanism be fitted to the fifth valve slide to facilitate its adjustment.

Another difference in five-valve systems is how the fifth valve is operated. On many tubas, an actuating lever is placed adjacent to the thumb ring with linkage connecting it to the fifth valve. Other models have a spatula attached directly to the fifth valve which is operated with the left hand. The disadvantage of the latter arrangement is that the left hand is not free to adjust valve slides when the fifth valve is in use. Roger Bobo has advocated a dual linkage which would enable the player to operate the valve with either hand, as desired.

THE AUTOMATIC COMPENSATING SYSTEM

An entirely different approach to the problem of low-register intonation is the compensating system, devised in 1874 by the English acoustician David Blaikley, which is incorporated in some baritones, euphoniums, and tubas.[2] In this system corrective lengths of tubing are automatically added when the fourth valve is used in combination with the other valves. While the Blaikley system does not solve all intonation problems, it works quite well. Thus far, however, it has only been available in top-action, medium-bore instruments. Tubas of this type are used almost exclusively in British orchestras, bands, and brass ensembles.

INTONATION

In addition to the intonation difficulties of the lower range, the tubist must also be prepared to cope with some problem notes in the middle and upper registers. No absolute rules can be set, for individual instruments vary in this respect. This is a fertile period in the development of the tuba, and one of the prime goals is improved intonation. The cardinal rule is for tubists to get to know their own instrument.

Faulty intonation is corrected by substituting an alternate fingering, moving a valve slide, or combining these measures. Whenever possible, it is preferable to adjust a note mechanically rather than with the lip because of the negative effect on tone and stability caused by forcing an off-center note into tune with the embouchure. Through careful practice, tubists learn to incorporate the necessary slide movements into their normal technique.

The current trend among manufacturers of high-quality tubas is to shorten the outer tubes of the valve slides (as is customary with the horn) to allow more room for slide adjustment. The chart below applies to this type of instrument. On older tubas, more use of alternate fingerings would probably be necessary.

2. The Blaikley system is discussed more fully in Chapter 6.

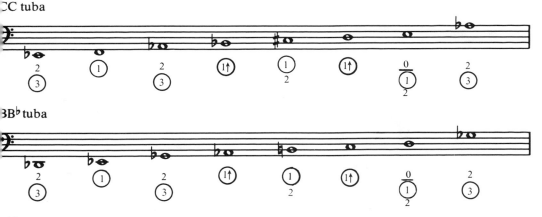

The fifth partial might be flat when played open.

it is, it may be played 1-2 while pulling out the first valve slide. The 1-2 combination tends to be sharp an octave lower and some adjustment of the slide will probably be necessary to correct it. An electronic tuner should be used to determine the best means of correction for other notes.

Regardless of how well the tubist can learn to play in tune with himself, he must be prepared to make further adjustments when performing in an ensemble. Within a brass section, the tubist must listen intently to the first trombone and first trumpet to provide a clear sense of pitch for the inner players to match.

BB♭ AND CC TUBAS

The preference of American orchestral tubists for the CC instrument is based on three factors. First, like the C trumpet, the CC tuba responds well in making "cold" entrances and is particularly flexible. Second, since orchestras frequently play in sharp keys, the awkward fingerings that would result if a BB♭ instrument were used is avoided. The third factor is that the timbre of the CC tuba projects with greater clarity. Some players find little difference in tone between the two instruments, but others, particularly German and Eastern European performers, have a definite partiality for the tone of the BB♭.

The BB♭ tuba remains the primary band instrument, but CC tubas are sometimes used in schools of music since tuba majors are accustomed to playing the CC as their principal instrument. It is important, however, that, when parts are doubled by more than one player, the same key instrument is used to avoid conflicts in intonation. At one time, bell-front or recording-bell tubas were often seen in large bands, but these have been replaced by standard upright bell models. The directionality of the forward-radiating bell tended to lose the characteristic roundness of the tuba's timbre.

E♭ AND F TUBAS

E♭ and F tubas are predominantly used as auxiliary instruments to the normal CC when high passages are encountered or when a lighter sound is desirable (Figs.

Figure 7.2. EE♭ tuba (Besson), played by the legendary British tubist, the late John Fletcher.
(Photo courtesy of Decca Records International)

Figure 7.3. F tuba (R. Meinl), played by Sco Mendoker, New York freelance artist.
(Photo courtesy of S. Mendok

7.2 and 7.3). In British orchestras and military and brass bands, a large-bo E♭ (EE♭) is commonly used as a principal instrument. (Brass bands have a pair BB♭s and EE♭s).

The first British tubists were former euphonium players who sought an instr ment that retained some of the euphonium's technical flexibility and response. small-bore piston valve tuba in F was developed and this provided an agreeab "bottom" to orchestral brass sections until the end of the second world war.[3] Up that time, smaller bore trumpets, trombones, and French-type piston valve hor were mainly in use. In the postwar years as brass sections adopted larger instr ments, British tubists changed to the brass band EE♭, which combines a fuller tor with much of the F's flexibility.

Rotary valve F tubas are often used on the European continent (particular in German orchestras), along with contrabass models. An important applicatio of the E♭ and F tubas is in the brass quintet, where their lighter timbres for a more effective balance than a contrabass. Unfortunately, in many quintets, th misbalance created by the consuming tone of the BB♭ or CC is accepted witho question.[4]

THE FRENCH SIX-VALVE C TUBA

Although practically obsolete today, the French C tuba is of interest because the large body of solo literature and orchestral parts by French composers writte

3. Ralph Vaughan Williams wrote his technically demanding *Bass Tuba Concerto* for the F tuba.

4. An idea of the degree of balance that can be achieved with an EE♭ may be gained by listening to the ma recordings of the Philip Jones Brass Ensemble. The superb player on these recordings was the late John Fletch principal tubist of the London Symphony Orchestra.

r it. In reality, it is an extended-range tenor tuba pitched one tone higher than
e euphonium. Through the addition of two sets of valves (one for each hand)
full four octaves is obtainable, from the lowest notes of the contrabass CC
to the normal euphonium range. Parts for this unusual instrument have caused
onfusion, since both the range and technical demands are not well suited to bass
d contrabass tubas. French solo literature is often neglected for this reason.

The concept of a tenor-sized bass for the brass section is not as peculiar as it
ay seem. French composers have always shown a predilection for mixtures of
early defined timbres rather than a blend of sound. The C tuba was well-suited
this aesthetic, while offering additional possibilities as a solo instrument. Such
rts, as are found in Stravinsky's *Petrushka, Rite of Spring,* and the *Bydlo* solo in
avel's transcription of Mussorgsky's *Pictures at an Exhibition,* are an indication
the capabilities of this unique instrument.

In French orchestras today, six-valve F or contrabass tubas in C are used for the
ajority of the repertoire, while the French C is reserved for the solos originally
tended for it.

THE TUBA MUTE

ichard Strauss was the first to write for the muted tuba in *Don Quixote* (1897).
ince composers now call for the muted timbre with some regularity, a mute is
ow considered a necessary part of the tubist's regular equipment. The problem
to find a mute that fits the bell taper accurately and plays in tune. Tuba mutes
e normally in straight-mute form, but a few of the other shapes (such as the
elvet-tone and practice mutes) have now become available.

NOTATION

acking any historical convention that the fundamental must be written as C
s the horn and trumpet), the BB♭, E♭, and F tubas function as nontransposing
struments with the player using the appropriate fingering to yield concert pitch.
/hen more than one tuba is used, such as the CC or F, the player must learn a
ifferent set of fingerings for each instrument. There are exceptions to this practice.
British brass bands, all instruments except the bass trombone are considered
ansposing instruments and read in the treble clef. The bass tuba in E♭ is treated
s a transposing instrument in much of the French solo literature, although parts
r the six-valve C tuba are usually included (in French C tuba parts there is some
se of the nontransposed treble clef). This is often the practice in French band
cores and in some of Verdi's operas.

In order to have access to a greater variety of study material, it is important
r tubists to develop the ability to read down an octave. This brings trombone
nd euphonium literature into a practicable range. It is also helpful to be able to
ead treble clef in order to perform etudes and solos written for trumpet and horn.

THE GOLDEN AGE OF THE TUBA

he last two and one-half decades have seen more activity in the tuba world
an in any period of its history. Today's generation of tubists are no longer
ontent to remain in the background and have broken through barriers that were
onsidered impassable even 30 years ago. There are now several internationally
ecognized soloists, but the most striking aspect of the movement is the incredibly
igh standard of playing which is now taken for granted. In fact, the point has been

reached where the best players feel limited by the instruments currently availab
Consequently, there is great demand for improved tubas and new developmen
are constantly appearing.

Many of these developments are concerned with improving the action of rota
valves through more direct linkages and lighter rotors. The bell, in particular, is t
subject of current research; differing rims, mid-bell bands, and various tapers a
flares are being tested. Intonation is another area of concern. Traditional yello
or gold brass remains the preferred material, but metallurgical research is no
being directed toward the influence of material on tone quality. Lacquer is usua
avoided because of its deadening effect on response.

Tubists are looking to the next decade to bring significantly improved tub
which will spur an even higher standard of performance.

RECOMMENDED LITERATURE[5]

Complete Methods

*Arban: *Famous Method for Slide and Valve Trombone and Baritone,* ed. Rand
and Mantia (read octave down) (C. Fischer)
*Arban: *Arban-Bell Method* (C. Colin)
 Beeler: *Method,* 2 vols. (Warner Bros.)
 Bell: *Complete Method* (Colin)
 Geib: *Method* (C. Fischer)

Elementary Methods

*Arban: *Method,* 1st and 2nd year, ed. Prescott (C. Fischer)
*Bell: *Foundation to Tuba Playing* (C. Fischer)
 Endresen: *Method for E♭ Tuba* (M.M. Cole)
 Hovey: *Rubank Elementary Method* (Rubank)
 Kuhn-Cimera: *Method* (Belwin)

Studies

Medium to Medium-Difficult

 Bell: *Blazhevich Interpretations* (C. Colin)
 Bordogni: *43 Bel Canto Studies,* transcribed Roberts (R. King)
*Concone: *Legato Etudes,* ed. Shoemaker (C. Fischer)
*Endresen: *Supplementary Studies* (Rubank)
 Fink: *Studies in Legato* (C. Fischer)
 Getchell: *Practical Studies,* 2 vols. (Belwin-Mills)
 Gower and Voxman: *Rubank Advanced Method,* 2 vols. (Rubank)
 Knaub: *Progressive Techniques* (Belwin)
 Little: *Embouchure Builder* (Pro Art)
*Parès: *Scales* (Rubank)
*Schlossberg: *Daily Drills and Technical Studies* (trom.) (M. Baron) (8va) (med. t
 diff.)
 Skornicka and Boltz: *Rubank Intermediate Method* (Rubank)
 Uber: *25 Early Studies* (Southern)

Difficult

 Bach: *Bach for Tuba,* transcribed Bixby and Bobo (Western International)
*Blazhevich: *70 Studies* (R. King)

---

5. Essential material is noted with an asterisk. For additional literature, see the *Brass Music Guide* (Robert King
Repertoire lists appear in the texts by Bell, Bevan, Griffiths, and Morris.

Cimera: *73 Advanced Studies* (Belwin-Mills)
Gallay: *30 Studies* (R. King)
Kopprasch: *60 Studies* (R. King) (med. to diff.)
Kuehn: *28 Advanced Studies* (Southern)
Kuehn: *60 Musical Studies,* 2 vols. (Southern)
Robinson: *Advanced Conditioning Studies* (Whaling)
Tyrrell: *Advanced Studies* (Boosey & Hawkes)
Uber: *Concert Etudes* (Southern)
Vasiliev: *24 Melodious Etudes* (R. King)

Unaccompanied Tuba

Difficult

Adler: *Canto VII* (Boosey & Hawkes)
Arnold: *Fantasy* (Faber)
Frackenpohl: *Studies on Christmas Carols* (Kendor)
Hartley: *Suite* (Presser)
Persichetti: *Parable* (Presser)
Persichetti: *Serenade No. 12* (Presser)
Tuthill: *Tiny Tunes for Tuba* (Presser)
Wilder: *Convalescence Suite* (Margun Music)

Tuba and Piano

Easy

Adams: *The Holy City* (Kjos)
Bach: *Air and Bourreé,* arr. Bell and Swanson (C. Fischer)
Bach: *Gavotte,* arr. Smith (Belwin-Mills)
Bell: *Melodious Etude* (Belwin-Mills)
Bell: *Gavotte* (C. Fischer)
Bell: *Jig Elephantine* (C. Fischer)
Bell: *Low Down Bass* (C. Fischer)
Bell: *Nautical John* (C. Fischer)
Bizet: *Toreador's Song,* arr. Holmes (Rubank)
Grieg: *In the Hall of the Mountain King,* arr. Holmes (Rubank)
Handel: *Honor & Arms from Samson* (Schirmer)
Kreisler: *Rondo* (Southern)
Schumann: *The Jolly Farmer* (C. Fischer)
Vekselblatt (ed.): *First Solos for the Tuba Player* (Schirmer)

Medium to Medium-Difficult

Beethoven: *Variations on a Theme by Handel,* arr. Bell (C. Fischer)
Benson: *Arioso* (Belwin)
Benson: *Helix* (C. Fischer)
Capuzzi: *Andante & Rondo* (Hinrichsen)
Davis: *Variations on a Theme of Robert Schumann* (Southern)
Fletcher: *Tuba Solos* (Chester)
Haddad: *Suite* (Shawnee)
Jacob: *6 Little Tuba Pieces* (Emerson Ed.)
Jacob: *Tuba Suite* (Boosey & Hawkes)
Ostling (ed.): *Tuba Solos,* 2 vols. (Belwin)
Ostrander (ed.): *Concert Album* (Editions Musicus)
Phillips: *8 Bel Canto Songs* (Shawnee)
Reed: *Fantasia a due* (Belwin)

Senaille: *Introduction and Allegro Spiritoso* (Hinrichsen)
Voxman (ed.): *Concert & Contest Collection* (Rubank)
Wekselblatt (ed.): *Solos for the Tuba Player* (Schirmer)

Difficult

Barat: *Introduction & Dance,* arr. Smith (Southern)
Bellstedt: *Introduction & Tarantella* (Southern)
Beversdorf: *Sonata* (Southern)
Boda: *Sonatina* (R. King)
Childs: *Seaview* (M.M. Cole)
Frackenpohl: *Sonata* (Kendor)
Gregson: *Concerto* (Novello)
Hartley: *Sonatina* (Fema Music)
*Hindemith: *Sonate* (Schott)
*Jacob: *Bagatelles* (Emerson Ed.)
Koetsier: *Sonatina* (Donemus)
Nelybel: *Concert Piece* (E.C. Kerby)
*Salzedo: *Sonata* (Chester)
*Vaughan Williams: *Concerto* (Oxford)
*Vaughan Williams: *6 Studies in English Folksong* (Galaxy)
*White: *Sonata* (Ludwig)
*Wilder: *Sonata* (Mentor)
*Wilder: *Suite No. 1* (Margun)

Books on the Tuba[6]

Bell, William. *Encyclopedia of Literature for the Tuba.* New York: Charles Col[
1967.
*Bevan, Clifford. *The Tuba Family.* New York: Scribner's, 1978.
*Cummings, Barton. *The Contemporary Tuba.* New London, Conn.: Whali[
Music, 1984.
Griffiths, John R. *The Low Brass Guide.* Hackensack, N.J.: Jerona Music, 198(
Little, Donald C. *Practical Hints on Playing the Tuba.* Melville, N.Y.: Belwin-Mil[
1984.
Mason, J. Kent. *The Tuba Handbook.* Toronto: Sonante, 1977.
*Morris, R. Winston. *Tuba Music Guide.* Evanston, Ill.: Instrumentalist Co., 197[
*Randolph, David Mark. "New Techniques in the Avant-Garde Repertoire for So[
Tuba." D.M.A. thesis, University of Rochester, 1978. UM 78-11, 493.
Rose, W.H. *Studio Class Manual for Tuba and Euphonium.* Houston, Tex.: Io[
1980.
Sorenson, Richard A. "Tuba Pedagogy: A Study of Selected Method Book[
1840–1911." Ph.D. dissertation, University of Colorado, 1972. U[
73-1832.
*Stewart, Dee. *Arnold Jacobs: The Legacy of a Master.* Northfield, Ill.: Instrume[
talist Publishing Co., 1987.

---

6. Many interesting articles appear in the *T.U.B.A. Journal* (published by the Tubists' Universal Brotherho[
Association) and other periodicals listed in Appendix C.

CHAPTER 8
More Brass

FLUGELHORN

The flugelhorn derives its name from the curved horn that was used for signaling by the *flügelmeister* during hunts in 18th-century Germany. Subsequently adopted as the *halbmond* (half-moon, denoting its shape) for military purposes, it was later modified to the bugle shape we know today (Fig. 8.1). In 1810, an English bandmaster, Joseph Halliday, fitted the instrument with keys, and in this form it was known as the Royal Kent bugle. In Germany, the instrument was known as the *Klappenflügelhorn*. When valves replaced the key system, the flugelhorn found its modern form; models are now made with both piston and rotary valves.

Piston valve flugelhorns are constructed basically in a trumpet format, but with a very widely wrapped bell section and with the mouthpipe going directly into the first valve. Models with rotary valves are played on the side in the manner of the rotary valve trumpet. Although the Bb flugelhorn covers the same range as the trumpet, its tone is almost totally opposite because of the broad conically shaped bell. The attractive, softly mellow timbre was used to haunting effect by Ralph Vaughan Williams in the opening of his Ninth Symphony. Other composers who have made effective use of the flugelhorn are Stravinsky in *Threni,* and Respighi in *The Pines of Rome,* where flugelhorns are used to recreate the sound of the Roman *buccina.*

Flugelhorns are used only when required by the score in American and British bands, but are a mainstay of European bands. An Eb flugelhorn is made in Europe; it is known as the *petit bugle* in France and the *pikkolo* in Germany. The flugelhorn is included in the standard instrumentation of British brass bands where it normally doubles the repiano[1] cornet and enjoys occasional solo passages. It is also widely used in German brass ensembles. In the jazz field, the flugelhorn has come into prominence as a solo voice and is considered a normal part of the trumpeter's equipment. There are several internationally known jazz soloists who play flugelhorn exclusively.[2]

ALTO (TENOR) HORN

The primary use today of the Eb alto horn (Fig. 8.2)—or as it is known in Britain, tenor horn—is in the brass band, where the standard instrumentation calls for a section of three.[3] It is also used to some degree in European and Russian military bands. Alto horns were once popular in American concert bands as a substitute for the French horn, but this is no longer the case. Bell-front versions were the principal alto-range brass of American marching bands—again substituting for the French horn. These have largely been replaced by derivative instruments such

1. In British brass bands this part has always been called repiano, not *ripieno.*
2. For additional information on the flugelhorn, see Frederick Allan Beck, "The Flugelhorn: Its History and Literature" (D.M.A. thesis, University of Rochester, 1979), UM 79-21, 124.
3. See Clifford Bevan, *The Tuba Family* (New York: Scribner's, 1978), pp. 24–35.

Figure 8.1. Flugelhorn (Besson).   *(Photo courtesy of the Boosey & Hawkes Group)*

as the marching mellophone[4] (actually an alto horn wrapped in flugelhorn shape with a more widely flaring bell).

The somewhat confusing designations for instruments of this family should be kept in mind:

	U.S.	*Britain*	*Germany*	*France*	*Italy*
E♭	Alto horn	Tenor horn	Althorn	Alto	Genis
B♭	Baritone	Baritone	Tenorhorn	Baryton	Flicorno Tenore
B♭	Euphonium	Euphonium	Baryton	Basse	Eufonio

Based on information in Bevan, *The Tuba Family*.

During the era when alto horns were used in concert bands, it was found that constructing the instrument in a round, horn-like shape would result in a better imitation of horn sound. The new instrument was termed the mellophone (in England, the tenor cor) and was equipped with right-hand piston valves, and a mouthpiece that was somewhat larger and more cup-shaped than the horn. Although easy to play, it lacked the true tone color of the horn and fell into disuse as horn players became more plentiful.

4. Substitutes for the French horn in marching bands are discussed below.

Figure 8.2. E♭ alto (tenor) horn, played by British soloist Gordon Higginbottom.
(Photo courtesy of G. Higginbottom)

German alto horns are usually constructed in the traditional oval shape with rotary valves and have a somewhat fuller tone. It was for this instrument that Hindemith composed his 1943 *Sonata für Althorn,* although it is now usually performed on the French horn.

BASS TRUMPET

Natural bass trumpets, usually in E♭ or B♭, were commonly found in German cavalry bands in the early 19th century. After the invention of valves, chromatic instruments continued to be a feature of mounted bands throughout the century. The chief interest in the bass trumpet today is that Richard Wagner, seeking a broader spectrum of timbres, wrote for it in *The Ring.* Modern bass trumpets are built in C or B♭, with rotary or piston valves (Fig. 8.3). Due to the size of its mouthpiece, the bass trumpet is always played by a trombonist rather than a trumpeter. The instrument produces a clearly defined tone, distinct from the trombone; it was this quality that was exploited in Wagner's scoring.

Figure 8.3. Bass trumpet (Bach).

(Photo courtesy of the Selmer Company, Elkhart, Indiana)

VALVE TROMBONE

Although greeted with interest when they made their appearance in the 1820
valve trombones (Fig. 8.4) ultimately failed to hold their own against the con
ventional slide instrument. The inherent intonation difficulties in the valve syster
and the lack of an effective means of correction (other than the lip) made the ir
strument unequal to the almost total pitch control afforded by the movable slid
The valve trombone also compared unfavorably in timbre. The valve trombon
did find acceptance in situations where use of a moving slide was inconvenien
such as cavalry bands. Deficiencies aside, some bands adopted the valve trom
bone for the technical facility it offered. Italian bands, in particular, were note
for dazzling technical displays by their all-valve brass sections. In the 20th cen

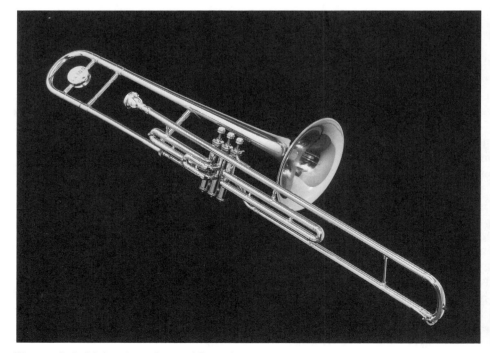

Figure 8.4. Valve trombone (Conn).

(Photo courtesy of Conn, a member company of United Musical Instruments, U.S.A., Inc.)

tury, the valve trombone has found an important niche in jazz, where its agility has made it a favorite solo instrument.

Valve trombones have been made with both piston and rotary valves. Rotary valve models sometimes have the bell angled upward to increase the directionality of the sound toward the audience.

CONTRABASS TROMBONE

Apparently an *octav-posaune* existed during the Renaissance, but how, and to what extent the instrument was actually used, remain obscure. Wagner called for a contrabass trombone in the score to *The Ring,* and an instrument was specially constructed an octave below the B♭ tenor trombone. This instrument utilized double tubing in its slide so that the feel would be similar to the tenor instrument. Contrabass parts also occur in operas by Verdi. Today, such parts are played on a double-valved version (sometimes called the *cimbasso*) in which the coupled valves convert the instrument to low B♭, or on one of the double-trigger bass trombones, often with an extension to C. At one time, contrabass trombones were made with rotary valves—one of these remains in use in the Vienna Philharmonic.

HISTORICAL BRASS

The past two-and-one-half decades have witnessed a phenomenal revival of instruments which had previously been unused for over two centuries or more. From the first uncertain attempts, performances of early music have grown to the point that today's leading groups routinely attain first-rate standards of precision, technique, and intonation (see Figs. 8.5, 8.6, and 8.7). The underlying principle in such performances is the desire to hear music as it would have been heard by the composer and audiences of his time. The cornerstone of the early music revival is the use of authentic instruments whose timbres differ markedly from their modern counterparts. Of equal importance is the employment of stylistic procedures that musicians of the time would probably have followed. In this way, historical performances attempt to convey a more faithful realization of the composer's intentions.

The success of this approach is demonstrated by the fact that new recordings of Baroque music made with modern instruments are becoming increasingly rare, and several early music groups have achieved international status. The movement has now reached forward to Berlioz, and one wonders just how far the quest for authenticity will ultimately extend.

Reconstructions of natural trumpets and horns are a feature of orchestras specializing in Baroque performance. There are a number of outstanding soloists active on the natural trumpet, including Michael Laird, Crispian Steele-Perkins, Friedemann Immer, Edward Tarr, and Don Smithers. Trumpeters no longer need to speculate as to how Bach's trumpet parts may have sounded in his time, but may choose from among several representative recordings. Excellent performances on natural horns can also be heard via recordings.[5]

In Renaissance music, the cornett[6] and sackbut are widely used in various types of consort. Through the efforts of Don Smithers, Michael Laird, the instrument maker Christopher Monk, and others, the cornett has regained its position as an

5. A most convincing demonstration of the hand horn is offered by Hermann Baumann's account of the Mozart horn concertos (Telefunken 6.41272).

6. Although the cornett is made of leather-covered wood and has finger holes, its method of tone production is that of a brass instrument.

Figure 8.5. Natural trumpet (William Bull, 1680), played by Crispian Steele-Perkins.

(Photo: John Edwards, courtesy of C. Steele-Perkins)

Figure 8.6. Natural trumpets, played by (l–r) David Staff and Michael Laird before a performance of Beethoven's Third Symphony at Queen Elizabeth Hall, London.   *(Photo courtesy of Michael Laird)*

Figure 8.7. Sackbuts and cornets, played by "His Majesties Sagbutts & Cornetts."

(Photo: Julion Nieman, courtesy of His Majesties Sagbutts & Cornetts, Jeremy West, Director)

agile solo voice in 16th- and 17th-century music. Consorts of cornetts and sackbuts bring a light, expressive character to pieces by the Gabrielis, Matthew Locke, John Adson, and others. Performers in modern brass ensembles can gain much stylistic insight by listening to such performances.

Along with the many achievements of today's early music movement, some difficulties might be noted as well. Problems of authenticity are more apparent in the brass than in other areas, such as the use of trombones with re-formed bells in place of genuine sackbuts. Due to their larger bore, such hybrids sound more

ke trombones than sackbuts. Authentic sackbuts are capable of great subtlety
1 blending with almost any instrumental combination and possess a near-vocal
mbre. These qualities are lost with the recycled modern instruments. Another
roblem of authenticity involves the use of finger holes ("clarino holes") which
re commonly incorporated in reconstructions of Baroque trumpets to correct the
itch of certain partials. These additions were unknown during 17th and 18th
enturies, when players were taught to lip the sharp partials into tune.[7] Baroque
orn parts, which were played with the instrument raised and no hand in the bell,
re commonly played on copies of early 19th-century horns using handstopping, a
echnique that did not become common until after 1750. The unevenness between
topped and open tones—while appropriate in later music—sounds particularly
nachronistic in Baroque music.

"Clarino holes" and handstopping are functions of the perceived need to
roduce intonation that is acceptable to modern audiences. In the author's view,
he natural intonation of the open partials contributes a certain rustic quality to the
Baroque horn, which is lost when handstopping is used. If authenticity is indeed the
oal, one might ask whether the natural trumpet should not be approached with
he same technique as the great 18th-century masters, such as Gottfried Reiche.
Compromises of this sort raise a more serious question: are we genuine in wishing
o hear music performed as it actually was in its own time, or must we have it
onform to 20th-century ears?

These issues aside, there are splendid historical performances available today,
nd they should be carefully studied by all brass players.

BRASS IN THE MARCHING BAND

Aside from military and community bands, marching bands in the United States
re in reality football and competition bands, specialized for performance in the
pen air. In Britain, bandsmen take the same instruments[8] on the march as they
lay in concerts, but the trend toward specialization in America has created a
demand for instruments specifically designed for outdoor performance. In earlier
ears, this took the form of bell-front baritones, alto horns, and Sousaphones to
ncrease the directionality of sound and provide a more equal balance. Today,
argely because of the drum corps influence, an entire range of new instruments
known as "marching brass" has been created.

Various alternatives to the French horn have been tried over the years, since the
orn is basically unsuited to the needs of school and college marching bands. The
Eb alto horn[9] served as a worthy substitute for the French horn, providing a horn-
ike timbre[10] and (with high-quality instruments) reliable intonation. Following
he stylistic trend toward the drum corps, however, many directors abandoned the
onally inconspicuous alto horn for more powerful instruments.

Trumpets built in low F or Eb were tried, but these were found to be unsatis-
actory in tone and intonation. Next came the circular, forward-facing mellopho-
nium and the frumpet, which combined the broad bell-throat of the horn with a
rumpet-shaped body. These continue to be used in many bands today. The latest
developments are the marching mellophone (in F), which is played bugle fash-
on, and the marching French horn. Pitched in F or Bb, the latter attempt to retain

7. A point raised by Don Smithers, Klaus Wogram, and John Bowsher in "Playing the Baroque Trumpet," *Scientific American* (April 1986), pp. 108–115.
8. French horns, cornets, and upright euphoniums and tubas are used in British military bands.
9. Some alto horns are pitched in F and supplied with an Eb tuning slide. The alto horn is also known as the ltonium.
10. Especially with instruments having upright bells.

more of the French horn's round construction and bell flare in a forward-radiating format. Each of the instruments mentioned has its advocates, and only careful trial and error will establish their relative merits. Intonation is the critical factor, and this is where most of the problems occur.

Regular horn mouthpieces may be used on marching French horns and frumpets, but a larger shank is required for the other instruments. In such cases, horn players can use shank adapters or try to play on the mouthpiece supplied with the instrument. While the instrument will function better with the supplied mouthpiece, the broad rim often has a negative effect on the hornist's embouchure. A better solution (if a mouthpiece maker is accessible) is to modify the original mouthpiece to incorporate the narrow horn rim and a more conical cup, while retaining the normal backbore and shank. It would be helpful if instrument manufacturers provided alternative mouthpieces of this type.

Again from the drum corps influence, several firms now produce compact bugle-shaped marching baritones and (valve) trombones. Some years ago, Sousaphones made of fiberglass made their appearance offering lower cost and lightness, but there is a definite sacrifice in tone in comparison to the usual brass instruments. Small upright tubas with convertible leadpipes are sometimes used in place of Sousaphones. These are played bell-forward, resting on the tubist's shoulder.

Suggestions to Marching Band Directors

Brass players in marching bands should strive for an unforced, well-articulated and sustained sound. A crisp and uniform attack gives sharpness and excitement to the sound and focuses it in the distance. Good balance and sustaining work together to bring resonance and fullness to the sound. Many bands actually lose sound by encouraging a heavy emphasis from note to note, rather than a consistent effort to "blow through the notes." Smaller bands can often convey an impression of greater size by using their sound well.

In addition to stressing the sustained approach, directors should emphasize that notes and chords be played as broadly as possible due to the absence of ambience in the outdoor environment. A good procedure is to make certain that notes do not diminish before their release, and to designate the beginning of the following beat as the release point. It is the combination of balance, sustaining, and a broad style that brings resonance and fullness to brass in the open air.

One of the most common problems in marching bands today is poor intonation and tone quality. Intonation difficulties are most obvious in the alto range with the various substitutes for French horn. In addition to careful tuning, the use of octave and chord studies as a daily warm-up will do much to improve the sound. These should be played at low- to medium-volume levels while concentrating on an unforced, balanced, and in-tune sound. Careful listening and matching will soon lead to an improved concept of sound that will carry over into the performance.

CHAPTER 9

Outlines of the Historical Development of Brass Instruments

The historical outlines that follow note the principal points in the development of the major brass instruments. The outlines are horizontally aligned to show concurrent developments in the four areas and to provide an overview of the development of the brass family.

Museum collections often give a rather incoherent picture by displaying instruments (like the omnitonic horn) that are interesting visually, but were little-used in actual practice. Written accounts, too, sometimes leave the reader in doubt as to which instrument is likely to have been used in an orchestra in a particular era. In the interest of space, the outlines have been kept as concise as possible while attempting to convey an accurate impression of the main instruments in use in each period. Important solo compositions are noted along the way. For those interested in pursuing the history of brass instruments, the following books are recommended (other sources are listed in the bibliography).

Baines, Anthony. *Brass Instruments: Their History and Development.* London: Faber and Faber, 1976.

Mende, Emilie. *Pictorial Family Tree of Brass Instruments in Europe Since the Early Middle Ages.* Moudon, Switzerland: Editions BIM, 1978.

Carse, Adam. *Musical Wind Instruments.* London: Macmillan, 1940. Reprint: Da Capo Press, 1965.

Bate, Philip. *The Trumpet and Trombone:* An Outline of Their History, Development, and Construction. 2nd ed. London: Ernest Benn, 1978. New York: Norton, 1978.

Bendinelli, Cesare. *The Entire Art of Trumpet Playing, 1614.* Nashville: Brass Press, 1975.

Eichborn, Hermann. *The Old Art of Clarino Playing on Trumpets.* Trans. by Bryan A. Simms. Denver, Colo.: Tromba Publications, 1976.

Enrico, Eugene. *The Orchestra at San Petronio in the Baroque Era.* Washington, D.C.: Smithsonian Institution Press, 1976.

Fantini, Girolamo. *Modo per imparare a sonare di Tromba: A Modern Edition of Girolamo Fantini's Trumpet Method.* Boulder, Colo.: Empire Printing, 1977.

Smithers, Don. L. *The Music and History of the Baroque Trumpet Before 1721.* London: Dent, 1973.

Dahlqvist, Reine. *The Keyed Trumpet and Its Greatest Virtuoso, Anton Weidinger.* Nashville: Brass Press, 1975.

Naylor, Tom. L. *The Trumpet and Trombone in Graphic Arts, 1500–1800.* Nashville: Brass Press, 1979.

Coar, Birchard. *The French Horn.* DeKalb, Ill.: Coar, 1947.

Coar, Birchard. *A Critical Study of the Nineteenth-Century Horn Virtuosi in Franc* DeKalb, Ill.: Coar, 1952.

Morley-Pegge, Reginald. *The French Horn.* London: Ernest Benn, 1973.

Fitzpatrick, Horace. *The Horn and Horn-Playing and the Austro-Bohemian Traditic from 1680–1830.* London: Oxford University Press, 1970.

Gregory, Robin. *The Horn: A Comprehensive Guide to the Modern Instrument and Music.* London: Faber and Faber, 1961.

Tuckwell, Barry. *Horn.* New York: Schirmer Books, 1983.

Gregory, Robin. *The Trombone, the Instrument and Its Music.* New York: Praege 1973.

Fischer, Henry George. *The Renaissance Sackbut and Its Use Today.* New Yor Metropolitan Museum of Art, 1984.

Smith, David. "Trombone Technique in the Early Seventeenth Century." D.M./ thesis, Stanford University, 1981.

Wigness, C. Robert. *The Soloistic Use of the Trombone in Eighteenth-Century Vienn* Nashville: Brass Press, 1978.

Bevan, Clifford. *The Tuba Family.* New York: Scribner's, 1978.

Trumpet and Cornet[1]	Horn	Trombone	Baritone, Euphonium, and Tuba
Antiquity Straight trumpets made of wood, bronze, and silver. Greek *salpinx,* Roman *tuba, lituus* and *buccina.* **Middle Ages** Trumpets reappeared during the crusades, probably derived from the Saracens. *Ca. 1300. Buisine, trumba, trombono, trombetta, trummet.* Medieval trumpeters played only on the lowest overtones.	**Antiquity** Scandinavian *lur* (bronze), Hebrew *schofar,* Roman *cornu* and various animal horns.		
Renaissance *Ca. 1400–1413.* The S-shaped trumpet was developed, followed by the folded trumpet and slide trumpet. The latter enabled the player to produce notes between the overtones by sliding the instrument in and out on the mouthpipe.	**Renaissance**	**Renaissance**	
Ca. 1500. Corps of trumpeters were maintained by the large courts. Eventually, such large ensembles played in up to five parts (but with little harmonic variety). Players began to specialize in high and low ranges.	Two types of hunting horn were widely used: the curved horn and the helical horn. The latter was made of coiled metal and is the immediate predecessor of the *cor de chasse.*	*Ca. 1450.* The trombone developed from the slide trumpet. Both the exact date and identity of the originator of the movable slide are unknown. The connected double tubes of the slide represented a significant advance over the awkward slide trumpet and reduced the distances between notes, greatly improving technique. The smaller slide movements also rendered tenor-range instruments practicable. These were known as the *saque-boute* or *trompone.* *Ca. 1540.* The earliest surviving instruments date from the mid-16th century. Three types were used in this period: an "ordinary" sackbut in B♭ (*gemeine-posaune*), an E♭ alto (*mittel-posaune*), and a bass (*grosse-posaune*), also known as *quart-* or *quint-posaune* indicating its intervallic distance from the B♭ *Gemeine-Posaune.* Trombones in other keys were sometimes made, probably for transposition, and were also identified by interval from the "ordinary" in B♭.	

1. The cornet is grouped with the trumpet in the interest of space. Actually, they have different origins. The cornet dates from ca. 1828 when Halary-Antoine added valves to the German posthorn. Since the period of Arban (1869–1889), the evolution of cornet and trumpet playing has been intertwined.

Trumpet and Cornet	Horn	Trombone	Baritone, Euphonium and Tuba

17th Century

Ca. 1600. Instrument makers centered in Nuremberg produced improved natural trumpets designed to function well on the upper overtones. The pitch was usually D or E♭ with terminal crooks added for lower keys. Lacking a tuning slide, natural trumpets were tuned by inserting small lengths of tubing to extend the mouthpipe.

Ca. 1600. Increasing use was made of trumpets in church music, frequently in combination with strings. Praetorius's *In dulci jubilo* (1618) calls for six trumpets.

1620. Florid parts in the high register were written by Samuel Scheidt in his setting of *In dulci jubilo* and Heinrich Schütz's *Buccinate in neomenia Tuba* (1629).

Ca. 1665–1700. Beginning with Maurizio Cazzati, composers associated with the basilica of San Petronio in Bologna produced an important body of works for solo trumpet and strings. The style reached its apex near the end of the century in the solo concertos of Giuseppe Torelli, Domenico Gabrielli, and Giacomo Perti. These works are widely performed today.

Ca. 1680–1695. The trumpet was widely used as a solo instrument in central Europe by composers such as Heinrich Biber and Johann Schmelzer. In England, Henry Purcell and others made extensive use of the trumpet in stage works. Purcell's *Sonata in D for Trumpet and Strings* (1694) is an important solo piece.

17th Century

Hunting horns were occasionally used on the stage in operas, usually depicting hunting scenes.

Ca. 1660. The hoop-shaped *cor-* or *trompe de chasse* became a feature of hunting tradition in France.

Ca. 1680. A larger-wound *trompe de chasse* made its appearance in France. This instrument had a circumference large enough to fit over the body for carrying on horseback.

1680–1682. Franz Anton, Count von Sporck of Bohemia, became interested in the *cor de chasse* during a visit to France. He had two of his servants, Wenzel Sweda and Peter Röllig, trained to play the instrument and established a tradition of hornplaying in central Europe.

17th Century

Ca. 1600. The same pattern continued during the 17th century with the addition of a contrabass instrument (*octav-posaune*), although it is unclear to what extent it was actually used. Sackbuts were regularly employed in all types of ensemble, from large court bands to small mixed consorts where it could blend with the softest instruments. A "vocal" style was cultivated which was free of any influence from the trumpet. The capacity to blend with voices caused the sackbut to be widely used in church music. It was also common in municipal groups along with cornett and shawms, or in a consort of 2 cornetts and 3 sackbuts. Venetian composers such as Gabrieli and Massaino wrote for the instrument with regularity, occasionally calling for exceptionally large forces.

Ca. 1685. A small trombone pitched an octave above the tenor made its appearance in central Europe and was used mostly for playing chorale melodies in trombone ensembles.

Trumpet and Cornet	Horn	Trombone	Baritone, Euphonium, and Tuba
18th Century	**18th Century**	**18th Century**	**18th Century**

Ca. 1716–1750. The Baroque trumpet reached its zenith in the works of Johann Sebastian Bach, who was well served by the Leipzig trumpeter Gottfried Reiche. In his portrait, Reiche holds a coiled instrument known as a *jägertrompete,* probably by the Nuremberg instrument maker J.W. Haas. Apparently, these were occasionally used in place of the more common long trumpet.

Ca. 1700–1710. Viennese instrument maker Michael Leichnambschneider was probably the first to produce terminal crooks to put the horn into different keys. The crooks consisted of various lengths of coiled tubing which were inserted between the mouthpiece and instrument. For lower keys, the crooks could be coupled together, although the instrument became farther away from the player. Once the crook was in place, the horn was played in accordance with the natural overtone series which sounded in the chosen key.

1705. Two horns were used in the orchestra for the opera *Octavia* by Reinhard Keiser.

Ca. 1717. Handel's *Water Music,* which included parts for a pair of horns, was performed. During the Baroque era, horn parts focused on the upper portion of the overtone series and were played without the hand in the bell.

Ca. 1750. Anton Joseph Hampel, a hornist of Dresden, advanced the technique of filling in the spaces between the notes of the overtone series by various degrees of handstopping, rendering the horn chromatic. The procedure is as follows:

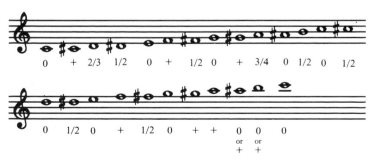

Although there was an unevenness of timbre between stopped and open tones, handstopping became the standard horn technique until well after the

Although there may have been diminished use of the trombone generally during the 18th century, the instrument continued to flourish in an important soloistic role (at least) at the Viennese Imperial Court. Following the pattern established in the 17th century by Antonio Bertali (1605–1669), composers such as Johann Joseph Fux (1660–1741), Marc' Antonio Ziani (1653–1715), Franz Tuma (1704–1774), and Georg Reutter (1708–1772) used the trombone in virtuosic fashion in vocal and instrumental works. The style reached its peak in the concertos of Georg Christoph Wagenseil (1715–1777) and Johann Georg Albrechtsberger (1736–1809). Concertos were also written by Salzburg composers Michael Haydn (1737–1806) and Leopold Mozart (1719–1787). This interesting chapter in the trombone's history is described in detail in C. Robert Wigness's *The Soloistic Use of the Trombone in Eighteenth-Century Vienna* (Nashville, Tenn.: Brass Press, 1978).

Ca. 1755. Concerto by Georg Christoph Wagenseil (alto trombone).

97

invention of valves. Placing the hand in the bell altered the tone, and a darker and softer timbre became accepted as traditional horn tone.

To improve on the limitations of terminal crooks, Hampel invented a new structural format which incorporated a fixed mouthpipe and located the crook in the middle of the instrument. The new instrument, made by Johann Werner (Dresden), was known as the *inventionshorn.*

Ca. 1760. The high clarino style of trumpet playing declined, not from lack of ability on the players' part, but as a function of broad changes in compositional style. Henceforth, trumpets played a supporting role in the orchestra, although there are two late concertos written in the earlier clarino style (Leopold Mozart, 1762; Michael Haydn, 1764).

Ca. 1762. Concerto by Leopold Mozart (alto trombone).
1763. Larghetto by Michael Haydn (alto trombone).
1764. Divertimento in D by Michael Haydn (alto trombone). [Solo movements also published under the title, Concerto].

1762. Horn Concerto No. 1 by Franz Joseph Haydn.
1750-1776. J. G. Haltenhof (Hanau am Main) developed the tuning slide which was applied to the *inventionshorn.*

Ca. 1777. Handstopping, first used on the horn in 1750 and by this time normal practice, was applied to the trumpet by Michael Wöggerl. Notes of the overtone series could be lowered a half or full tone by covering the bell with the hand, although a veiled tone resulted. Stop trumpets were curved or made quite short to increase the bell's accessibility; they followed the *inventionshorn* in locating the crook in the middle of the instrument thereby eliminating terminal crooks.

1769. Concerto by Johann Georg Albrechtsberger (alto trombone).

1780. The Parisian instrument makers Joseph and Lucien-Joseph Raoux brought out a structurally improved *inventionshorn,* calling their new model *cor solo.* Designed for solo playing, it had crooks only for the common solo keys: G,F,E,Eb, and D.
1781-1791. Concertos for Horn—Wolfgang Amadeus Mozart: *Rondo in Eb,* K.371, 1781; *Concerto in Eb,* K.417, 1783 (No. 2); *Concerto in Eb,* K.447, 1786 (No. 3); *Concerto in Eb,* K.495, 1786 (No. 4); *Concerto in D,* K.412, 1791 (No. 1).

Ca. 1780. The trombone began to be used in opera to lend dramatic effect to certain scenes—as in Mozart's *Don Giovanni* and *Magic Flute.*

1795. Trumpeter's and Kettledrummer's Art by Ernst Altenburg was published. This is an important source concerning the natural trumpet and clarino style (see translation by Edward Tarr [Nashville: Brass Press, 1974]).
1795. The Viennese trumpeter Anton Weidinger gave solo appearances, performing on a keyed trumpet of his own design. Haydn's Trumpet Concerto (1796) was composed for him as was the concerto by Hummel (1803).

Ca. 1795. Terminal crooks once again became popular with orchestral players, but with individual crooks for each key instead of the cumbersome practice of coupling crooks together for the lower keys. English players, however, continued to use the earlier system of terminal crooks and couplers; their instruments were fitted with tuning slides.

Trumpet and Cornet	Horn	Trombone	Baritone, Euphonium, and Tuba
19th Century	**19th Century**	**19th Century**	**19th Century**
a. 1800. The natural trumpet flourished in England later than elsewhere (through most of the 19th century) due to John Hyde's invention of a tuning-slide mechanism which allowed the instrument's fundamental pitch to be lowered a half or whole tone without affecting the timbre. An active tradition of performing Handel's clarino parts on the natural trumpet was thereby maintained.	*1800. Horn Sonata,* Op. 17, by Ludwig van Beethoven. Written for the virtuoso Giovanni Punto (Jan Václav Stich). *Ca. 1800.* Prior to the invention of valves, there were attempts to construct a chromatic horn. These included the keyed horn and omnitonic horn. Neither gained wide acceptance, and the hand horn continued as the primary orchestral and solo instrument with players specializing in either high or low ranges. *1806. Concertino for Horn* by Carl Maria von Weber; revised 1815. The cadenza includes horn chords.	*Ca. 1800–1850.* During the early 19th century, composers increasingly called for 3 trombones in the orchestra. Parts were included in Beethoven's 5th and 9th symphonies. The normal trio of E♭ alto, B♭ tenor, and F bass began to give way as alto parts were often performed on the tenor. A large-bore trombone in B♭ was occasionally substituted for the bass in F. The alto trombone was retained (as it is today in central Europe) for parts requiring a high tessitura and light balances.	(The valved low brass have no direct predecessors. The instruments they replaced were the serpent [the bass of the cornetto family and its more developed form, the bass horn] and the ophicleide, which was derived from the keyed bugle.)

THE DEVELOPMENT OF VALVES

In 1788, Charles Clagget was granted a patent for a "chromatic trumpet" which in fact consisted of two instruments, each with its own fundamental and a switching mechanism to direct the single mouthpiece to one side or the other. Although the invention was demonstrated, it failed to achieve any acceptance and should not, therefore, be considered a stage in the development of the valve.

The history of the valve begins with an article in the *Allgemeine musikalische Zeitung* of May 3, 1815, by G. B. Bierey, which reported on a new invention by the horn player Heinrich Stölzel. Through the use of two "levers," a chromatic scale of almost three octaves could be obtained. The author described the timbre of the valve notes as "clear and strong," comparable to the natural tones. By 1818, Stölzel had joined the court orchestra in Berlin when Friedrich Blühmel turned up claiming that the invention was his. A joint ten-year patent was granted to Stölzel and Blühmel; we will probably never know which of them was responsible for the original idea.

The joint patent of 1818 was for both a tubular and a square-shaped (box) valve. In the tubular valve (Stölzel's), the air column was directed downward through the valve tube and out the bottom. Valves of this type were popular during the first half of the century and were known as Stölzel valves. The square valve (Blühmel's) had the advantage of more direct windways, but was slower in action.[2]

In 1828, Stölzel and Blühmel were unsuccessful in obtaining patents for rotary valves. Of similar design, the valves were apparently developed quite early, but, for some reason, Stölzel and Blühmel chose not to include them in the 1818 patent. Wieprecht stated that the rotary valve was immediately improved in Prague, a

2. An important source of information on the early development of the valve is the account by the Prussian band-master, Wilhelm Wieprecht (1845), who knew both Stölzel and Blühmel. Relevant passages are translated in Anthony Baines, *Brass Instruments* (London, Faber and Faber, 1976), pp. 207–212. The most detailed study presently available is Herbert Heyde's series of articles, "Zur Frühgeschichte der Ventile und Ventilinstrumente in Deutschland 1814–1833)," *Brass Bulletin,* 24 (1978), pp. 9–33; 25 (1979), pp. 41–50; 26 (1979), pp. 69–82; 27 (1979), pp. 51–59 translations in English and French are included).

comment that lends credence to a story found in the papers of the instrument maker Karl Nödel that credits the hornist Joseph Kail with the invention of the rotary valve rather than Josef Riedl, who patented it in 1832.[3] According to Nödel, his father (also an instrument maker) and other old Viennese makers always maintained that Kail, a professor at the Prague Conservatory, had invented the rotary valve in 1827, having gotten the idea from a beer tap. Kail apparently made the mistake of describing his idea to Josef Riedl during a visit to Vienna and Riedl proceeded to manufacture the valves, eventually securing a patent.[4]

Another valve in use today (but only on the Vienna horn) is the double-piston valve, which was patented in 1830 by the Viennese instrument maker, Leopold Uhlmann, as an improved version of an earlier design by Christian Friedrich Sattler of Leipzig. With attached twin pistons, the air column flows from the bottom of one piston (like the Stölzel valve) and, after going through the requisite length of tubing, reenters the bottom of the second piston. This action is believed to contribute to the exceptionally smooth slurs and free tone of the Vienna horn.

In 1835, Wieprecht and the instrument maker J. G. Moritz introduced improved piston valves known as *Berliner-Pumpen,* which featured unconstricted airways. Although they had a rather slow action, they were widely used in military bands in Germany and northern Europe (particularly on low brass instruments) and continued to be made into the present century.

There were other experiments, such as the transverse spring slide by John Shaw and disc-type valves by Halary-Antoine, Shaw and Köhler, but these had no significant impact on the development of the valve.

The final stage of development was reached in 1839 when François Périnet, a Parisian instrument maker, brought the piston valve into the form we know today. Thus the three modern valves—piston, rotary, and Vienna—were developed in the 1830s and have come down to the present era essentially unchanged.

Following this momentary interruption, the historical outlines continue on page 101.

3. Nödel's statement is reproduced in Bernhard Brüchle and Kurt Janetzky, *Kulturgeschichte des Horns* (Tutzing: Hans Schneider, 1976), pp. 252–253.

4. Another source, T. Rode, writing in the *Neue Berliner Musikzeitung* in 1860, says that Kail improved the rotary valve in 1829. Whether there is any connection between the Stölzel and Blühmel rotary valve and the Kail valve, or (if the Nödel story is true) is a case of independent conception remains unclear. Another early type of rotary valve was made by Nathan Adams of Boston, Mass., as early as 1825.

Trumpet and Cornet	Horn	Trombone	Baritone, Euphonium, and Tuba
1826. Spontini brought German valve trumpet to Paris where it gained acceptance and was copied. Berlioz was the first to use the new instrument in the overture *Les francs-juges* of the same year. During this period, valve trumpets were often used beside natural trumpets. As the valve trumpet developed during the 19th century, instruments were produced with Stölzel, piston, rotary, and Vienna valves. The usual key was F or G, and crooks were added for lower keys. *Ca. 1828.* Jean-Louis Antoine (Halary)[5] modified the (round) German post horn to become a valve instrument, calling it *cornet à pistons.* Two Stölzel valves were fitted, and it was wound (in B♭) so that the bell projected forward. The cornet gained rapid popularity as a solo instrument because of its chromatic agility, and it was often used (in a pair) along with trumpets in works by French composers.	*Ca. 1825.* Although valve horns made their appearance, players preferred to use hand technique whenever possible on the new instruments. The valves were used to avoid the most obvious inequalities of timbre inherent in the hand horn technique. French instrument makers often produced horns with removable valves, and a third valve was considered unnecessary. *1835.* Halevy's *La juive* was the first score to call for valve horns. A pair of hand horns and a pair of valve horns was customary.	As trombones were being increasingly used in orchestras, several trombonists attained fame as soloists. The first of these was Friedrich August Belcke (1795–1874). *Ca. 1828.* The new valve trombone was introduced, and, while it received some acceptance in bands, it was little used in orchestras. Following in the virtuoso tradition of Belcke were Karl Traugott Queisser (1800–1846) and Antoine Guillaume Dieppo (1808–1878). The latter taught at the Paris Conservatory and produced a *méthode complète* in 1840. *1837. Concertino* by Ferdinand David (1810–1873). *1839.* C. F. Sattler of Leipzig introduced the first B♭ -F trombone. The change to the F attachment was (as it is today) made by a rotary valve.	*Ca. 1828.* Tenor- and baritone-range instruments with valves appeared in German military bands during the late 1820s. These may be considered the first versions of the modern German *tenorhorn* and *baryton.* *Ca. 1835.* The first tuba, a five-valve (Berliner-pumpen) instrument in F, was invented by the Berlin bandmaster Wilhelm Wieprecht and instrument maker Johann Gottfried Moritz. *1838.* Moritz produced a tenor tuba in B♭. *1842–1845.* The Parisian inventor, Adolphe Sax, produced his complete family of saxhorns, receiving a patent in 1845. These typically ranged from the E♭ soprano to the B♭ contrabass. Aside from the quality of their construction, the saxhorns' success can be attributed to their adoption by the French Army and by the famous Distin family quintet (who popularized them in England, where they were taken up by the developing brass band movement). Modern low brass instruments with piston valves are in general developed from the saxhorn.

J.-L. Antoine took over the Halary business and adopted the name. His son Jules-Leon Antoine later joined him as a partner.

Trumpet and Cornet

Ca. 1850–1890. Possibly due to the influence of the B♭ cornet, with its advantage of more widely spaced harmonics, trumpeters gradually moved away from the long F and G trumpets toward instruments built in B♭ or C. Stölzel valves declined in popularity, and instruments were made with 3 piston or rotary valves.

1864. Jean-Baptiste Arban's *Grande méthode complète pour cornet à pistons et de saxhorn* was published in Paris. Arban's influence as performer and teacher had wide impact on both cornetists and trumpeters, which extends to the present. His method forms the basis of most modern teaching of the instruments.

1871. Julius Kosleck, Professor at the Berlin *Hoch-Schule,* gave a demonstration of clarino playing which aroused interest in reviving this art. Later, in 1884–1885, he caused a stir by performing the Bach parts on a 2-valve straight trumpet in A. English players had similar instruments made by G. Silvani. Teste, of the Paris Opera, performed the *Magnificat* on a 3-valve G trumpet (1885) made by Besson. Mahillon produced a successful D trumpet in 1892, and Alexander an F for the *2nd Brandenburg Concerto* in 1894. The various high trumpets were often called "Bach trumpets."

Horn

1848. Jules-Léon Antoine (Halary), hornist and son of the instrument maker Jean-Louis Antoine (Halary), devised the ascending 3rd-valve system, still in use in France and Belgium.

1849. Robert Schumann was an important early advocate for the valve horn. His *Adagio and Allegro* for solo horn and piano and *Konzertstück* for 4 horns and orchestra demand the full capacity of the valve instrument.

1865. Trio for Violin, Horn, and Piano, op. 40, by Johannes Brahms.

Ca. 1865. During the second half of the 19th century, horns were typically built (in Germany) in F with three rotary valves and either terminal or slide crooks. Players preferred to use the high-B♭,A,G,E, and E♭ crooks when in those keys in order to retain the timbre of the open tones and avoid awkward fingerings. Henri Kling, in his *Horn-Schule* (1865), cited examples for the use of crooks and disparaged the practice of trying to play everything on the F crook, which was now theoretically possible through the use of valves. In France, horns with terminal G crook and ascending 3rd valve (which put the horn in F) were preferred, and English players used French instruments with descending 3rd valve and F crook. Uhlmann's ca. 1830 Vienna horn with double piston valves and terminal crook was (and still is) standard in that city.

1882–1883. First Concerto for Horn, op. 11 by Richard Strauss.

Trombone

Ca. 1850. From the middle of the 19th century, German trombones became larger in bore and bell and took on their traditional wide-bow construction. French trombones of the Courtois type retained a smaller bore and bell taper. Large bass trombones in F or B♭/F became the rule in German sections. A smaller bass trombone in G was used in brass bands and orchestras in England for almost a century.

1876. A contrabass trombone in B♭ with double-tubed slide was constructed for Wagner's *Ring* (composed 1848–1874; performed, Bayreuth, 1876).

Baritone, Euphonium and Tuba

1843. The *Euphonion* was introduced by Sommer of Weimar. A similar instrument, identified as the *Sommerophone,* was exhibited in 1851 at the Crystal Palace in London.

1845. Contrabass tubas in B♭ and C with rotary valves rather than *Berliner-pumpen* were manufactured by the Bohemian firm of Cervény. The tuba was rapidly accepted in orchestras in Germany but the ophicleide maintained its place in France and England until late in the century. Tubas found acceptance in bands everywhere.

Ca. 1840–1880. Berlioz and Wagner were early champions of the tuba. The latter wrote for it in *The Flying Dutchman* (1843) and it was included in Berlioz's *Damnation of Faust,* composed three years later. The bass tuba in F was normally used, but the contrabass was occasionally specified, as in Wagner's *Ring.* In France, a small C tuba (pitched above the F bass) with 6 valves finally replaced the ophicleide.

1874. A compensating system (still in use) to correct intonation when valves are used in combination was invented by David Blaikley of Boosey and Co. This significantly improved low brass instruments used in England and is a contributing factor to the high quality of British brass bands.

Ca. 1880. Cerveny introduced a very large bore tuba known as a *kaiserbass.* This became the prototype for most modern rotary valve orchestral tubas in C and B♭.

Trumpet and Cornet	Horn	Trombone	Baritone, Euphonium, and Tuba

a. 1890. The modern rm of the orchestral umpet became tablished. Piston valve umpets were generally und in France, England, d the U.S.; rotary valve umpets in Germany, ustria, and Italy. struments in C were vored by French and iennese trumpeters, while the ♭ was common elsewhere. he long F trumpet rvived into the early 20th ntury in England.)

1897. Edmund Gumpert and Eduard Kruspe developed the first F-B♭ double horn, a compensating type which was soon followed by the full double. (The idea had been partially anticipated by Gautrot, who designed a compensating system to correct intonation in 1865.)

Ca. 1890–1920. During these years, small-bore Courtois-type trombones were popular in France, England, and in bands in the U.S. Players in American symphony orchestras preferred large-bore German instruments, and these influenced the development of the modern American symphonic trombone (which combines the best features of French and German instruments).

20th Century

20th Century

a. 1905. The Belgian firm Mahillon constructed a ccolo B♭ trumpet tended for Bach's *2nd randenburg Concerto*.

a. 1929. Larger-bore ston valve trumpets based the Besson model placed smaller struments in American chestras. Through the fluence of Georges Mager, incipal trumpet of the oston Symphony 920–1950), the C umpet became creasingly common. By e late 1940s, it had rgely replaced the B♭ as e standard orchestral strument.

a. 1959. Improved high umpets were developed, inging the Baroque erature into the sphere of gular orchestral players, ther than specialists. *a. 1960.* French virtuoso laurice André brought the umpet into a new era as a pular solo instrument rough worldwide pearances and cordings.

20th Century

At the beginning of the century, single F, B♭ and double horns were in simultaneous use.

Ca. 1928. The hornist Louis Vuillermoz developed a compensating double horn (piston-valve) based on the ascending 3rd-valve principle. This became the standard orchestral horn in France and parts of Belgium.
1942. Second Concerto for Horn by Richard Strauss.
Ca. 1945–1950. In England, French-type piston valve horns were gradually replaced by German single B♭s, and doubles (a change regretted by many).
Ca. 1950–1957. English horn player Dennis Brain achieved world renown as a soloist, establishing the horn as a major solo instrument.
Ca. 1958. The first practical B♭-F alto double descant horn was developed by Richard Merewether. Double descants are also made in F-F alto and B♭-B♭ soprano. Single descants are most commonly built in F or G alto.

20th Century

Ca. 1939. The trombone gained widespread popularity through the influence of bandleaders such as Tommy Dorsey and Glenn Miller and its use in jazz. Tommy Dorsey, in particular, left his mark on all trombonists.
Ca. 1948. American-type orchestral trombones became standardized throughout the world, in some cases (as in England) displacing traditional small-bore instruments. In Germany and Austria, however, German trombones continued their independent line of development.
Ca. 1950. Several American bass trombonists were frustrated by the limitations of the B♭-F instrument in producing good notes immediately above the pedal range. They experimented with an additional length of tubing connected to the F attachment by a second rotor which lowered the pitch to E. This was later altered to E♭ or D, and the double-trigger bass trombone soon became standardized.

20th Century

1900–present. German low-brass instruments continued in the 20th century essentially unchanged from their 19th-century counterparts. Band instruments, such as the E♭ *althorn, tenorhorn,* and *baryton* (the latter two equivalent to the baritone and euphonium), were wrapped in an oval form with rotary valves and remain the same today. German tubas became accepted in many countries as the standard orchestral instrument. In England, however, an agile piston valve tuba in F (Ralph Vaughan Williams wrote his *Bass Tuba Concerto* [1954] for this instrument) was favored up to the second world war. Since then, the brass band-type E♭ is standard, with occasional use of a B♭ contrabass for certain works. The small French C tuba was used for some years, but has now given way to more conventional instruments in Parisian orchestras, usually a German-type 6-valve F or contrabass. The C instrument is still employed for high solos, as in Mussorgsky-Ravel's *Pictures at an Exhibition* and Stravinsky's *Petrouchka.* German tubas were widely used in American orchestras (though not in bands) from the late 19th century

Trumpet and Cornet	Horn	Trombone	Baritone, Euphonium and Tuba

Ca. 1961. Performances on natural trumpets were revived to lend an authentic timbre and style to Baroque music. The standard of performance has now risen to a very high level, and there are several internationally recognized soloists on natural trumpet. Replicas of Baroque instruments are readily available.

1965. Richard Merewether introduced the triple horn in F-B♭-F alto.

onward. Some large-bore piston valve tubas were made by domestic firms early in the century and a greatly prized today. American tubists established the trend of using the C contrabass as the primary instrument, reserving the bass in F for high-register passages, an this pattern has been followed elsewhere (although the B♭ contraba is preferred in some countries). At present, the is interest in reviving the large-bore piston valve tu for orchestral use. In rece decades, orchestral-type rotary-valve tubas have become the rule in bands the U.S. Marching bands use the Sousaphone. British-type Euphoniums are preferred in American concert bands, while traditional narrow-bore baritones and alto (tenor) horns are now only used i brass bands. At present, brass bands, modeled on the British tradition, are gaining popularity. There also some use of "American-bore" baritone (larger), usually as substitutes for the euphonium.

Present. Trumpet sections composed of C trumpets are now standard in American orchestras, but the B♭ is used in certain situations. English and German players generally prefer the B♭, while C trumpets are widely used in France and Austria. Trumpets with piston valves are most common, but rotary valve instruments are the mainstay of orchestras in Germany and Austria, and have been adopted by American players for certain repertoire. B♭ cornets and trumpets are invariably used in bands. Baroque parts are now usually played on the piccolo B♭/A trumpet. Present-day trumpets are available in the following keys: B♭, C, D, E♭, E, F, G, (piccolo) A, B♭, C. Some are built in one key with slides for other keys, e.g.: D/E♭, G/F/E, and piccolo B♭/A.

Present. The F-B♭ full double is the standard orchestral instrument today. Exceptions are the single F horn used in the Vienna Philharmonic (there is renewed interest elsewhere in this horn) and the occasional single B♭ or triple horn. Compensating doubles are favored in certain parts of Europe. Double or triple descant horns are usually employed for high-register work. The ascending 3rd-valve system is still dominant in France, although rotary valve models utilizing this system now compete with traditional piston valve types.

Present. Large-bore tenors with and without F attachment and in-line double-rotor bass trombones are used in orchestras and bands today. While small-bore trombones are rare, medium and medium-large bores are widely used by students and in the jazz and recording fields. Alto trombones are employed for certain repertoire (particularly in Germany). Modern versions of traditional German trombones are preferred in Central Europe. The valve trombone is now only found in jazz, where it is an important solo instrument. Parts for contrabass trombone are usually played on the bass trombone, due to the increased capability of the in-line double-rotor instrument, but there is increased use of modern forms of the contrabass instrument.

PART TWO

PEDAGOGY

CHAPTER 10

Tone Production

All good brass players have one characteristic in common: a free production of sound. Whether in the high or low ranges, loud or soft, notes respond easily and reliably with a full, clear tone. This is the result of good fundamental procedures and the way in which the instrument is approached.

Tone production is not a complex activity in which each muscular function must be analyzed and consciously controlled. On the contrary, it consists of a few basic techniques which, when established, allow the player to concentrate on the sound and the music. Brass students sometimes become obsessed with an analytical approach, usually with destructive consequences. This has been aptly termed "paralysis by analysis" by Adolph Herseth (principal trumpet of the Chicago Symphony Orchestra). The finest teaching emphasizes a relaxed, natural approach to the instrument, stressing basic fundamentals and focusing on musical results.

It is important that the basic techniques be presented simply: it is impossible to concentrate on the sound and simultaneously conceptualize an elaborate process. Therefore, in the following pages, the elements of tone production are presented in practical terms as concisely as possible. Theoretical discussions of the operation of each element are omitted, as these tend to encourage an analytical approach rather than the result-centered process advocated by the author. A discussion of common problems is included at the end of the chapter which should serve as a reference if difficulties arise.

EMBOUCHURE FORMATION

Tone is generated by the vibration of the embouchure. Vibration is caused not only by the air passing through the embouchure, but also by pressure fluctuations within the mouthpiece created by standing waves from the instrument's bell flare.[1] The instrument and embouchure work together to promote vibration at a particular frequency. It follows that the embouchure should be as flexible as possible inside the mouthpiece rim and that the facial muscles outside the rim must support the embouchure so that free vibration can take place.

Of prime importance is the aperture—this is the opening between the lips through which the air passes and where the vibration occurs. The aperture must be open in all ranges—high and low. There are, however, subtle changes in size as the embouchure adjusts to favor vibration at different frequencies. Any restriction or flattening of the aperture will tend to impede vibration. The shape of the aperture is oval. This can be seen if the embouchure is viewed through an embouchure visualizer[2] or transparent mouthpiece.

The vibratory area of the embouchure is within the circle defined by the mouthpiece rim. The lower lip serves primarily as a seat for the mouthpiece. While both lips vibrate, the important part of the embouchure is the central area

---

This process is described in Chapter 1.

The embouchure visualizer consists of a mouthpiece rim (without cup or shank) with a handle. By placing it the embouchure and looking into a mirror, the player can observe the aperture.

Figure 10.1. The TRU-VU transparent mouthpiece demonstrated by Peter Su? van, trombonist with the Orchestre symphonique de Montréal.

(Photo courtesy of L-S Music Innovatio?)

of the upper lip that is brought into vibration by the motion of the air to crea? sound.

This process can be clearly observed through the use of a TRU-VU transpare? mouthpiece,[3] a new development of the greatest pedagogical importance. Devis? by Ellis Wean, principal tubist of the Montreal Symphony Orchestra, the TRU-V? enables brass players to see for the first time the vibration of the embouchure ? sound is being produced on the instrument. This is of enormous help in guidi? the player in the formation and control of the embouchure.

In starting a tone, as seen through the TRU-VU mouthpiece (Fig. 10-1), t? upper lip is driven forward (into the mouthpiece) by the air, setting it into vibrati? and creating the oval-shaped aperture. (The vibrations correspond to the numb? of cycles per second of the pitch being produced.) Observed in slow motion, f? each vibration, the upper lip is blown forward until it reaches the limit of its stretc? it then snaps back to its starting position. The return action is aided by pressu? variations that occur in the mouthpiece (see Chapter 1).

The jaw should be brought forward so that the upper and lower teeth are mo? or less aligned. With the trumpet, this will result in the instrument being held rath? straight or slightly downward. The horn is an exception: the lower teeth must ? back a bit from the upper teeth to accommodate the more downward flowing a? stream required by the horn mouthpiece's depth.

The facial muscles, particularly those within the lower cheeks,[4] support t? formation inside the mouthpiece rim. It is often said that the main point ? support is at the mouth corners. Actually, the point is felt somewhat beyond t? corners, which are themselves supported by the musculature of the lower cheek? Consciously contracting the corners tends to make the embouchure too rigid ? vibrate easily. In general, the embouchure should have a relaxed feel, with on? enough support from the facial muscles to resist any tendency for the embouchu? to pull outward (as in a smile). If the latter is allowed to happen, the apertu?

3. TRU-VU mouthpieces are available from L-S Music Innovations, Inc., 1896 Lionel-Groulx, Montréal, Québ? H3J 2P5 Canada. A videotape showing embouchures in action is also available.
4. Specifically, the buccinator, depressor anguli oris, and risorius.

ends to close, the lips become tense and resistant to vibration, and there is a corresponding loss in tone and response.

To form the embouchure, the lips should be brought inward toward the center so that an oval-shaped aperture is formed in the middle. This is often referred to as a "puckered formation." The lower lip as well as the upper must be gently puckered. At the aperture, the center portion of the upper lip should be slightly forward so that it can vibrate without hindrance. Forming the lips as in the sound of the letter "p" ("puh" or "pa") will encourage the aperture to open and the upper lip to vibrate freely. The jaw should be dropped so that a space is made between the teeth for the air to pass through (this also opens the aperture). The chin should be gently drawn downward, following the outline of the lower jaw. It is quite common for beginners to tense the embouchure, inhibiting vibration. Instead, the player should think of supporting the puckered formation and relaxed tissue inside the mouthpiece rim with the musculature within the lower cheeks. The aperture must remain open (see Figs. 10.2 and 10.3).

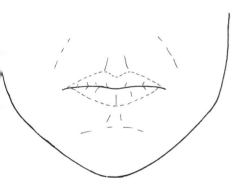

Figure 10.2. Natural lip formation.

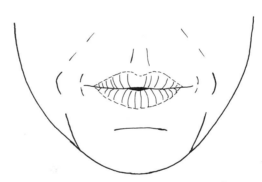

Figure 10.3. Embouchure formation.

MOUTHPIECE PLACEMENT

The embouchure should be formed *before* placing the mouthpiece on the lips. Mouthpiece placement is an important consideration since difficulties often stem from an improper placement. The mouthpiece rim should be centered horizontally on the embouchure. Although this is generally the preferred position, many successful players play slightly off-center due to variations in dental structure. The vertical placement is more critical.

Vertical placement is usually expressed as proportions of upper and lower lip within the mouthpiece rim. These differ with the various instruments. An embouchure visualizer or transparent mouthpiece is helpful in determining the optimum placement for a specific instrument. Modern trumpet playing favors an equal proportion of upper and lower lip in the mouthpiece, although some players prefer a slightly higher placement. In earlier periods, a one-third upper–two-thirds lower placement was advocated, but this is generally not encouraged today. Horn players have always been in complete agreement that the only workable placement for their instrument consists of two-thirds upper lip and one-third lower lip. The bottom of the rim should rest on the line between the "red" and "white" portions of the lower lip, or slightly on the "red." Trombone, euphonium, and tuba players normally use a fairly high placement, but not necessarily as high as the horn. Figures 10.4 through 10.7 illustrate typical placements for each instrument.

Figure 10.4. Mouthpiece placement: trumpet and cornet.

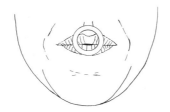

Figure 10.5. Mouthpiece placement: horn

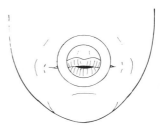

Figure 10.6. Mouthpiece placement: trombone and euphonium.

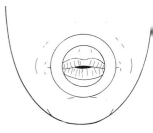

Figure 10.7. Mouthpiec[e] placement: tuba.

EMBOUCHURE ADJUSTMENT

To play the full range of the instrument, the embouchure must adjust to facilitate vibration at different frequencies. The jaw and tongue, in particular, must move when ascending and descending.

For example, when the player slurs the following arpeggio, the jaw moves upward in minute degrees for each change of pitch as the line rises, and downward as it descends.

This allows the aperture to adjust for optimum vibration at each frequency. Similarly, the tongue, which works with the jaw, rises within the mouth, concentrating the air stream and redirecting it in a more downward course in ascending; the tongue flattens in descending. Brass players often think of changing from an "ah" syllable to an "ee"[5] when passing from low to high ranges to encourage the appropriate tongue motion. The upper lip comes downward within the mouthpiece to accommodate the more downward-flowing air in the upper register.

The importance of the proper jaw and tongue position can be seen by playing a middle- or upper-register note and consciously lowering the jaw or tongue. Only one position will yield an accurately centered sound and pitch.

Along with the subtle, almost unconscious movements of jaw and tongue, there are fine adjustments made by the lips within the mouthpiece rim. The great tubist of the Chicago Symphony Orchestra, Arnold Jacobs, has suggested that embouchure adjustment can best be accomplished by thinking of very gently *rotating the lips inward upon themselves* when moving upward in range. This provides slightly greater resistance to the wind, causing faster vibrations. The muscles within the lower cheeks also increase their support by degrees as the range goes higher. This is mainly in response to a surge in air pressure which must accompany the ascending pattern and to resist any outward pull; the greater support also enables the aperture to focus more centrally for the upper tones. In the descending pattern, the muscular support decreases.

Beginners are sometimes under the mistaken impression that they must consciously tighten their lips when ascending and loosen them in descending. The

5. "Ah"–"ee" or "ah"–"oo"–"ee" are primarily trumpet syllables. Hornists and low brass players often use "oh" or "ah"–"oo." Once proper tongue motion is established, many players do not consciously think of forming syllables as they play.

mbouchure becomes inflexible as a result and resists vibration. Actually, the primary changes in muscular tension are the subtle increases and decreases in support the lower cheeks which allow the tissue inside the mouthpiece rim to remain relaxed, promoting free vibration.

A beneficial practice and warm-up technique followed by many brass players to play melodies and exercises on the mouthpiece alone. By locating exact itches without the assistance of the instrument, the embouchure becomes more roficient in centering notes and intervals with the instrument in place. Sometimes is helpful to place the index finger over part of the end of the mouthpiece nank or to cup the hand around the shank to make the mouthpiece respond more asily. (A device known as a Buzz Extension and Resistance Piece [B.E.R.P.],[6] which pproximates the same resistance as that offered by the instrument, is particularly seful. The unit fits into the instrument's leadpipe so that it may be used in playing osition while employing the appropriate fingering or slide position.) In addition its warm-up value, the mouthpiece can be used to play first lines of studies or roblematic passages at various points during the practice session. In this way, ue player will gain greater control of the embouchure movements necessary in djusting for different frequencies.

THE AIR

iscussions of breathing as it applies to brass playing often center only on king the air in, when, in reality, two distinct processes are involved: inspiration nhalation) and expiration (exhalation). Of the two, expiration tends to be more ritical since it is where most problems occur.

The primary consideration in taking in the air is that the body remain relaxed. uring inspiration, the diaphragm moves downward, and the waist and rib cage xpand as the lungs are filled. Any muscular rigidity or tension will obstruct this rocess. Sometimes residual tension remains from the expiration process when a ew breath is taken. Therefore, a conscious effort should be made to relax during spiration.

Inexperienced players frequently take shallow breaths from the chest, resulting an insufficient quantity of air to sustain a full tone and relaxed tone production. he lungs are shaped so that the largest area occurs from the middle downward. o ensure an adequate air supply, *the player should think of filling the lungs from ie bottom upward.* Actual quantities can vary from around one quart in a shallow reath, to five and a half quarts in a deep breath.[7] Tone production is most efficient hen the lungs are full. Once the habit of taking a relaxed breath has become stablished, the player should plan his breathing points in accordance with the hrases of the music being performed.

The expiration process should focus on moving the air by creating *wind.*[8] It is ue movement of the air through the embouchure, causing it to vibrate, which enerates sound. A common problem is a conscious flexing of the waist and bdominal muscles, bringing the body into a state of tension in exhaling the air. lthough such a procedure is often recommended in the interest of "support,"

The Buzz Extension and Resistance Piece is available for all brass instruments from Musical Enterprises, P.O. ox 1465-N, Pacific Palisades, Calif. 90272.

See Paul Lewis and David Rubenstein, *The Human Body* (New York: Bantam Books, 1972), pp. 32–37.

The concept of moving the air as wind in brass playing is one of a number of significant pedagogical inciples to emerge from the over 40 years of research and teaching of Arnold Jacobs, principal tuba of the hicago Symphony Orchestra. Jacobs's work has had wide-ranging influence on modern brass playing. See . Dee Stewart, *Arnold Jacobs's: The Legacy of a Master* (Northfield, Ill.: Instrumentalist Co., 1987); Kevin Kelly ith Arnold Jacobs and David Cugell, M.D., "The Dynamics of Breathing," *The Instrumentalist,* December 1983, . 6–12; Bill Russo, "An Interview with Arnold Jacobs," *The Instrumentalist,* February 1973. (The latter two ticles are reprinted in the Stewart book.)

it actually restricts the free outflow of air. Players who adopt this approach mistakenly associate muscular effort with airflow, creating an almost "isometric" tension within their bodies, yet the actual flow of air is small.

Borrowing an analogy from string playing, Arnold Jacobs has compared the above approach to a bow that will not move. It is the movement of the bow that causes the string to vibrate, producing sound. In order to move the air effectively there must be an absence of bodily tension. In addition, it is best *not to think* about the muscular activity involved in the process, but to *concentrate solely on the movement of the wind itself.* Air, being essentially weightless, can be expelled naturally and freely by focusing on movement rather than muscular tension. By thinking of creating *wind,* the movement of the air is assured.

In the shift from the middle to the upper range, the intensity of the airflow must increase. The low range requires both greater quantity and force to retain an even volume. In loud playing, one should think of relaxing and moving more air. The tone will tend to become strident if the increased effort required in loud dynamics is not accompanied by a definite feeling of relaxation.

In all dynamic levels and ranges any irregularity of the sound and pitch should be steadied by the movement of the wind. In general, fast wind should be used rather than slow wind; the latter lacks the force necessary for stable vibration of the lips.

The least disturbance to the embouchure will occur if, when the breath is taken, the player releases the pressure on the lower lip and drops the jaw slightly to allow the air to flow inward. This method of taking in the air differs from the commonly recommended procedure of breathing through the corners of the mouth. While many players use the latter approach effectively, the process of opening the corners tends to pull the embouchure into a slight smile, thereby thinning the lip surfaces resting within the mouthpiece rim. By dropping the jaw for the breath, the player keeps the corners in their usual position and maintains the necessary embouchure pucker.

ATTACK AND TONGUING

The sound is initiated primarily by the motion of the air, rather than the action of the tongue. However, the tongue does provide a clear beginning to the sound and allows different styles of attack to be used in starting a note. It is of vital importance that inspiration, expiration, and attack be approached as a continuous action. Inspiration should flow smoothly into expiration with no hesitation at the changeover point. It is equally important that the outward motion of the air column not stop at the tongue before an attack is made. Such an interruption of the air flow places the thorax (the chest cavity) and throat in a state of tension which resists the free outflow of the wind. The proper role of the tongue is to assist the motion of the air column in starting a note. With a transparent mouthpiece, one can clearly see the upper lip being driven forward into vibration by the wind on each attack.

The placement of the tip of the tongue varies with individual players. The most common location is in the upper front corner of the mouth at the gum line of the front teeth. Some players prefer a lower placement, at the middle or bottom of the upper teeth (Fig. 10.8).

Beginning method books usually suggest the use of an attack syllable, such as "du," "tu," "da," or "ta," to develop the correct tongue movement in starting a note. After the pattern is established, most players do not consciously pronounce syllables into the instrument when tonguing. Rather, the sound of the passage is visualized or heard in the "mind's ear," and the player reproduces the desired sound on the instrument.

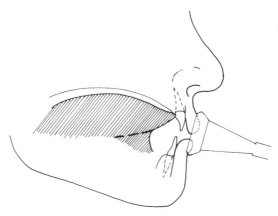

Figure 10.8. Tongue placement.

The "du" and "tu" syllables are helpful in getting across the concept of hard
and soft attack. The sound at the beginning of a note can be modified from pointed
to smooth (as is appropriate to the context of the piece being performed). There is
a wide range of possible sounds, and players usually think not only of the style of
attack, but of the note's overall shape as well. Figure 10.9 illustrates three basic
examples. The first "rectangular" shape might be used for general purposes. It
promotes an equality of sound at the beginning, middle, and end of a note. The
second applies to repertoire in which a sharp, bell-like quality is appropriate. The
last example provides a soft beginning followed by a swell in the sound, which
can be used to good stylistic effect in certain 19th-century compositions.

The way in which the tongue moves in creating articulation must be considered
carefully. The motion should be limited to the tip of the tongue, and its direction
must be more vertical than forward and back. The latter requires too much mass of
the tongue to be moved thus hindering rapid tonguing. A more serious consequence
of using more than the tip of the tongue is that the jaw tends to follow the
tongue motion causing a disturbance to the embouchure at the beginning of each
articulation.[9]

A word should be said about the so-called tongued release. Beginners occasionally develop the habit of stopping the sound by replacing the tongue in its attack
position while the note is still sounding. This creates an audible release which is
detrimental to good tone. The correct way of ending a note is to stop blowing.
The tongued release does have its place, however. Professional players often use
this technique in staccato passages where it produces a degree of crispness that
can be obtained in no other way.

This can impede the development of the low register of the horn, for example. In this range, jaw movement
tends to unsettle the mouthpiece on the embouchure. This will be avoided if the player visualizes a vertical
motion of the tip of the tongue.

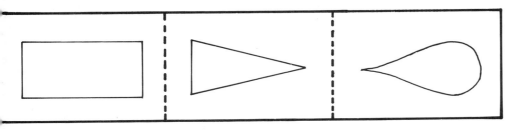

Figure 10.9. Diagram of various styles of attack.

DOUBLE AND TRIPLE TONGUING

If normal single tonguing cannot cope with the pace demanded by a passage or sounds labored, a special technique is required. By utilizing the rear portion of the tongue for the second or third repetition, tonguing speed can be increased dramatically. The syllables "tu-ku," "ta-ka," and "tu-tu-ku," "ta-ta-ka" are most often recommended for this purpose.[10] The main difficulty in double and triple tonguing is achieving sufficient evenness that compares favorably to single tonguing. The tendency to inequality is caused by a certain weakness of the "k" syllable.

This can be remedied in two ways. By substituting the syllables "da-ga" and "da-da-ga" for "tu-ku" and "ta-ta-ka," a player can produce a stronger "k" syllable. If double and triple tonguing are practiced *slowly* and in direct comparison with single tonguing, the syllables will gain in clarity and strength, promoting equality.

single tongue   da ga da ga da   single tongue   da ga da ga da   etc.

Each measure or pattern in an exercise should first be single-tongued, then immediately repeated using double or triple syllables. The goal is to be unable to detect an important difference between the two approaches.

SLURRING

Slurring on brass instruments may be defined as moving between notes without the use of the tongue. This can be done on the harmonic series, known as the lip slur, or with the valves. The primary consideration in executing a slur is that the connection between notes be smooth and without any break in the sound. It is essential to keep the air in motion between notes, and it is helpful if the slur is approached as one continuous sound going into another.

Any interruption to the air flow or sound in the space between two slurred notes will negatively affect the quality of the slur. Valve slurs are particularly prone to this problem; care should be taken to "blow through" the valve change. It is also important that the valve motion be quick. By keeping the sound moving between notes, a player is assured of good continuity and achieves a feeling of raising or lowering one note to the level of another. All slurs must be carefully timed to provide a clean, almost imperceptible change. Through great mastery of timing, German and Viennese hornists produce long, expressive "glides" from note to note in the romantic repertoire.

In order to retain an evenness of volume between slurred notes, it is necessary to increase the wind pressure for ascending notes to compensate for the smaller aperture and slightly greater resistance that is encountered on the upper note. The air flow must also rise for descending notes to accommodate a more relaxed embouchure and larger aperture. As was noted under "Embouchure Adjustment," a movement of the jaw and tongue must accompany the shift in air pressure in executing slurred intervals. Sometimes it is useful (particularly in ascending) to crescendo on the *lower note* and let the momentum carry the sound to the higher note.

10. In certain passages, professional players occasionally rearrange the order of triple tongue syllables to: "ku-ku-tu," "ta-ka-ta," or "da-ga-da."

TROMBONE LEGATO

Because the medium for changing notes is a movable slide, the subject of legato on the trombone must be treated separately. Actually, the only true slurs available on the trombone occur with the lip slur (moving between two different partials of the harmonic series), and when the slide motion is opposite to the direction of the notes. The rest of the time the trombonist must depend on a refined legato tongue to create the effect of slurring. In practice, all of these methods are used within one integrated technique.

What has been said concerning slurring in general applies to the trombone, particularly with lip slurs which take place in the same position. When the slide is moved, the problem of avoiding unwanted sound between notes becomes paramount. Quick slide motion is essential to avoid the slide's natural tendency to glissando.[11]

It is possible to achieve a clean slur between adjacent positions if the move involves a change from one set of partials to another (a set of partials consists of the seven positions of one partial of the harmonic series). For example, a slur can be made from A at the top of the bass staff (2nd position, 4th partial) to D above (1st position, 5th partial), without using the tongue, if the slide motion is quick. Another approach is through the direction of the motion of the slide in relation to the direction of the notes. A smooth slur may be achieved if the notes move downward as the slide is brought inward. The reverse—notes ascending, outward slide motion—is only effective in the upper register.

Legato tonguing must be cultivated through the use of a soft syllable, such as "du," "thu," "loo," or "roo," and perhaps by placing the tip of the tongue on the roof of the mouth. To achieve a smooth legato it is vital to keep the air stream moving. Students sometimes hesitate with the air between notes to avoid a glissando when the real problem is sluggish slide motion.[12] A number of teachers advocate that the legato tongue should almost always be used in performance and that natural slurs be reserved for practice.

SUSTAINING AND CONTINUITY

The related concepts of sustaining and continuity are underlying principles of all good brass playing. It is important that notes retain an evenness of volume. Any "erosion" of a note detracts from the tone and reflects a poor mastery of style. Ensemble problems are created with balance and intonation, as well.[13] Another error is to allow the note before a breath to decrease in volume (unless the musical context calls for a diminuendo). This creates a rough end to one phrase and upsets the continuity between phrases. Care must be taken in practicing to develop the habit of sustaining up to the breathing point and then beginning the next phrase

11. Slide movement is discussed in Chapter 5.

12. Several books of studies on trombone legato may be recommended: Joannes Rochut, *Melodious Etudes,* vol. 1–3 (Carl Fischer); André LaFosse, *Méthode Complète de Trombone a Coulisse* (Alphonse Leduc); Reginald H. Fink, *Studies in Legato for Trombone* (Carl Fischer); Blazevich, *30 Legato Studies* (International).

13. The importance of sustaining in ensembles is discussed in Chapter 8 under "Suggestions to Marching Band Directors" and in Chapter 14.

with a minimum of interruption. The beginnings and ends of phrases must b carefully shaped.

The concept of sustaining must be applied to phrases as well as individu notes. Brass players often speak of the need to "blow through the notes." The a stream must remain constant through the phrase, with the player resisting ar tendency to allow air pressure to drop when notes are tongued or changed durir a slur.

Continuity is a function of sustaining and is concerned with the coheren of the line or phrase. In legato and slurred passages, each new note shou flow from the one before it without interruption. This can be accomplished b approaching the phrase as one long tone. In his complete method, the 19th-centur cornetist Saint-Jacome presented legato tonguing under the heading, "tonguing o the sound."[14] This reflects a very clear concept of continuity: continuous sour uninterrupted by the tongue. Saint-Jacome's maxim might be diagrammed in th following way:

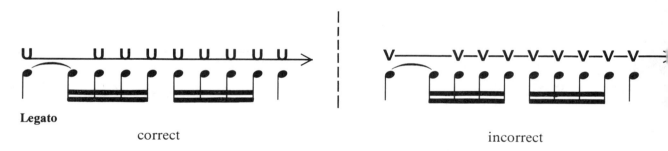

Legato

correct   incorrect

Tonguing on the sound.

CONCEPT OF SOUND

A concept of sound is developed through careful listening. In the early stages, th teacher should lose no opportunity to play for and with the student. In this wa elements of the teacher's tone will be transferred to the student. While every grea player has a unique and recognizable timbre and style of playing, many influence have contributed to this individual quality. The process through which a person sound is developed is enriched by studying a variety of models.

It is inaccurate to think of sound as a single entity. Actually, players mus modify their timbre according to the repertoire being performed. What may b appropriate in one context may not be in another. By meticulous observatio of how representative players and brass sections approach specific literatur (via recordings, concerts, and broadcasts), one's overall concept of sound an interpretation will develop.

14. Louis Antoine Saint-Jacome (1830–1898), *Grand Method for Trumpet or Cornet* (New York: Carl Fische 1894), p. 110.

Mental imagery plays a vital role in this process. By having a clearly realized image of the sound one is trying to create present in the mind, the physical aspects of tone production are guided to reproduce that sound.[15]

VIBRATO

Vibrato should be viewed as a means of bringing added color to the sound. There are some contexts where it applies, and some where it does not. For example, in the author's view, the horn should never be played with vibrato, since it adds nothing to the expressiveness of the timbre and robs the horn of its purity and natural beauty. With other members of the brass family, vibrato can add character and sensitivity when used in specific areas of the repertoire, but the majority of the literature should be played with a pure, vibratoless tone.

There are four types of vibrato currently in use: hand, diaphragm, slide, and lip/jaw.

Hand vibrato, which is only effective on the trumpet and cornet, is created by a gentle forward and backward movement from the right thumb resting on the bottom of the leadpipe. Because of its ease of control, it is the preferred means of vibrato on the cornet and trumpet.

Diaphragm vibrato consists of pulsations in the air stream (similar to that used on the flute). Although it can be effective, it tends to be difficult to control and consequently is only rarely used on brass instruments.

Slide vibrato is commonly employed by trombonists in the jazz and studio fields and it is also occasionally used by symphonic players in certain passages. Less subtle than vibrato produced by the lip and jaw (which is more commonly used on the trombone), it is produced by moving the slide slightly inward and outward according to the desired speed.

Lip/jaw vibrato involves a subtle movement of the embouchure and jaw. It is the principal type of vibrato used on low brass instruments. Although it can also be applied to the trumpet, it tends to be heavy and less easily controlled than hand vibrato. Symphonic trombonists generally prefer lip/jaw vibrato for most of their work, but have a perfected slide vibrato available when needed.

When it is used, vibrato can bring differing expressive effects to the appropriate literature according to its speed. These may range from a quick vibrato and a bright timbre in French works, to a slower, more vocal style in Verdi. Germanic composers such as Brahms or Bruckner are best served by a pure, round tone without any hint of vibrato.

SPECIAL EFFECTS

Composers sometimes call upon brass players to produce specialized sounds. Two of the most common are the flutter tongue and the glissando. The flutter tongue is produced by thinking of rolling an "r" and allowing the tongue tip to vibrate as the air passes into the instrument. It is most effective in the middle range.

On valved brass instruments, when an obvious glissando effect is called for, lowering the valves halfway and sliding upward or downward will usually give the best results. Composers sometimes indicate when a valve glissando is to be used. Expressive glissandi of shorter duration can be rendered by elongating a slur, or, if a less subtle effect is desired, by allowing the valves to come up with a deliberately slow action. Trombonists are frequently required to produce a slide glissando; this technique is discussed in Chapter 5.

15. See William H. Trusheim, "Mental Imagery and Musical Performance: An Inquiry into Imagery Use by Eminent Orchestral Brass Players (Ed.D. dissertation, Rutgers University, 1987). See also Stewart, *Arnold Jacobs*.

New effects are occasionally found in the works of contemporary composers. These include singing or hissing through the instrument, playing with the water key open, and raising or lowering the pitch from the hand in the horn bell, among others.

COMMON TONE PRODUCTION PROBLEMS

1. *Restriction of the Exhalation Process.* By far, the most frequently encountered tone production problem is restriction of the exhalation process. This can stem from several causes. Players who bring their body into a state of tension attempting to create support often suffer from this difficulty. Despite the muscular effort, the *flow* of air is meager. The body must remain relaxed if an unimpeded outward flow of air is to be achieved. A related hindrance is attempting to expel the air by consciously controlling specific muscles. Both of these problems can be eliminated if the use of the air is seen as *movement* by creating *wind.* The body has known how to expel air from the lungs from birth so the correct procedure will automatically be employed in brass playing if the player concentrates solely on moving the wind freely. Problems of this sort are often wrongly attributed to the embouchure or to an insufficiently large breath. In fact, tension is sometimes created by taking overly large breaths (see "The Air," above).

2. *Impedance at the Mouthpiece.* The exhalation process is occasionally restricted within the mouthpiece. If the portion of the lips inside the mouthpiece rim is flexed or otherwise brought into a state of tension, the embouchure will resist vibration. It is essential that this area retain maximum flexibility. The musculature of the lower cheeks provides the necessary support so that the pliable formation within the rim can vibrate freely. Similarly, the aperture must remain open and oval in shape. Using a formation similar to the letter "P" will help the aperture to open. Any constriction of the aperture will obstruct the air stream and inhibit vibration. This problem is also the principal cause of tightness in the throat (see "Embouchure Formation," above).

3. *Interrupting the Breath.* Students sometimes develop the habit of stopping the breath at the peak of inhalation and restarting the air on the exhalation phase. This puts the body into a resistive state of tension which interferes with the free outflow of the air. Inhalation and exhalation should be approached as a continuous action, with no interruption at the point where one becomes the other. Another error is to hold back the air by attempting to build up air pressure behind the tongue before an attack. Tension is again generated causing a constriction of the throat (see "Attack and Tonguing," above).

4. *Stretching the Embouchure.* Brass players must always be on guard against any tendency for the lips to pull outward (as in smiling). If this occurs, the tissue inside the mouthpiece rim becomes tense and the aperture tends to close, hampering a free tone production. Beginners occasionally make the fatal mistake of stretching back the lips in forming the embouchure. Others develop this difficulty as a temporary means of reaching the upper register. The muscles of the lower cheeks must prevent any inclination of the lips to pull outward through adequate support of the embouchure formation. Another ruinous habit is to allow the cheeks to inflate, rendering their vital muscles useless (see "Embouchure Formation" and "Embouchure Adjustment," above).

5. *Incorrect Mouthpiece Placement.* Embouchure difficulties can occur if the mouthpiece placement is too low. If the edge of the rim contacts the "red" of

the upper lip it will interfere with its vibration and affect the aperture. Lateral placement is less crucial, and only if the mouthpiece is distinctly off-center should any change be made (see "Mouthpiece Placement," above).

6. *Rigid Jaw or Tongue.* Some students try to play with limited movement of their jaw or tongue. This causes reduced flexibility and range since the embouchure is limited in its ability to adjust for vibration at different frequencies. (see "Embouchure Adjustment").

7. *Excessive Pressure.* While no viable non-pressure system exists, brass players should always be alert to any indication of excessive mouthpiece pressure. A certain minimal pressure is required, and undue pressure can best be prevented by good habits of tone production.

HOW TO WARM UP AND PRACTICE EFFECTIVELY

The warm-up is an important element in brass playing. This is the time when all of the playing functions are brought into proper condition before being applied to the demands of the literature. The warm-up should be extended, whenever time allows, to include basic exercises covering all phases of playing to aid one's general development and to prevent problems from arising. To plunge straight into a rehearsal or performance situation without adequate preparation is to invite difficulties.

The most effective warm-up is a flexible one. This allows players to vary their material according to the condition of the embouchure and the time available. To force the embouchure through a fixed series of exercises when it does not feel up to it (due to heavy playing or a layoff) is destructive. In such cases, it is better to work slowly and patiently, bringing the embouchure into condition gradually. When there is too little time to go through the set routine, the player often must begin the rehearsal or concert with a feeling of not being completely warmed up—a frame of mind not conducive to confidence.

Warm-up material may be selected from various studies, melodies, intervals, scales, and arpeggios, or be improvised. The general procedure is to warm up the middle range first, and then progressively work outward to include the lower and upper range. By the end of the warm-up period, the entire compass should have been covered. With certain instruments, particularly the horn, playing in the low register early in the warm-up period is especially beneficial. Playing on the F side of the double horn during the warm-up period is also helpful. The overall goal of the warm-up is to get the wind moving freely and notes throughout the range responding with a full, centered sound and relaxed tone production.

At the beginning of the warm-up, some exercises or melodies should be played on the mouthpiece alone. This helps center the sound and stimulates a free tone production. The mouthpiece might also be buzzed every so often during the warm-up and practice session. The use of a transparent mouthpiece at the beginning of the warm-up is also useful in reminding oneself of the essential elements of tone production.

Practice should be tied to an organized program of development. This should consist of daily work on basic skills,[16] such as slurring, tonguing, scales and arpeggios, flexibility, and so on, with any weak areas singled out for special attention. The second part of the practice session might be devoted to systematically working through important study literature for the instrument. There is immense value

16. Studies such as those found in Schlossberg, *Daily Drills and Technical Studies* (M. Baron) are helpful in developing good practices of tone production, control, and endurance. With minor adjustments, the Schlossberg studies can be used with all brass instruments.

in etudes, many of which were written by great players of the past. The variety of technical and musical challenges presented will expand one's ability to play the instrument in a way no other literature can. The final portion of practice may include study of solo works, transposition, orchestral or band excerpts, and sightreading.

Again, flexibility is the key to successful practicing. The order of the three sections may be varied or portions omitted. Practice may be lengthened or shortened as necessary. At all times, the player should work patiently, stressing good tone production as the primary goal. While accuracy can only be developed through repetition, it is of no use to practice beyond the tiring point. The best results will be achieved by working in a relaxed but thorough manner, always concentrating on building one's confidence.

CHAPTER 11
Playing Position

In the early stages of playing, the importance of the playing position is not always recognized. Actually, how a player positions his or her body when playing a brass instrument is the starting point of good tone production.

There are two vital factors that must be considered. First, if there is to be free movement of the air during inhalation and exhalation, the body must be situated in such a way that no restriction is placed on the expansion of the lungs. A curved posture will interfere with the breathing process and will create tension, which significantly reduces the quantity of air that can be taken in. The second factor is the need for relaxation in the exhalation process. An upright but relaxed posture is essential in promoting unencumbered exhalation.

THE TRUMPET AND CORNET

The trumpet and cornet are supported by the left hand, which lightly grips the valve casings (see Figs. 11.1–11.4). The third or little finger should be placed in the ring on the third valve slide. The tips of the fingers of the right hand are located over the valve caps. In order to press the valves straight down, the fingers must be curved. The right thumb should be turned upward and rest on the bottom of the leadpipe. Better valve action will be achieved if the little finger is kept free of the ring on the leadpipe.

The instrument should be held fairly straight or at a *slight* angle. Only the minimum effort necessary to hold the instrument should be used and the arms must remain as relaxed as possible. When seated, it is best for the player to sit in an upright position, not leaning against the back of the chair. Practice time should be divided between sitting and standing.

Young players often point the instrument directly into the music stand and attempt to read over the bell. Aside from the negative effect on the sound, this practice tends to cause the trumpet to pull downward and the jaw to recede, and thereby affects the embouchure. The solution is to place the stand slightly to the side or lower it so that does not obstruct the radiation of sound from the bell.

THE HORN

Of all the brass, the horn is the most prone to poor playing positions. The bell can easily be blocked by the body; this results in a dull, unresonant timbre. With the bell resting on the thigh, there can be a tendency to slump over the horn, which would diminish the player's air capacity.

There are two methods of holding the horn. Many American horn players rest the bell on the right thigh, while European players usually hold the bell free at the side. The popularity of the latter position is rapidly growing in the United States, however, and it is now used in several major orchestras, notably the Chicago Symphony (Fig. 11.5). By resting the bell, more of the higher overtones are absorbed by the body, and a darker and rounder timbre is produced. With the bell free, the tone is more pure, although slightly brighter in color. Barry Tuckwell

Figure 11.1. Playing position (trumpet): Charles Schlueter, Principal Trumpet, Boston Symphony Orchestra. *(Photo courtesy of the Boston Symphony Orchestra.)*

Figure 11.2. Playing position (trumpet): British trumpeter Philip Jones.
(Photo courtesy of Decca Records International.)

Figure 11.3. Playing position (trumpet): trumpet soloist Crispian Steele-Perkins.
(Photo courtesy of C. Steele-Perkins)

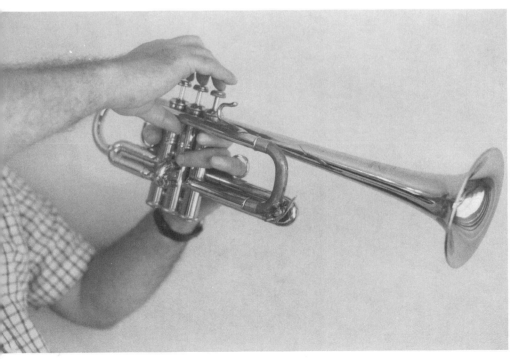

Figure 11.4. Hand position (trumpet).

Figure 11.5. Two views of playing position (horn): Dale Clevenger, Principal Horn, Chicago Symphony Orchestra.
(Photos: Jim Steere)

Figure 11.6. Playing position (horn): horn soloist Barry Tuckwell.

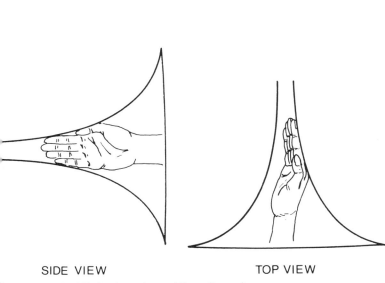

SIDE VIEW   TOP VIEW

Figure 11.7. Right-hand position (horn).

Figure 11.8. Right-hand position (horn).
(Photo: Joseph Hetman)

Fig. 11.6) has pointed out that the free-held position has the advantage of greater freedom in breathing.[1]

In developing a good playing position, the player should try turning the chair about 30 degrees to the right. This allows the right leg to be brought back to a point where the bell rim can rest comfortably on top of the thigh. Turning the chair also aids the free-held position. In both methods of holding the horn, it is essential that the entire circumference of the bell clear the body so that the sound can project rearward without obstruction.

The first three fingers of the left hand should be curved over the valve levers (the little finger may rest in the hook provided). The left thumb should rest on the $B\flat$ valve lever on double horns, or in the ring on single horns.

The right-hand position is of vital importance in influencing tone and intonation. The hand should be slightly cupped, with the thumb resting *on top of the fingers* (see Figs. 11.7 and 11.8). This is crucial in forming an acoustically effective duct within the horn bell. Any space between the fingers should be sealed. Students often rest the thumb alongside the fingers, which causes problems with intonation and tonal center.

Placing the hand vertically into the bell, the player should have the backs of his fingers resting against the bell's far wall. (Some advocate that the tips of the fingers should cross the bell throat.) The free space between the palm of the hand and the near wall can be closed down or opened to control intonation and change the tone from a more covered quality to a brighter timbre.

There are several problems frequently encountered among horn students. Aside from an incorrectly formed right hand position, the hand often unconsciously shifts away from the outer bell wall, causing a muffled tone. Another common problem occurs when the horn is held in such a way that the mouthpipe approaches the embouchure at too straight an angle. On the horn, the air stream is directed downward; for good tone production, the mouthpiece and mouthpipe must assume a downward angle. By holding the horn so that the bell is perpendicular, or tilted only slightly backward, the player will automatically achieve the proper angle

. Barry Tuckwell, *Playing the Horn* (London: Oxford University Press, 1978), p. 6.

of the mouthpipe. Sometimes the horn is simply too large for a youngster to hold correctly. The only solution is to gradually perfect the position as the student grows, although it would be helpful if manufacturers would construct student instruments in a more compactly wound pattern.

It should be noted that horn players are now expected to stand when playing a solo, as the tone can be projected more clearly and a better visual impression is created. It is wise, therefore, to practice standing periodically. Care should be taken that the right-hand position does not change, however.

THE TROMBONE

The full weight of the trombone must be supported by the left hand and arm so that the right arm will be free of tension and able to move the slide quickly from position to position. The left index finger should rest on the mouthpiece shank or receiver with the remaining fingers formed around the inner slide brace and the cork barrel. The left thumb grasps the bottom of the bell brace, or the rotary valve on instruments fitted with F attachments.

The outer slide brace is held at its base between the right thumb and first two fingers. Usually, the third and fourth fingers curl under the lower portion of the slide. The slide is controlled through a combination of finger, wrist, and forearm motion.

Figure 11.9. Two views of playing position (trombone): Jay Friedman, Principal Trombone, Chicago Symphony Orchestra.
(Photos: Jim Steere)

Figure 11.10. Hand position (trombone). *(Photo: Joseph Hetman)*

The most natural playing position for the trombonist is with the instrument held at a slight downward angle. Sometimes there is a tendency to lean the head to one side or the othe. This can be avoided by keeping the head erect and bringing the trombone to the embouchure rather than adapting the body to fit the instrument. (See Figures 11.9 and 11.10.)

Music stands often cause difficulties. The best location for the player and the slide is to the left of the stand. The music can be read by looking to the right. The tone will project more resonantly with the bell clear of the stand as well.

LOCATING THE POSITIONS

The trombone slide has been compared to a violin string. Continuously variable in pitch, the exact placement of a position must ultimately be determined by careful listening. Some basic visual guidelines may be offered as a starting point, but these should not be taken as absolute since there are variations between instruments and individual players.

Some of the positions are more clearly defined on the slide than others. The 1st, 3rd, 4th, and 6th positions are fairly easy to locate. Less obvious are the 2nd, 5th, and 7th positions, which require even greater reliance on the ear to place them precisely. (See Figs. 11.11–11.17.)

There is some tendency to place the 2nd position sharp, particularly when it occurs on a leading tone. The 5th position is rather awkward and depends heavily on the ear to find its exact center. Intonation problems are sometimes encountered in ensemble playing with this position. Advanced players usually play the notes produced by the 6th and 7th positions in 1st and (altered) 2nd position on the F attachment. It is, however, unwise for students to develop a dependency on the F attachment: comparable ease and confidence should be sought on the longer positions as on the shorter ones.

Figure 11.11. Trombone: 1st position—slide fully in, lightly touching the corks or springs.

Figure 11.12. Trombone: 3rd position—brace slightly above the bell rim.

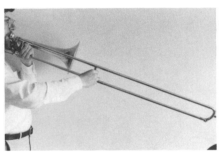

Figure 11.13. Trombone: 4th position—top of outer slide below the bell rim.

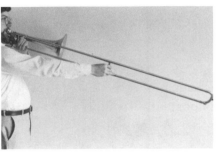

Figure 11.14. Trombone: 6th position—a comfortable arm's length.

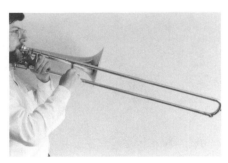

Figure 11.15. Trombone: 2nd position—approximately one-third the distance between positions 1 and 3.

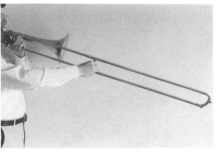

Figure 11.16. Trombone: 5th position—approximately halfway between positions 4 and 6.

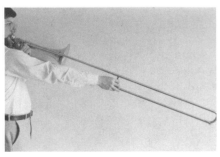

Figure 11.17. Trombone: 7th position—a stretched arm's length, exposing the slide stocking (boot).

Figure 11.18. Playing position (euphonium): SSgt. Steven Kellner, Principal Euphonium, United States Marine Band.

(Photo courtesy of "The President's Own" United States Marine Band, Washington, D.C.)

Figure 11.19. Playing position (euphonium): Brian Bowman, euphonium soloist, United States Air Force Band.   *(Photo courtesy of Dr. Brian Bowman)*

THE BARITONE AND EUPHONIUM

The baritone or euphonium is held diagonally across the body with the lower bow pressed in to the waist to provide stability (Figs. 11.18 and 11.19). It is important for the mouthpiece to be brought upward to the embouchure rather than allowing the instrument to rest on the lap or chair. If the instrument is too low, breathing will be restricted. If necessary, a pillow, folded towel, or specially made stand should be used to bring the instrument to the correct height. Mouthpiece pressure must also be monitored to make certain that the embouchure is not being used to help support the instrument.

On euphoniums with side-action valves, the right arm reaches to the front of the instrument while the left hand grasps the left side of the top bow. If rings are provided on the tuning or valve slides to adjust intonation, the left hand may rest on one of these.

The right hand is placed under the top bow on instruments with top-action valves. The fingers should be rounded over the valve caps. The left arm must reach across the lower bow and grip the tubing on the right side. When a fourth valve is located on the side, the left index or middle finger is used to depress the valve.

Figure 11.20. Two views of playing position (tuba): Arnold Jacobs, Principal Tuba, Chicago Symphony Orchestra.   *(Photos: Jim Steere*

THE TUBA

The tuba should rest on the lap or the front of the chair and be stabilized by the left arm and a gentle tension between the thighs (Fig. 11.20). On tubas with top-action valves, the right-hand fingers are rounded over the valve caps beneath the top bow. The left hand should grasp any tubing that can be comfortably reached on the right front of the instrument.

The right arm must reach around to the front of rotary and side-action piston tubas, where the fingers rest on the valve levers or caps. The thumb should be placed in the ring; it is important that no tension (resulting from weight) be felt at the thumb, hand, or arm in order to promote good finger dexterity. The left hand grasps the first valve slide, which will be moved in controlling intonation.

Some students have difficulty reaching the mouthpiece of the larger tubas; in such cases, the player should use a cushion or some other means of achieving alignment between embouchure and mouthpiece. There should be no tendency to lean back into the chair or curve the torso. Some tubists feel that leaning the instrument slightly forward assists the free movement of the air and provides a greater feeling of control.

CHOICE OF CLOTHING

Before leaving the subject of playing position, some comments on appropriate clothing might be useful. Tight-fitting concert attire should be avoided since breathing might feel restricted. There should be ample room for expansion at the waist and chest. Women hornists and tubists generally find slacks more conducive than skirts to a good playing position.

CHAPTER 12

Getting Started

TEACHING YOUNG BEGINNERS

An important factor in beginning instruction is to make certain that students are provided with good instruments and mouthpieces. Too often a youngster has to struggle with equipment that would present difficulties to an advanced player. At any level, brass players are dependent on their equipment. Mouthpieces, especially, are a vital concern, and those provided with rental instruments are often less than adequate. This is particularly the case with horn mouthpieces: some commonly recommended models simply will not produce good results under any circumstances. The teacher should specify the mouthpieces that will be provided with rental instruments, and, if necessary, the school should purchase a set to be loaned to students. It is also advisable to provide parents with a list of appropriate mouthpieces before they purchase an instrument.

In selecting mouthpieces suitable for beginners, the main considerations are that the mouthpiece responds easily and that it produces a characteristic tone. Mouthpieces of medium-cup diameter and depth are best for this purpose. Excessively small or large mouthpieces should be avoided at this stage. The following mouthpieces can be specifically recommended:

Trumpet	Cornet	Horn
Bach 7, 7C, or 6C Schilke 9 or 11 Denis Wick 4	Denis Wick 7 or 5B Bach 7 or 6	Giardinelli C12 or S15 Schilke 27 or 30 Denis Wick 7N Holton MDC

Trombone	Baritone or Euphonium	Tuba
Bach 12C, 12, or 11 Denis Wick 12CS or 9 BS Schilke 46	Denis Wick 6BY, 6BM, or 6BL Schilke 46D Bach 6-1/2 A, or 6-1/2 AL	Schilke 62 Bach 25 Denis Wick 5 Mirafone H2 Giardinelli 25

Additional information on mouthpieces is provided in Chapter 2.

The teacher should carefully check each instrument that will be used in the class to determine if it is in acceptable condition and of reasonable quality. The following is a checklist that the teacher may follow in making this assessment:

1. Is the mouthpiece among the recommended models? If not, is it suitable for a beginning student and is it of adequate quality?
   a. The throat and backbore should be clean. Instructions for cleaning brass instruments are presented in Chapter 13.
   b. There should be no dents at the bottom of the shank.
   c. There should be no scrapes or gouges on the mouthpiece rim.

    d. The plating should be in good condition.

    e. The shank must fit the instrument's receiver.

2. The valves should be checked to see that they move freely.

    a. If the instrument does not play, check to see if each piston is in the correct valve casing.

    b. Valve casings should be free of dents.

    c. If the instrument plays, but the response and tone are uneven, valve alignment should be checked. This is especially important on rotary valve instruments. Valve alignment is discussed in Chapter 13.

    d. Frayed or broken strings on rotary valves should be replaced.

    e. The height of rotary valve keys should be adjusted to fit the students' hands. See Chapter 13.

    f. The valves should be oiled.

3. Tuning and valve slides should move freely. All slides should be lubricated.

4. The trombone slide should move smoothly without binding and be free of dents.

5. There should be no dents in critical areas of the tubing such as the leadpipe.

6. The spring and pad of the water key should be checked to be certain that it forms an effective seal.

7. Instrument cases must provide adequate protection.

Above all, the teacher should play each instrument to evaluate both condition and quality. The first consideration is whether the instrument's air seal is adequate. Excessive wear on the valves and slides will cause leaking, which affects the instrument's response and tone. This can usually be detected as the instrument is played. A sluggish response, particularly in the upper register, combined with a dull and uneven tone are indications that the instrument may be leaking excessively (although faulty valve alignment or a leaking water key can also cause these symptoms). This condition can be corrected, but it represents a major repair. If all of the previous criteria have been successfully met, the teacher should examine the instrument for quality by testing its intonation, response, tone quality, and evenness from register to register. Once the teacher is confident that the instruments to be used by the class are reasonably serviceable, instruction may begin.

Classes composed of the same instrument are generally more successful at the elementary level than classes of mixed instruments. The size of the class should be kept small because of the need for individual attention. In programs where private lessons can be offered as part of the regular curriculum, it is advisable to start students in pairs to take advantage of the positive motivation stimulated by interaction between students.

Although some texts give a great deal of attention to the selection of students for instrumental classes, it is difficult to predict with accuracy whether a student will be successful on a particular brass instrument. Aside from reasonable pitch discrimination, the primary considerations are lip size and tooth formation. Students who have a thick lip structure are usually better suited to the low brass rather than the horn or trumpet, but there are exceptions. Perfectly even teeth are not essential, but protruding or missing teeth can cause problems.

The First Lesson

No rigid plans should be set for the first few lessons. Better results will be gained if the teacher is free to approach each lesson flexibly, following his or her own individual teaching style and the needs of the students. The first lesson might begin by showing the students how to assemble the instrument correctly. This procedure is outlined below. Next, a good playing position should be established following the instructions presented in Chapter 11. The teacher should then show the students how to form an embouchure and demonstrate correct mouthpiece placement for that instrument using the guidelines established in Chapter 10.

Producing Sound

The foremost goal of the first lesson is to have the students produce sound. With the mouthpiece, the teacher should demonstrate a buzz and have each student try to imitate that sound. It is not important what pitch is produced at this point or even that it is a good sound. *The objective is to have the students experience that sound is produced by vibration, and that vibration is caused by the motion of the air through the lips.*[1]

Occasionally, a student is found who has difficulty making a sound on the mouthpiece. In such cases, the teacher should demonstrate how to buzz the lips alone and ask the student to imitate that sound. Once the student can buzz his lips, he should have little difficulty in transferring the feeling of vibration to the mouthpiece. (Buzzing the lips without the mouthpiece as a general procedure is not recommended since the lips function differently when the mouthpiece and instrument are used.) Placing the tip of the index finger slightly over the end of the mouthpiece shank also helps the student achieve a buzz more easily. Some time should be spent with the students freely buzzing the mouthpiece following the lead of the teacher. It should be stressed that *each sound must be held as long as possible.* The teacher should gradually guide the buzzing toward middle-register pitches, especially these tones:

Changing Pitch

After the students are able to make a reasonably stable sound on the mouthpiece, the teacher should demonstrate changing pitch on the mouthpiece by sliding upward and downward with a glissando effect. The students should try to imitate this. Again, specific pitches are not important. This is an appropriate time to introduce the idea of starting the sound with the tongue, using a "da" or "du" syllable. In presenting this skill, however, it is essential to re-emphasize that it is *the air* that starts the sound; the tongue only assists in making a clean attack. The tongue should not be used to stop the sound since this makes an audible sound at the end of the note. The correct method of ending a note is to cease blowing.

Transferring Sound Making to the Instrument

The next step is to transfer the sound making to the instrument. A very common error is to insist that students begin on predetermined pitches. While the notes shown above are good starting tones, if students seem inclined to produce higher or lower pitches, it is better to work with these notes than to force them to play a specified pitch. As with the mouthpiece, the teacher should demonstrate a sound on the instrument for each student and have him or her try to imitate it. Again, each note should be held as long as possible. This portion of the lesson should be concerned with having the students play as many notes as possible. The use of transparent mouthpieces is extremely helpful at this point. The teacher should

1. Some very useful advice on teaching beginning brass players was presented in two lectures by Arnold Jacobs at the Second International Brass Congress at Indiana University in 1984. Texts of the lectures appear in M. Dee Stewart, *Arnold Jacobs: The Legacy of a Master* (Northfield, Ill.: Instrumentalist Co., 1987), pp. 127–143. Many of the ideas presented here are based on concepts of Mr. Jacobs.

demonstrate a sound while allowing the students to observe the vibration taking place within the mouthpiece. Where possible, transparent mouthpieces should be made available for loan to students.

Aural Imagery

One of the most important processes involved with learning to play a brass instrument is the formation of aural images. The research on mental imagery and brass performance has shown that sound memory and imitation are powerful tools which guide the development of the player.[2] Therefore, the teacher should attempt to demonstrate a poor sound on the instrument and follow it with a good sound. This initiates a "sound image" in the students' minds which can be recalled when they attempt to produce their own sound. By imitating the teacher's sound, the student's mental sound image functions like a guidance system which directs the physical aspects of sound production. It is most beneficial to use the technique of demonstration-imitation frequently in beginning classes. When the teacher demonstrates both a satisfactory and unsatisfactory sound, students gain a more clearly defined picture of what to strive for.

Correct Breathing

At this point in the lesson, it is desirable to demonstrate and explain correct breathing. In beginning classes, all explanations should be as brief as possible and presented in terms students can understand. Technical terms should be avoided. For example, rather than discuss the operation of the diaphragm in the respiratory process, it is better to demonstrate a deep breath as opposed to a shallow, chest breath. Have the students place their hands on the sides of their waists and feel the expansion taking place in this area as they inhale. By showing the students—and having them experience—both a correct and an incorrect breath, the concept of diaphragmatic breathing will usually take root. A more detailed explanation of the breathing process can be presented later. Before leaving the subject of breathing, the need to relax when inhaling and the idea of filling from the bottom upward should also be stressed. It might be worthwhile to reinforce the basic concept that sound is produced on a brass instrument by the vibration of the lips in the mouthpiece. To cause this vibration, a stream of air must pass through the lips. *The breathing process as it applies to brass playing is concerned with moving air in and out of the lungs and through the lips into the instrument.*

Associating Sound with Notation

Toward the end of the lesson, some attention should be given to connecting the sounds being produced with their notation. After giving an assignment for the next lesson, the teacher should review embouchure formation and mouthpiece placement. If these important topics are repeated at the end of the lesson, students will tend to keep them in mind during practice. The lesson may conclude by demonstrating the proper method of lubricating the valves or trombone slide (see Chapter 13), removing accumulated condensation, and disassembling the instrument and placing it correctly in the case. (Instructions for the latter two procedures are given below.)

The Second Lesson

The second lesson should begin with a very brief review of the points covered in the first class. It is important to have the students play early in the lesson

---

2. See William H. Trusheim, "Mental Imagery and Musical Performance: An Inquiry into Imagery Use by Eminent Orchestral Brass Players (Ed.D. dissertation, Rutgers University, 1987).

to take advantage of their natural eagerness to make sound. At this lesson, the teacher should carefully check every individual in the class to determine if the fundamental procedures are correct and to watch for obvious problems. Potential problems to check are the following:

1. Incorrect mouthpiece placement
2. Stretched embouchure
3. Incorrect playing position
4. Interruption of the breath
5. Excessive pressure

These and other problems are discussed in Chapter 10. Instructions for correct playing position are given in Chapter 11.

The principal objectives of the second lesson are to add more notes, to change pitch, and to begin to learn simple tunes. Using the technique of demonstration-imitation, the teacher should have the students play various notes on the mouthpiece, holding each note as long as possible. More middle-range notes should be added to those attempted in the first lesson. Next, the teacher should demonstrate changing pitch with the mouthpiece and call upon each student to imitate this sound. The principle of altering pitch syllables ("ah-ee" or "oo-ee") which was discussed in Chapter 10 should be established at this point. Once the students are able to change pitch to some degree, simple tunes in the middle register can be introduced. Buzzing melodies on the mouthpiece is of great value; this practice should continue through the most advanced stages. After spending some time with the mouthpiece, a similar procedure can be followed with the instrument.

During the last third of the lesson, it is useful to restate the basic processes of tone production—playing position, embouchure formation, mouthpiece placement, starting the sound, breathing—in a more thorough presentation than the brief review at the beginning of the class. The remaining portion of the lesson could be concerned with attempting to play familiar melodies and basic instruction in reading music. One of the elementary methods listed at the end of each instrumental chapter (Chapters 3–7) could be used for this purpose, or the teacher could create some original exercises. At the conclusion of the lesson, the teacher should observe how each student disassembles the instrument and places it in the case, offering any necessary corrections.

Subsequent Lessons

Subsequent lessons should focus on establishing good tone production, exploring the instrument, expanding the students' ability to read, and steadily developing tone, technique, and range. Every lesson should contain some form of reinforcement of the basic concepts of tone production, perhaps using different words, and each student's progress must be carefully monitored by the teacher. It is essential that each individual play alone during some portion of the lesson so that progress in mastering these principles may be observed. Sometimes, students will play the notes of an exercise correctly, but with an incorrect approach to tone production. Teachers must be alert to this type of occurrence and center their evaluation on whether a student is developing correct procedures of tone production rather than on getting the notes.

As a general procedure, each tune or exercise should be played first on the mouthpiece and then on the instrument, with the teacher demonstrating frequently. In discussing tonguing, it is helpful for the teacher to ask the student to hold a note and try moving the tongue around in the mouth without interrupting the airflow or stopping the sound. This encourages a continuity of sound in tonguing and can be followed with some simple exercises consisting of repeated notes. The emphasis ould be on keeping the air moving and on following the brass player's maxim, low through the notes."

New material should be introduced at each lesson. Students will realize a eater feeling of accomplishment by progressing through a number of exercises d tunes which accomplish similar things, than by remaining on the same material om class to class. Motivation is intimately linked to a sense of accomplishment. miliar melodies and folk tunes are especially important since students uncon- iously focus their thought patterns on the melodic sequence of the tune instead on the mechanical aspects of producing sound. Melodic material should remain part of the students' study routine throughout all levels. Melodies can be used help students explore the instrument and develop a feel for different keys. It is so productive to encourage students to try to play as many notes as they can in e harmonic series of each valve combination/slide position as well as bugle-like elodies.

It is equally important to begin systematic work in one of the method books r the instrument. In this way, steady development will be assured. Unfortunately, ethod books are not always organized in the most practical sequence, and it is nost always necessary to supplement the primary method with additional studies om other books or material written by the teacher. Teachers should adapt both e study material and their approach to the needs of the students.

Above all, teachers should strive to develop a concept of sound in the students playing and demonstrating whenever possible. It is also worthwhile to play cordings of brass artists for the class and to occasionally bring in advanced dents to perform. As early as possible, duets, trios, and quartets should be empted in order to begin to cultivate a sense of ensemble.

One of the main reasons students give up their study of a brass instrument is feeling of lack of progress. In the early stages, progress must be made rapidly. youngsters advance in their ability to play, a sense of pride in this special skill velops and their motivation increases. Discouragement sets in if the process ems to be standing still. This is why the importance of correct principles of tone oduction and the need for a definite practice routine cannot be overstressed. nstant infusion of new material is also essential in stimulating progress. It is al that students participate within a course of study that has been systematically ganized to ensure progress over a period of time. Students' work should be aluated regularly to make certain that they are developing at a prescribed rate.

In spite of the best efforts, however, a student will sometimes encounter oblems with a specific instrument. In such cases, the teacher might consider commending a change to a different instrument. There are many successful ofessional players who began their study of music on a different instrument.

After a certain stage has been reached, it is of great benefit for students to ve an opportunity to play in an elementary band or orchestra in addition to eir weekly lesson(s). Membership in such a group offers a wealth of positive periences and boosts motivation as well as providing an opportunity to learn w skills.

ASSEMBLING BRASS INSTRUMENTS

e following procedures should be observed in assembling brass instruments. The uthpiece should be carefully inserted into the receiver and given a very gentle n to lock it in position. It must never be forced or tapped into the receiver. In mbone assembly, the slide should remain locked to prevent it from accidentally ling out and becoming dented. The bell section is held firmly with the left hand. e right hand should grip the slide by both braces and insert the end into the l lock receiver. The slide should be rotated so that an angle of 90 degrees (or slightly less) is formed and the lock nut tightened. Particular care must be taken i removing trombones from their cases since the slide rests in the case lid. The cas should be laid flat and the lid opened evenly from end to end to avoid twisting th slide. With each instrument, it is important to remember to pull the main tunin slide out a half inch or so before beginning to play.

REMOVING CONDENSATION

Condensation forms as warm breath is blown into the instrument. If this is n removed every so often, a gurgling sound will occur. The water can be remove almost silently by forming the lower lip around the mouthpiece rim and blowin lightly with the water key open. One or more of the valve slides may requir clearing as well, and these should be removed as necessary.

Removing water from the horn is slightly more involved. With the instrume resting on the left leg and held vertically so that the valves are downward, th horn should be rotated to the right allowing any accumulated water to collect i the main tuning slide. The tuning slide should be removed and the water poure out. Next, the horn should be returned to the inverted position so that water in th valve slides will run downward into the valves. The valves should be depresse to allow the water to enter the valves. With the third valve depressed, the hor should again be rotated to the right to direct the water into the third valve slid which should be removed and emptied. Draining the valve slides will be easier the water is poured in the opposite direction from the loop (Fig. 12.1).

The same procedure can be applied to the double horn, except that the F tunir slide must also be emptied. In clearing the valves, the player should acquire th knack of grasping both the F and B♭ third valve slides and emptying them togethe

THE COLLEGE BRASS METHODS COURSE

The study of secondary instruments is one of the most vital aspects of a prospe tive instrumental teacher's preparation. To be successful today, teachers need have extensive knowledge of all the instruments and be able to convey effecti principles of playing technique to their students. Considering the highly specia ized and developed nature of brass playing today, greater demands are now place on the college brass methods course than ever before. There are two fundament goals of the course: to provide detailed knowledge of the brass instruments ar contemporary brass playing; and to prepare students to teach brass effectively giving them a firm grasp of correct tone production and technique, both conce tually and practically. In meeting the first need, the content of the course can enriched by incorporating information from the first nine chapters of this boo The chapters on tone production, playing position, and the studies and ensembl presented in the present chapter are directed toward the second goal. Ultimatel however, it is the student's own effort in learning to play each instrument that w determine his or her effectiveness as a brass teacher.

In the class material that follows, Section A consists of progressive studies to played in unison with some easy ensembles added at various points. The instruct should move at whatever pace seems appropriate and remain on any material long as necessary. The choice of tempos is also totally at the discretion of th instructor; these will undoubtedly vary according to the ability level of each clas Typical classes are made up of both brass players learning the other instrumen and non-brass players. The brass-playing students will obviously develop at somewhat faster rate, so the instructor must attempt to balance the pace betwee the two groups. There is enough material here for both groups to feel challenge

Figure 12.1. "Removing water from the horn is
slightly more involved."

...d it is organized to ensure a comfortable rate of progress for all. Most studies
...ould be played first with the mouthpiece alone, and then on the instrument. In
...is way, students learn to center pitches accurately and their advancement will
... faster. Mouthpiece playing has been aptly termed "lip solfège."

In general, the horn should play the lower notation where possible, since
...aying in the lower range forms the foundation of the hornist's embouchure and
...ne. If necessary, however, exercises can be played up an octave. Beginning
...th exercise 89, common alternate positions are noted in the trombone part
...here appropriate. In learning fingerings and positions, students should mentally
...actice the fingering/position charts contained in Appendix D. Although 16th
...tes frequently appear in the notation after exercise 129, the tempo should be
...ry slow and can be subdivided where necessary.

Section B presents a series of ensembles which progress from easy to medium
...vels of difficulty. The instructor may wish to integrate these into Section A, or
...rk through this section as a unit. All ensembles appearing in this book have
...en scored for maximum flexibility of instrumentation so that they may be easily
...ed in any brass class. The part number (1–4 or 1–5) of each line is shown as
... circled number at the left. Trumpets are divided into two parts. The horn

part usually doubles either the second trumpet or the trombone/euphonium li
Trombones and euphoniums may be used interchangeably. The bottom part
played by the tuba(s), but, in the event that no tuba is present in the class, t
part has also been notated at the octave so that it can be played by a euphoni
or trombone.

Section C is made up of 50 individual exercises for each instrument. The
are intended to supplement the unison studies and ensembles used in class and
provide some additional material for the student to practice at home. In order
be able to include more exercises, an abbreviation has been used in notating so
of the studies. In such cases, the student should repeat the study by starting on
(stemless) note shown and playing in that key. (See, for example, number 28
trumpet-cornet.) This procedure has the added benefit of challenging students
explore the instrument, a process that significantly develops control, technique, a
confidence. The author was trained in this manner and can attest to its effectiven
as a pedagogical procedure.

In addition to providing learning material for the college brass methods cour
the studies and ensembles presented in Sections A, B, and C can be used on
elementary and secondary levels, where they should also prove of value.

Unison Studies and Easy Ensembles
for Class Use

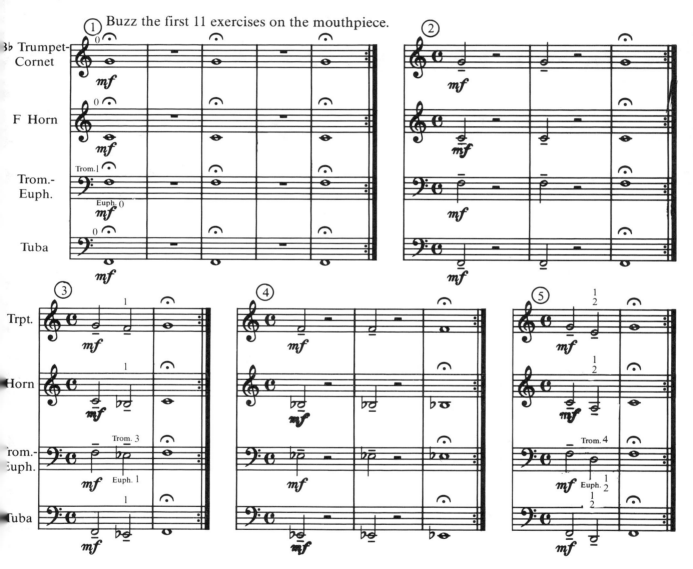

Strive for a clear, freely produced sound on the mouthpiece.
Concentrate on in-tune pitches.

Repeat the first 11 exercises with instrument

(12) Buzz exercises 12–23 first on the mouthpiece; then play with instruments.

Stabilize the sound and the pitch by moving the air.

Remember to sustain the sound and blow through the notes.

(20) Hymn: *Abide with Me*
Legato

21 *The Prince of Denmark's March* Jeremiah Clarke (ca. 1674–1707)
Marcato

(25) *Chester* William Billings (1746–1800)

(26) Think of creating *wind* in moving the air outward.

To perform No. 27 as a round, parts should be identified as 1, 2, 3, or 4.
To develop independence, parts should be changed.

(32) Chromatic Scale
Slowly

(33) Arpeggio Study

(36) From the *Ninth Symphony* Ludwig van Beethoven (1770–1827)

From the *Third Symphony* Ludwig van Beethoven (1770–1827)

Lip Slurs   Use the syllables ee–ah or oo–ah in descending,
and ah–ee or ah–oo in ascending. (See Chapter 10.)

Trombone Legato. In addition to the lip slur, a slur can be made
when changing from one set of partials to another: Position:

The positions must be adjacent, however.   Partial number:

Trombone legato is discussed in Chapter 10.
(See also the harmonic fingering/position charts in Appendix D.)

A slur can also be made when the slide motion is opposite to the
direction of the notes. For example:

Slide motion *inward,* direction of notes *downward:*

or

Slide motion *outward,* direction of notes *upward:*
(This is more effective in the upper register.)

In all other instances, the trombonist must use an exceptionally
smooth legato tongue to create the illusion of a true slur:

thu thu thu   loo loo loo   roo roo roo   du du du

thu
loo
roo
du } Use whichever syllable produces the smoothest sound.

Trombone Legato Studies

6

Remember to keep the air moving between notes when slurring.

Welsh Folk Song: *All Through the Night*
Andante

English Folk Song: *Early in the Morning*
Slowly (in 4)

Largo from the *New World Symphony (No. 9)* Antonín Dvořák (1841–1904)

From number ⑥⑥ onward, all exercises should be taken in four as slowly as necessary.
As the ability of the class develops, these exercises should be repeated in a faster four or ¢

or 8va lower

A Also play No. 67 with these articulations:

Pilgrim's Chorus from *Tannhäuser* Richard Wagner (1813–1883)

Play No. 70 with these articulations:

Scottish Folk Song: *Ye Banks and Braes*
Sadly (slowly in 6)

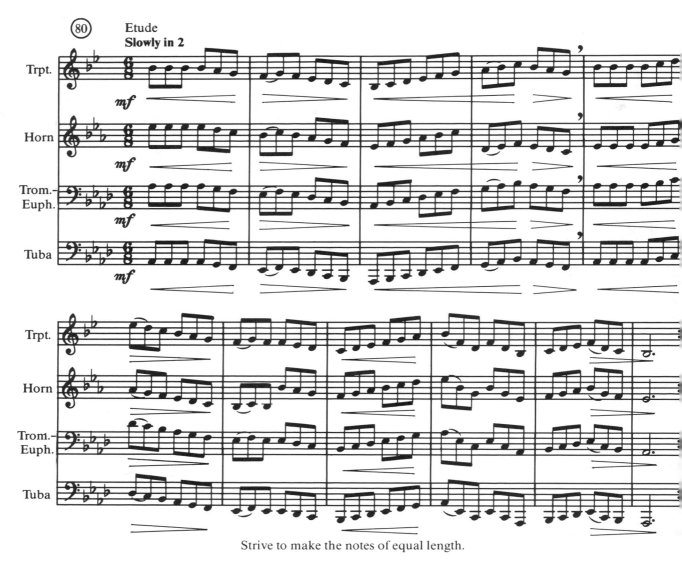

Strive to make the notes of equal length.

*In all ensembles the part number is shown by the circled numeral next to the instrument designation.

Alternate Positions for Trombone

mf Try to achieve an equality of sound between the normal and altered position.

Maintain the direction of slide motion where
possible by substituting alternate positions. (See Chapter 5.)

(96) Arpeggio Study

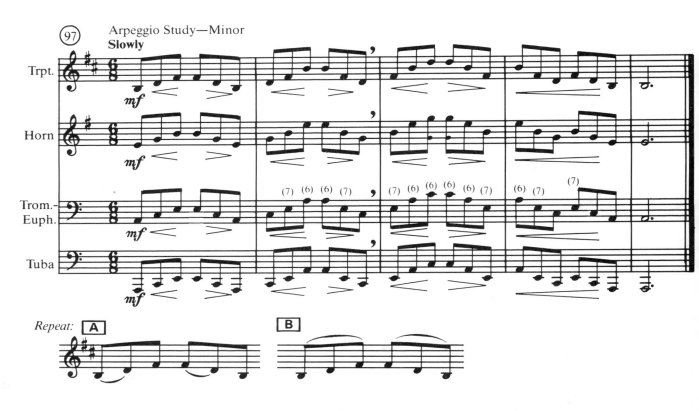

97 Arpeggio Study—Minor
Slowly

Repeat: **A**   **B**

98 Etude *In the style of a minuet*
In 3, but with a feeling of one

99 Agnus Dei from *L'Arlesienne* (adapted) Georges Bizet (1838–1875)

Lip Slur Study
Slowly

Now is the Month of Maying (adapted) Thomas Morley (1557–1602)

Since First I Saw Your Face (Abridged) Thomas Ford (d. 1648)

Studies in Staccato

Remember to keep the air moving in staccato playing.

Sea Chanty: *The Drunken Sailor*

The British Grenadiers

March tempo

Studies in Marcato

Sea Chanty: *Haul Away, Joe*

Welsh Folk Song: *Men of Harlech*

Studies in Legato Tonguing

English Folk Song: *The Wraggle–Taggle Gipseys*

French Christmas Carol
Slowly in 2

129

Sea Chanty: *Rio Grande*

All studies from this point forward should be played as slowly as necessary and may be subdivided.

(130) Major Scale
Slowly

Also play with these articulations.

(131) Relative Minor (melodic)
Slowly

Use articulations for No. 130.

(132) Arpeggio Study
Slowly

Also play with these articulations.

Also play with these articulations:

Repeat in all valve combinations:
2, 1, 1–2, 2–3, 1–3, 1–2–3; positions: 2, 3, 4, 5, 6, 7

Repeat in all valve combinations:
(omit 1–2–3)

All studies may be subdivided as necessary.

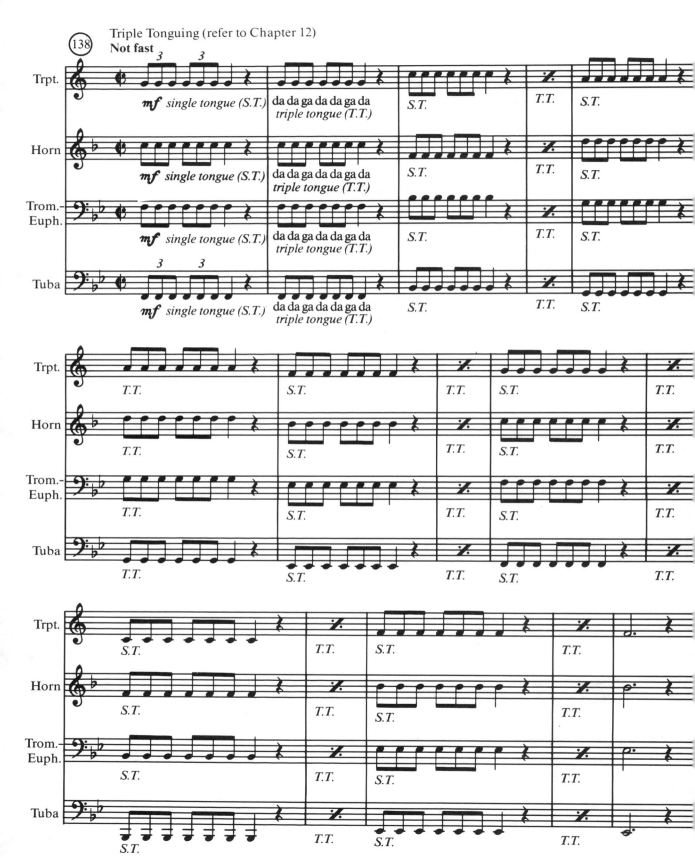

Exercises for double and triple tounging may also be practiced single-tongued.

(143) Interval Study

(144) Lip Slur Study

Repeat in all valve combinations

Repeat in all valve combinations (omit 1–2–3).

(149) Double tonguing

Exercises for double and triple tonguing may also be practiced single-tongued.

Scottish Folksong: *Loch Lomond*

(160) *Rondeau* Jean Joseph Mouret (1682–1738)

Exercises for double and triple tonguing may also be practiced single-tongued.

Nos. 173 and 174: Use articulations for No. 161.

Use articulations for No. 16

(188) Irish Folksong: *The Minstrel Boy*
Slowly

(189) Major Scale

(190) Relative Minor (Harmonic)

Use articulations for No. 16

Use articulations for No. 16

Nos. 193 and 194: Use articulations for No. 161

British Sailing Song: *Portsmouth*

Nos. 197–200 may be omitted.

Additional Scales

Progressive Ensembles

The Queen's Funeral March Henry Purcell (ca. 1659–1695)

* Parts are indicated by the circled number adjacent to the instrument designation.

Pavanne d'Angleterre Claude Gervaise (fl. 1540–1560)

La Mourisque Tylman Susato (ca. 1500–1561)

Bransle de villages Michael Praetorius (1571–1621)

L'arboscello ballo Furlano (1578) Giorgio Mainerio (fl. 16th cent.)
Moderato *broad, but not legato*

17 *L'arboscello* (cont.)

Danse du Roy Tylman Susato (ca. 1500–ca. 1561)

Courtly Masquing Ayre John Adson (ca. 1585–1640)

Tourdion (1547) Pierre Attaingnant (ca. 1494–ca. 1552)

Canzona (from the *Queen's Funeral Music*) Henry Purcell (ca. 1659–1695)

Courtly Masquing Ayre John Adson (ca. 1585–1640)

Gagliarda La Traditora Anonymous, ca 1520

Ballet Michael Praetorius (1571–1621)

Galliard Anthony Holborne (1584–1602)

Intrade Johann Pezel (1639–1694)

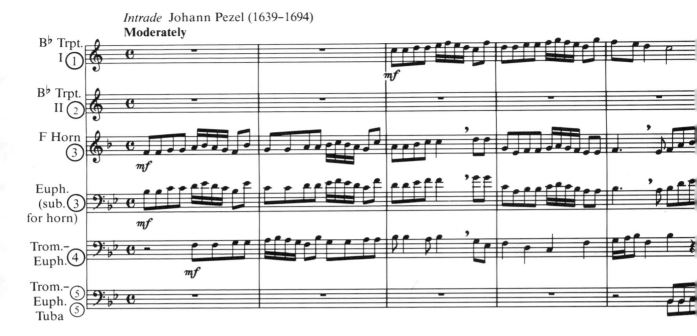

Intrade (cont.)

The tuba should play the upper octave if possible.

Bransle Simple Claude Gervaise (fl. 1540–1560)

SECTION C
Studies for Individual Practice

Trumpet and Cornet

Play all exercises on mouthpiece before playing on instrument.
Repeat often

Play on each of the previous notes.

Stay on each exercise as long as necessary before moving on.

28 Exercises should also be played in the keys of the notes indicated.

30 Exercises from 30 onward are more advanced.

slur and tongue

Horn

Play all exercises on the mouthpiece first.
All F Horn

29   Exercises should also be played in the keys of the notes indicated.

Exercises from 30 onward are more advanced.
30   Use double horn as desired.

Trombone and Euphonium

Play all exercises on the mouthpiece fir

Euphonium players should also play the exercises for trumpet and cornet.

Stay on each exercise as long as necessary before moving o

Exercises should also be played in the keys of the notes indicated

Tuba

Play all exercises on the mouthpiece first.

Exercises from 30 onward are more advanced.

Exercises should also be played in the keys of the notes indicate

39 *also slur*

CHAPTER 13

Instrument Care

WHY GOOD CARE IS IMPORTANT

Brass instruments are complex acoustical devices, and the process that takes place inside the tubing will function optimally only as long as the instrument remains in good condition. Most critical are the conical portions of the tubing, which must maintain an exact taper. If these become altered at certain points, because of grime or dents, the instrument's internal acoustical functions may be affected. Also, it is of primary importance that all moving parts work freely. Premature wear of valves and slides due to inadequate lubrication will ultimately lead to a deterioration of the air seal and a subsequent decline in the instrument's playing quality. Dents on a trombone slide create high spots that accelerate wear and ruin the smooth motion of the slide. Given adequate care, brass instruments will last for many years. A number of professional players have used a single instrument (with periodic servicing) for the majority of their careers.

CLEANING

Grime collects most frequently in the instrument's mouthpiece and leadpipe: these should be cleaned regularly at two- or three-week intervals. A tapered mouthpiece brush and a flexible cleaner (preferably plastic-coated) may be used for this purpose. The mouthpiece and leadpipe should be flushed with water before and after cleaning.

More complete attention is necessary every couple of months. The valves and slides should be removed (rotary valve instruments may be cleaned with the valves in place) and the instrument placed in a large sink or bathtub filled with warm slightly soapy water (dish soap or other light liquid soaps are good for this purpose). The water level should be high enough to penetrate all portions of the tubing, and the temperature must not exceed lukewarm or the lacquer might be damaged. Valve and tuning slides may also be placed in the water.

After approximately 15 minutes of soaking, a flexible brush should be pushed through as much of the tubing as possible, including the slides. The interior of the valve casings of piston valve instruments can be wiped with a cleaning rod covered with a lint-free cloth (the rod must be completely covered to avoid damage to the valve casings). Some valve oil added to the cloth will act as a solvent. All parts should be thoroughly rinsed and dried with a soft cloth. Double horns should be rinsed by holding the bell under the tap and allowing it to fill. Each valve should be depressed in turn to allow the water to flow through every section of tubing.

Trombone slides require special handling to avoid damage. After separating the slides, the outer slide may be cleaned with a flexible brush or a rod thoroughly wrapped with cloth.

A common way to clean the interior of the inner slide is to use a long cloth attached to a string and weight (a fishing line and sinker work well). The weight is dropped through the stocking end and pulled toward the cork barrel. Alternately, a flexible brush may be used. The slide's exterior should be carefully wiped. Old slide lubricant tends to collect in the cork or spring barrel and can be removed with a small brush.

The danger in handling the inner and outer slides is that the parallel tubes might be sprung out of alignment. This will be avoided if the slide is held by the same side as is being cleaned.

LUBRICATION

Piston Valves

Piston valves should first be wiped with a soft cloth moistened with valve oil to remove any residue. After applying a light coat of valve oil, the piston may be inserted into the casing following the alignment of the valve guides. These fit into the groove(s) on the side of the casings. The valve should not be turned or the piston surface will be scratched. The pistons are stamped with the appropriate number to avoid inserting them into the wrong casing.

Rotary Valves

In lubricating rotary valves, it is important to use oil that has been specifically formulated for this type of valve. Piston valve oil is too light and will not provide good results. With the instrument laid flat, the valve caps can be removed and a drop of oil placed on the ends of each rotor shaft. The valves should be moved to encourage the oil to seep down between the shaft and the top bearing plate. After the caps are replaced, the instrument should be turned over and some oil applied to the gap between the stop-arm hub and the lower bearing plate. Again the valves should be rotated several times. Next, each moving part of the valve activating linkage should receive some oil. The valve levers turn on a rocker shaft, therefore some oil should be applied to the shaft through the springs and at each end. (See Fig. 13.1.)

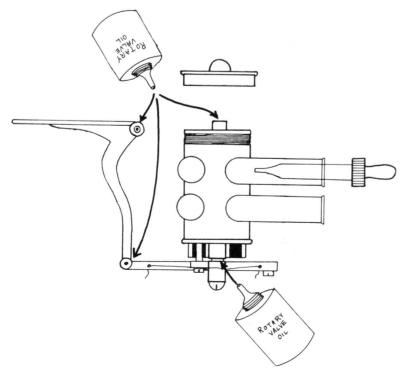

Figure 13.1. How to oil rotary valves.

The above procedure should be followed weekly. Every so often, it will be necessary to apply oil directly to the rotors. Since this is done through the valve slides, care must be taken to prevent grease (the oil acts as a solvent) from washing down into the valves, slowing their action. The horn should be held with the bell upward and the valve slides removed. A long eyedropper may be inserted into the open tubes to apply oil directly to the rotors. One should then replace the slides and turn the instrument to various positions while rapidly depressing the valves.

The Trombone Slide

One of the special silicone lubricants should be used on the trombone slide (although some players still prefer cold cream). The inner slide should be cleaned before applying new lubricant. After cleaning, small spots of cream are placed along the slide, including the stockings, and then spread evenly over the slide surface. Next, the slide is gently wiped so that only a light film remains. A fine mist of water is periodically sprayed on the slide surface to maintain good action (plastic sprayers of the type available at garden stores may be used for this purpose).

Tuning and Valve Slides

Since the instrument's air seal is maintained by these slides as well as the valves, it is important to prevent wear by keeping them well lubricated. Anhydrous lanolin yields the most satisfactory results. Petroleum jelly and gun grease are also used, but they must be replaced much more frequently than lanolin. For slides that must be moved often in playing, such as trumpet third-valve slides, petroleum jelly offers a freer motion than lanolin.

On older instruments, slides tend to become loose and should be tightened by a repairman. In severe cases, the slides can be replated, but, like valve replating, this should only be attempted by a skilled craftsman. In a complete overhaul, it is advisable to have both valves and slides replated to reclaim the instrument's original air seal.

Before lubricating, the slide must be wiped with a clean cloth to remove any residue. Only a light coating of lanolin should be applied. The slide should then be replaced and any excess lubricant removed. *Valves must always be depressed when inserting or withdrawing valve slides.*

MISCELLANEOUS

Removing Stuck Mouthpieces and Slides

Jammed mouthpieces are a common occurrence in school bands, so it is advisable to have a mouthpiece puller available. This is an inexpensive tool which will remove the mouthpiece quickly and safely. The leadpipe or receiver can be damaged if any other method of removal is attempted. Frozen slides should generally be referred to a repairman.

Piston and Rotary Valve Alignment

The valve ports of the piston must remain in correct alignment with those of the casing if there is to be minimal disturbance to the vibrating air column as it passes through the valves. On piston valve instruments, both vertical and radial alignment must be considered. The latter is maintained by the valve guides, which keep the piston from turning within the casing. Radial misalignment can occur only if the guides or keyways become worn.

The vertical alignment of piston valves is dependent on the thickness of the cork and felt bumpers. These become compressed with use and must be renewed periodically. Usually there is a mark on the valve stem that indicates the correct

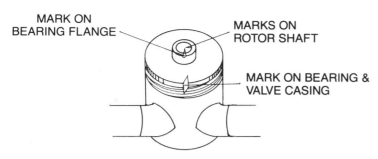

MARK ON
BEARING FLANGE

MARKS ON
ROTOR SHAFT

MARK ON BEARING &
VALVE CASING

Figure 13.2. Rotary valve alignment: one of the marks on the end of the rotor shaft must be aligned with the mark on the bearing flange. (Also note the mark on the edge of the bearing and valve casing; this must be in alignment when replacing the bearing after removing the valve).

height of the bumpers. If no mark can be found, or in cases of radial misalignment, the instrument should be sent to a repairman.

Rotary valve alignment is maintained by the neoprene or cork bumpers located on the cork stop plate. To check this, the top valve cap should be removed and the bearing examined to see if one of the marks on the end of the rotor shaft lines up with the mark on the flange of the top bearing with the valve at rest (closed). With the valve depressed (open), the other mark on the shaft should align with the bearing mark. If this is not the case, the bumper(s) must be replaced (or trimmed, if a high bumper is found). New neoprene or cork bumpers should be pressed into the cork stops and trimmed as necessary with a razor (Fig. 13.2).

Removing Rotary Valves

Sometimes corrosion and accumulated grease from the slides slow the action of rotary valves to the point that oiling will not help. In such cases, the inside of the casings and rotors must be cleaned and oiled. In general, because there is a risk of damaging the valves in the removal process, this work should be left to the specialist. If this is not possible, the following procedure may be used: After taking off the strings, the top valve cap is removed and the instrument turned so that the stop arm hub and screw are upward. The stop arm screw should be turned outward several times. While keeping the hand underneath the top bearing plate (to catch it when it falls), the head of the screw should be lightly tapped with a leather or wooden hammer (alternatively, a block of wood could be placed between a metal hammer and the screw). The instrument should be supported with the arm to absorb any shock. As the rotor is forced downward, the top bearing plate will drop into the hand; the stop arm screw and hub can then be taken off and the rotor removed. The interior of the casing and the rotor may be cleaned with a small amount of metal polish and a soft cloth (all traces of the polish must be removed after cleaning). After the rotor and casing are oiled, the rotor may be replaced. The next step is critical: the mark on the top bearing plate must be aligned with the mark on the casing. The plate may then be started into the casing and the bearing (the raised flange in the center) should be carefully tapped until the plate is fully seated. The rotor should be checked for free rotation. If the plate is tilted even slightly, the rotor will bind. The stop arm can then be replaced and the screw tightened.

Restringing Rotary Valves

The restringing procedure can be seen in Figure 13.3. It is best to begin with the middle valve to make the adjustment of the valve keys easier. Special cord designed for the purpose should be used. If this is unavailable, 20 to 27 pound test fishing line may be substituted (linen or dacron line is preferable to that made

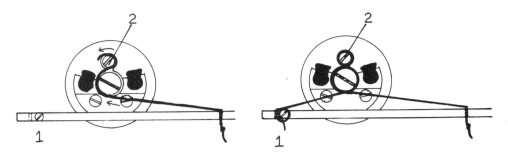

Figure 13.3. Restringing rotary valves.

from nylon). One end of a 6-inch length should be knotted and threaded in a figure-8 pattern.

Once the string is correctly threaded, it should be pulled taut and set-screw number 1 tightened. To adjust the height of the valve keys, the key should be pressed to the desired position and set-screw number 2 secured. To change the height, it is only necessary to loosen set-screw number 2. The height of the other valve keys should be adjusted to match the middle valve.

Water Keys

Periodically, water keys should be checked to make certain that the spring has not weakened and the cork makes an adequate air seal. Worn corks and springs should be replaced. A new cork of the exact size should be pressed into the water key cup (a slightly irregular cork can be secured with a drop of glue). It would be helpful if schools maintained a supply of the correct springs and corks for each instrument. In an emergency, a worn cork can be turned upside down to form a temporary seal.

Using Piston Valves

On piston valve instruments, it is important that the valves are pushed straight down with the fingertips. If the middle part of the finger is used, pressure tends to be exerted on one side of the valve casing, causing its diameter to go out of round and accelerating wear to that side of the piston.

Dents

Dents are a constant concern. Tubing dents can cause poor response, intonation, and other problems. Dents in the valve casing will affect valve action and seriously damage the piston or rotor. Aside from careless handling, many dents occur within the case. Loose mouthpieces can be particularly destructive. Well-designed hard cases should be provided with every instrument. During rehearsal breaks, the instrument must never be left on a chair and should be returned to its case. It is prudent for trombonists to acquire a stand since the slide is particularly vulnerable to dents.

Advice on Repairs

A less-than-competent repairman can do more harm than good to a brass instrument. Every effort should be made to locate a skilled craftsman. Professional players can usually recommend such a person, but, if none can be found locally, it might be advisable to send the instrument to a specialist. Also, manufacturers will often take their own instruments in for service. Repairs vary in complexity: valve replating, problems with trombone slides, and dent removal that entails taking the instrument apart, should only be attempted by an expert. Horns, in particular, require special skills that are often beyond the average repairman.

CHAPTER 14

Notes For Conductors

HOW THE BRASS SECTION IS ORGANIZED

The brass section is organized around a group of principal players who have the responsibility of directing all aspects of the section's performance. Since full rehearsals offer little opportunity for concentrated work on intonation, balance, precision, and uniformity of style, a prime duty of the principal is to oversee sectional rehearsals to develop these qualities. The principal is responsible to the conductor for the work of his or her individual section. Principals also communicate with each other to promote better ensemble playing within the brass section as a whole.

In orchestras, the third or fourth trumpeter usually serves as an assistant first, playing the less important works on the program and providing relief to the principal.

There are usually three cornet and two trumpet parts in bands. The first cornet part includes most of the solo work, so this should go to the principal. The trumpets often perform independently of the cornets, and the first trumpet and cornet parts are frequently doubled. For this reason, the second-most-advanced player after the principal should be assigned the first trumpet part, with the remaining players filling out the lower parts. In scores which specify three or four trumpets in place of cornets, the first cornetist and first trumpeter should take the two highest parts. Band conductors must know the scoring of each composition in order to assign parts to the best advantage.

In horn sections, the two best players should be assigned the first and third parts. This is because horn sections are composed of two pairs of high and low players, and horn writing follows that pattern of notation. Sometimes the pairs are called upon to perform separately, or the third may double the first. When all four play together, the usual voicing from upper to lower is 1–3–2–4. A similar pattern is followed in bands.

Professional players usually specialize as high or low players, and this is usually reflected in the material used for auditions. Fourth horn players, in particular, must develop a strong low range and cannot be expected to perform in the upper register in the same manner as a first or third player.

The third trombone part is conceived for the bass trombone. Bass trombone parts frequently diverge from the other two parts; the instrument should be treated more or less as a solo voice.

ACHIEVING A GOOD BRASS SOUND

The best results will be achieved if the conductor approaches the brass section as a brass ensemble within the orchestra or band, rather than as autonomous sections. Balance is of primary importance since it determines to a large extent the quality of the sound that will be produced by the section. A sense of balance is also vital in developing good intonation, since problems that might otherwise be masked are clearly revealed, making correction easier.

Each player must develop the habit of listening to the highest voice and matching its dynamic level precisely. When individual sections perform alone, players on the lower parts should adjust to the principal. The first trumpet sets the volume level for the complete brass section, and the low brass must match the principal trombone when playing alone. In a fine brass section, there is an equality of sound from top to bottom.

Volume is another factor that affects intonation. There is a far greater margin of error at high volumes, where faults tend to be covered up by the quantity of sound, than at medium levels. When a passage sounds out of tune, a good corrective procedure is to repeat it slowly at a mezzo-forte level. This affords the players both an opportunity to hear more clearly and sufficient time to make corrections. It is also a good practice to single out any chords needing improvement. In extreme cases, the root might be played, and then the fifth and third added.

Another factor that strongly influences the quality of sound is sustained playing. This contributes continuity and direction to musical lines and encourages a refined and balanced sound. Attention must also be given to making certain that the length of notes, attacks, and releases are uniform.

To insure that the full resonance of the brass section is heard by the audience, trumpeters and trombonists should hold their instruments so the bells are clear of the music stand. Individual playing angles should also be reasonably compatible since significant variations can alter the balance as it is heard from a distance.

SEATING PROBLEMS

It is regrettable that in many ensembles little thought is given to the best way of seating brass players so that they can adequately hear themselves and each other. Playing in such groups is both unpleasant and unrewarding. Among the worst and most frequent errors is to place the trumpets in front of the trombones. The first trumpeter can hear very little other than the sound radiating from the trombone bell in back of his head, and the first trombonist, who must balance and tune with the first trumpet, has difficulty hearing him. It is even worse to position the horns in front of trumpets or trombones.

The poorest location for the horns is in the center of the ensemble, another common placement. The horn bell is low and to the side of the player where its rear-directed sound is absorbed by the clothing and bodies of the players seated behind. In such a set-up, the horn player can barely hear his own sound and cannot judge volume or intonation accurately. The most satisfactory position for the horns is at the rear or side of the ensemble where their sound is unimpeded and can be reflected by one of the stage walls.

Because the horn bell goes to the player's right, it is customary for the principal to be seated on the left end of the section so that the players to his right can hear his sound clearly.[1] This arrangement is not universal, however. Some prefer the greater sense of support from the lower parts that is gained by sitting to the section's right. The latter format is currently in use in the Vienna Philharmonic and was favored by the great English horn players Aubrey and Dennis Brain. A third approach is to place the 3rd and 4th horns immediately behind the 1st and 2nd; this plan provides for good aural control and affords a viable alternative when a lateral layout is impracticable.

The trombone section requires similar consideration. The principal trombonist normally sits on the right of the section so that his bell, rather than his slide, is closest to his colleague to the left. In this way, the principal's sound can be heard across the section. The bass trombonist should be next to the tuba since their parts are often doubled.

---

1. All suggestions for lateral placement refer to "stage" left or right; that is, from the players' perspective, looking outward from the stage toward the conductor and audience.

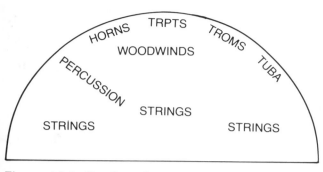

Figure 14.1. Seating chart: orchestra.

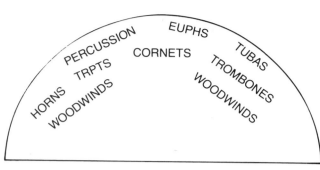

Figure 14.2. Seating chart: band.

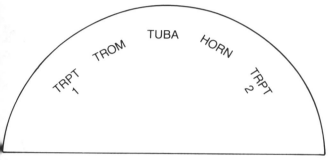

Figure 14.3. Seating chart: brass quintet.

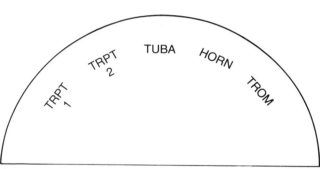

Figure 14.4. Seating chart: brass quintet (alternate).

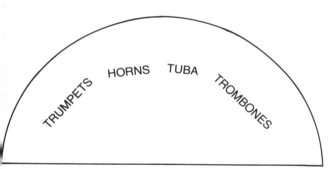

Figure 14.5. Seating chart: brass ensemble.

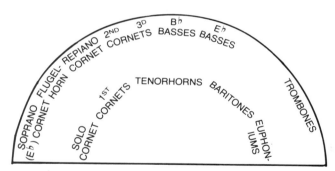

Figure 14.6. Seating chart: brass band.

Suggested seating plans for various types of ensemble are shown in Figures 14.1 through 14.6. Following these plans will allow members of the brass section to hear each other with reasonable clarity and project a well-balanced and vibrant tone quality to the audience.

CONDUCTING BRASS PLAYERS

A basic problem for the conductor is securing the arrival of sound from various distances at the point when the beat is felt. Given experience, brass players usually develop the knack of focusing their sound to the conductor's beat while compensating for any lags caused by distance. This process is aided if conductors refuse to accept late attacks and provide feedback to guide their players. To avoid ragged attacks, it is helpful if the conductor gains eye contact with the brass and breathes on the preparation beat.

Inexperienced conductors often create difficulties by demanding excessively soft dynamics. There is a minimum volume necessary for tone and security on brass instruments, and notes may fail to respond if this point is passed. High passages, in particular, require a certain effort and will be placed at risk if too low a dynamic is requested. Also, it should be recognized that the very best brass players miss notes occasionally.

Brass players respond positively to conductors who are knowledgeable about their instruments and ask for more than the notes. By attempting to bring out varied stylistic and tonal concepts of brass playing as they apply to the literature, the conductor will generate interest and commitment and the subsequent performance will have greater stylistic validity. To take an obvious example, a more brilliant timbre and sharper attack should be used in Berlioz than in Brahms, which requires a dark, round tone and milder attack. Similarly, the full, sonorous sound one strives for in Bruckner is totally wrong in the works of Stravinsky.

The question of vibrato must also be considered by the conductor. In general, a pure, vibratoless sound is to be preferred. However, certain compositions, such as works by Debussy, Ravel, and other French composers, derive color and style through the use of a light, rather quick vibrato. There are other instances in the literature where the use of vibrato will enhance the expressive and stylistic effect of a composition.

The choice of instruments can also contribute to the effectiveness of a performance. Rotary valve trumpets lend a rounder sonority to works by Wagner, Bruckner, and other Germanic composers. The use of cornets in *Le Carnaval Romaine* and *Symphonie fantastique* provide the contrast (to the trumpets) that Berlioz intended.

To gain an understanding of the various concepts and styles of brass playing, the conductor should make a study of representative recordings and seek out live performances, carefully analyzing the approach of each brass section to specific areas of the literature.

The World of Brass

ORCHESTRAL BRASS

Figure A.1. Chicago Symphony Orchestra: trumpets, trombones, horns (note the use of rotary valve trumpets and an alto trombone).

(Photo courtesy of the Chicago Symphony Orchestra)

Figure A.2. London Symphony Orchestra: trumpets and trombones.

(Photo courtesy of the London Symphony Orchestra)

Figure A.3. Vienna Philharmonic: trumpets and horns (note the use of rotary valve trumpets and single F Vienna horns).

(Photo: Vivianne Purdom

Figure A.4. Vienna Philharmonic: trombones and tuba (the two trombonists nearest the tuba are using traditional German trombones).

(Photo: Vivianne Purdom

Figure A.5. Orchestre symphonique de Montréal: trumpets, trombones, tuba.

(Photo: reproduction authorized by the Orchestre symphonique de Montréal)

Figure A.6. Royal Philharmonic Orchestra, London: horns.

(Photo courtesy of the Royal Philharmonic Orchestra)

BRASS ENSEMBLES

Figure A.7. Philip Jones Brass Ensemble (quintet).   *(Photo courtesy of Philip Jones)*

Figure A.8. Chicago Chamber Brass.   *(Photo courtesy of Chicago Chamber Brass)*

Figure A.9. Philip Jones Brass Ensemble (large ensemble).

(Photo courtesy of Philip Jones)

BRASS BAND

Figure A.10. John Foster Black Dyke Mills Band (brass band): musical director,
Major Peter Parks.   *(Photo courtesy of John Foster & Son, PLC)*

BANDS

Figure A.11. The United States Marine Band, "The President's Own": director, Colonel John R. Bourgeois.

(Photo courtesy of "The President's Own" United States Marine Band, Washington, D.C.)

Figure A.12. The Central Band of Her Majesty's Royal Air Force: principal director of music, Wing Commander Eric Banks, M.B.E., F.L.C.M., L.R.A.M., L.G.S.M., R.A.F.

(Photo: Crown Copyright-Ministry of Defense)

Figure A.13. Rutgers University Wind Ensemble: trumpets, euphoniums, tubas, trombones; Dr. Scott Whitener, conductor.

Figure A.14. Central Band of Her Majesty's Royal Air Force: trumpeters.

(Photo: Crown Copyright-Ministry of Defense)

Figure A.15. Band of the Grenadier Guards: director of music, Major R.J. Parker,
T.C.L., A.R.C.M., p.s.m.   *(Photo: Crown copyright-Ministry of Defense)*

Selected Brass Recordings

NOTE: The abbreviation "mc" and "cd" indicate that the recording is available
cassette and compact disc, respectively. For additional listings, see the *Schwar*
record catalogs, particularly the Artist Issue.

Since the introduction of the compact disc, LPs have been deleted at a
unprecedented rate. Many of these will undoubtedly reappear in CD form, whi
others will remain out of print. Given the uncertain conditions presently prevailir
within the record industry, it has been thought best to include all recordings deeme
to be of significant artistic and pedagogical value, without consideration of curre
availability. Deleted records (noted with an asterisk) can often be found in librarie
and secondhand record shops.

SOLO TRUMPET

Maurice André:
  Angel 4DS-38067, mc, "An Evening with Maurice André"
  Erato ECD-88081, cd, "La Belle époque"
  RCA CRL-2-7002, 2 rec., "Great Concertos"
  Angel 4XS-38068, mc, "Trompetissimo"
  Nonesuch 71132, Telemann
  RCA RCD-1-5864, cd, Albinoni, Handel, Tartini, Haydn
  Angel DS-37984, cd CDC-47012, Stölzel, Vivaldi
  Erato 75026, cd ECD-88007, Hummel, Neruda, Telemann
Armando Ghitalla:
  Cambridge 1819, Albrechtsberger, Hummel, Molter
  Cambridge 2823, Copland, M. Haydn
  Cambridge 2710, Scarlatti, Bach
Ludwig Güttler:
  Pro Arte S-608, mc, Corelli, Legrenzi, Stradella
  Pro Arte 621, mc, "The Splendor of the Baroque Trumpet"
  Pro Arte S-605, mc, Telemann, Torelli
Hakan Hardenberger:
  Bis 287, cd CD-287, "The Virtuoso Trumpet"
  Philips 420203, mc, cd, Haydn, Hummel, Hertel, Stamitz
Adolph Herseth:
  DG 415104, mc, cd, Haydn Concerto
Walter Holy:
  *Turnabout 34684, L. Mozart Concerto (natural trumpet)
Friedemann Immer:
  MD&G L 3271, cd, "Trompetenkonzerte des Barock" (natural trumpet)
  L'Oiseau-Lyre 701, Telemann Concerto for 3 Trumpets (natural trumpet)
  L'Oiseau-Lyre 417610, mc, cd, Haydn Concerto (keyed trumpet)
Crispian Steele-Perkins:
  MCA MCAD-5844, cd, "Trumpet Spectacular"
  Hyperion A 66145, cd, Biber Sonatas (natural trumpet)
  EMI 476642, mc, cd, "Shore's Trumpet" (natural trumpet)
  Priory PRCD 189, cd, "The King's Trumpeter"

Thomas Stevens:
  Crystal S-361, Stravinsky, Carter, Hindemith
Alan Stringer:
  *Argo ZRG-543, Haydn Concerto
  CRD 3308, cd, "Trumpet and Organ at Liverpool Cathedral"
Edward Tarr:
  Nonesuch 71279, 71290, 71356, mc, "Baroque Masterpieces"
  Christophus CD 74524, cd, "Chorale Preludes of Bach Pupils for Trumpet &
    Organ" (natural trumpet and slide trumpet)
  Nonesuch 71415, "Spanish Golden Age" (natural trumpet and cornett)
Helmut Wobisch:
  Bach Guild 5041/HM-63, 2 rec., "Virtuoso Trumpet"
John Wallace:
  Nimbus 5017, cd, "Italian Baroque Music"
  Nimbus 5010, cd, Haydn Concerto
  Nimbus 5065, cd, "Trumpet Concertos and Fanfares"

SOLO CORNET

Herbert L. Clarke:
  Crystal S-450, cornet solos
Phillip McCann:
  Chandos BBRD-1029, mc, cd, "The World's Most Beautiful Melodies"
  Chandos 8513, cd, "More of the World's Most Beautiful Melodies"
James Shepherd:
  Look Records (U.K.) LK/LP-6487, cornet solos

SOLO HORN[1]

Hermann Baumann:
  Teldec 641272, mc, Mozart Concertos (natural horn)
  Telefunken 6.42321, Mozart, Bach, Beethoven (natural horn)
  Philips 412737, mc, cd, Mozart concertos
  Philips 412237, mc, cd, Strauss concertos
Aubrey Brain:
  Opal 805, various solos & Brahms Trio (French horn, F crook)
Dennis Brain:
  *Seraphim 60040, Beethoven Sonata, Schumann: Adagio & Allegro
  BBC 22175E, Brahms Trio, Mozart Quintet
  EMI CDC-7 47834 2, cd, Strauss & Hindemith concertos
  *Angel S-35491, Hindemith Concerto
  *Angel 35092, mc, cd, CDH 7610132, Mozart concertos
  *Angel 35496, cd, CDC-7 47834 2, Strauss concertos
  Arabesque 8071, "Unreleased Performances"
  EMI RLS-7701, 3 rec., "The Art of Dennis Brain"
  London 417183, mc, Britten Serenade
Timothy Brown:
  L'Oiseau-Lyre 417610, mc, cd, Haydn Concerto #1 (natural horn)
Alan Civil:
  *Angel RL-32132, Brahms Trio
  Angel AE-34410, mc, Mozart concertos
  Philips 420709, cd, Mozart concertos and Concert Rondo

See Michael Hernon, *French Horn Discography* (New York: Greenwood Press, 1986).

Dale Clevenger:
   Teldec 8.42960, Haydn concertos
   DG/PSI 2531 199, Britten Serenade
   DG 415104, mc, cd, Mozart Concerto No. 3
   CBS MK 42324, cd, Mozart concertos
Philip Farkas:
   Coronet 1293, various solos
Lowell Greer:
   Coronet 3100, various solos
Norbert Hauptmann:
   Denon 7229, cd, Mozart Quintet
Gunther Högner:
   London 410114 Brahms Trio (Vienna horn, F crook)
   DG 413792, cd, Mozart concertos (Vienna horn, F crook)
Ifor James:
   Phoenix (U.K.) DGS1220, "Pot-pourri"
   Phoenix (U.K.) DGS 1002, "Sonatas" (reissued as KNEW CD201)
Jean Rife:
   Titanic 94, Beethoven Sonata (natural horn)
Gerd Seifert:
   *Vox SVBX-580, 3 rec., Beethoven Sonata
   DG 419057, cd, Mozart concertos
Michael Thompson:
   Nimbus 5010, cd, Haydn concertos
   Nimbus 5018, cd, various concertos
Barry Tuckwell:
   London 414128, cd Brahms Trio
   Angel AM-34730, mc, Haydn concertos
   *Angel S-36996, various concertos
   Decca 410283, 3 rec., Mozart: complete horn music
   London 410284, cd, Mozart concertos
   *Angel SZ-37781, Punto concertos
   *London CS 6519, Strauss concertos
   London 417406, cd, "Baroque Horn Concertos"
   EMI Eminence EM X-2095, cd, Rosetti concertos

SOLO TROMBONE[2]

Miles Anderson:
   Crystal S-385, various solos
Ronald Barron:
   Boston Brass 1001, "Le Trombone Française"
Ronald Borror:
   Crystal 388, various solos
Keith Brown:
   Golden Crest S-7043, various solos
Stuart Dempster:
   Olympic 104, 2 rec., "American Sampler"
John Kitzman:
   Crystal S-386, Hindemith, Pryor, Creston

2. See Edward Richard Bahr, "A Discography of Classical Trombone/Euphonium Solo and Ensemble Mus on Long-Playing Records Distributed in the United States" (D.M.A. thesis, University of Oklahoma, 1980) U 80-16, 922.

onald Knaub:
  Golden Crest 7040, Adler, Stevens, Wilder
hristian Lindberg:
  Bis 258, cd, Hindemith, Martin, Berio, Pryor
  Bis 298, cd, mc, "Romantic Trombone"
rthur Pryor:
  Crystal 451, "Solos with the Sousa Band"
alph Sauer:
  Crystal S-381, Milhaud, Persichetti, Pergolesi
  Crystal 384, Serocki, Haydn, Larsson
ranimir Slokar:
  Claves D-902, Trombone & Organ
  Claves D-707, L. Mozart Concerto, Albrechtsberger Concerto
  Claves D-8407, Wagenseil, David, Tomasi concertos
  Claves D-906, "Romantische Musik für Posaune und Orchester"
enry Charles Smith:
  Coronet 1711, Hartley, Haydn
ohn Swallow:
  GM Recordings, Schuller, Berio, Milhaud

SOLO EUPHONIUM[3]

rian Bowman:
  Crystal 393, Adler, Capuzzi, Boda
red Dart:
  Coronet 1054, various solos
aul Droste:
  Coronet 3026, various solos
eonard Falcone:
  Golden Crest 7001, 7016, 7036, various solos
aymond Young:
  Golden Crest 7025, Recital

SOLO TUBA

oger Bobo:
  Crystal S-125, Hindemith, Kraft, Wilder, Barat
  Crystal S-392, "Botuba"
  Crystal S-398, Kupferman, Subotnick
loyd Cooley:
  Crystal 120, Bach, Brahms, Zindars
  Avant 1020, "Romantic Tuba"
ex Conner:
  Coronet 1259, various solos
ohn Fletcher:
  RCA LSC-3281, Vaughan Williams: Concerto for Bass Tuba
  Claves DPF600, Flight of the Bumblebee (with Philip Jones Brass Ensemble)
oby Hanks:
  Crystal S-395, various solos

For additional listings, see Denis W. Winter, "The Band Directors' Guide to Euphonium Recordings," *The instrumentalist*, May 1981, pp. 27–28; also Bahr, "A Discography of Classical Trombone/Euphonium Solo and ensemble Music."

Michael Lind:
  Bis 95, Marcello, Hindemith
Daniel Perantoni:
  Ubres 101, Hindemith, Stevens
Harvey Philips:
  Golden Crest 7018, Persichetti, Wilder
  Golden Crest 4147, Wilder, Heiden
Abe Torchinsky:
  CBS M2-33971, 2 rec., Hindemith Sonata

BRASS ENSEMBLES

Bengt Eklund's Baroque Ensemble:
  Bis-217, cd, "Courtly Trumpet Ensemble Music" (natural trumpets)
Berlin Philharmonic Brass Ensemble:
  *DG 2531 298, Gabrieli, Scheidt, Zelenka
  *DG 2536 394, Christmas Music
Canadian Brass:
  CBS IM-39035, mc, cd, "Brass in Berlin" (with Berlin Phil. Brass Ensemble
  RCA ARL-1-4733, mc, cd, "Greatest Hits"
  RCA ARL-1-4574, mc, cd, "High, Bright, Light, & Clear"
Chicago Chamber Brass:
  Crystal CD-430 (cd), Christmas music
  Pro Arte Sinfonia 616, mc, cd, "Fireworks"
Chicago, Cleveland, & Philadelphia Brass Ensembles:
  CBS MP-38759, mc, Gabrieli
Eastman Brass Quintet:
  MMG 1139, mc, "Best of Brass"
Empire Brass Quintet:
  Angel DFO-37353, mc, cd CDC-4739, Bach program
  Digitech 102, "Renaissance Brass"
Equale Brass:
  Nimbus 5004 (cd), "Bacchanales" (Arnold, Warlock, Poulenc)
Eight Bayreuth Festival Hornists:
  Acanta 40.23 533, cd, Wagner
German Brass:
  Angel Ds-38288, mc, cd, "Bach 300"
  EMI CDC 7 47692 2, cd, "Samuel Scheidt 1587-1654"
Haarlem Trumpet Ensemble (natural trumpets):
  Teldec 6.42977, cd, "Baroque and Brass"
His Majesties Sagbutts and Cornetts (cornetts and sackbuts):
  Meridian E4577077, Brade, Locke, Adson, Holborne
  Meridian CDE 84096, cd, "Music from 17th Century Germany"
Philip Jones Brass Ensemble:
  Argo/London 414470, mc, "Golden Brass"
  MMG 1139, mc, Locke, Purcell
  London 411930, cd, "Handel"
  Claves DPF-600, "In Switzerland"
  Claves D-8503, cd, "Lollipops"
  London 411955, mc, cd, "Brass Splendour"
  Chandos ABRD 1190, mc, "PJBE Finale"
  *Argo ZRG-823, "Renaissance Brass"
  *Argo ZRG-731, "Classics for Brass"
  *Argo ZRG-576, "Voices & Brass"

*London LDR 71100, "A Celebration of Brass"
*London CS 7221, "Battles for Brass"
*Argo ZRG 644, "Strings and Brass"
*Argo ZRG 870, "Fanfare"
*Argo ZRG 912, "Festive Brass"
*Argo ZRG-898, "Baroque Brass"
*Argo ZRG 655, "Just Brass"
*Argo ZRG 851, "Divertimento"
*Decca SDD274, "Brass Now and Then"
*Argo ZRG-906, "Modern Brass"
*London ZRDL-1000, "Hindemith Concert Music"
*Argo ZRG-928, "Romantic Brass"
*London ZRDL-71081, "Gabrieli in Venice"
London 417 524, cd, "Music for the Courts of Europe"
Argo 417 468, cd, "The Glory of Venice"
Edward Tarr Brass Ensemble:
  Nonesuch 71385, "Baroque Brass Festival Music"
Locke Brass Consort (Stobart):
  Chandos 1002, Strauss for symphonic brass
  CRD CRDD 1102, "Symphonic Marches"
  RCA RL 25081 (U.K.), "Jubilant Brass" (fanfares by Bliss & others)
  Unicorn RHS-339 (U.K.), "Contrasts in Brass" (vol. 1)
  Unicorn UNI-72012 (U.K.), "Contrasts in Brass" (vol. 2)
  Chandos ABRD 1038, mc, "Miniatures for Brass"
London Brass:
  Teldec 8.43923, cd, "Intrada"
London Festival Brass:
  London 417101, mc, "Baroque Brass"
London Gabrieli Brass Ensemble:
  Nonesuch 71414, mc, "Heralding of Battles and Ceremonies" (Clarke, Pezel,
    Stanley, Scheidt)

BRASS BANDS

Besses O' Th' Barn (Evans & Newsome):
  Chandos BBR 1002, "Besses in Australia"
  Chandos BBRD 1016, "Hymns and Things"
Black Dyke Mills Band (Parkes):
  Chandos 8558 (cd), "150 Years of Black Dyke Mills Band"
  Chandos BBR 1007, "Kings of Brass"
  Chandos BBR 10011, "A Russian Festival"
  Chandos 1021, cd, "Black Dyke Plays Rossini"
London Brass Virtuosi (Honeyball):
  Hyperion A 66189, cd, "Music for Brass & Percussion"
London Collegiate Brass (Stobart):
  CRD 1134, cd, mc, Holst, Ireland, Elgar, Vaughan Williams
Various brass bands)
  Chandos CBRD 1009, "The Chandos Sound of Brass"

APPENDIX C

Sources

INSTRUMENT MANUFACTURERS[1]

Adaci: Gerwigstrasse 29, D-7500 Karlsruhe 1, W. Germany.
Alexander: D-6500 Mainz, Bahnhofstrasse 9, Postfach 1166, W. Germany. [Horns and Tubas].
Ankerl: Haberlgasse 11, 1160 Vienna, Austria [Vienna horns].
B&S: (information through Demusa, see below).
B&S-Perantucci and B&S-Sanders: (dist.) Tuba World-Custom Music Co., 1414 S. Main St., Royal Oak, Mich. 48067 [tubas].
Bach: [trumpets & trombones] (see Selmer Co.).
Benge: (see King). [trumpets & trombones].
Blackburn: Rt. 1, Box 175-A, Decatur, Tenn. 37322 [trumpets, leadpipes].
Blättler: Dorfbachstrasse 21, CH-6430, Switzerland [alphorns].
Blessing: 1301 W. Beardsley Ave., Elkhart, Ind. 46514.
Boosey & Hawkes (Besson): 1925 Enterprise Ct., P.O. Box 130, Libertyville, Ill. 60048. U.K.: Deansbrook Rd., Edgware, Middlesex, England HA8 9BB.
Bohm & Meinl: (tubas: see DEG Music Products; rotary valve trumpets, sackbuts: see Antique Sound Workshop, below).
Burri: Morillonstrasse 11, 3007 Bern, Switzerland.
Burbank Trumpets: (dist.) Roche Thomas, P.O. Box 129, San Bernardino, Calif. 92402.
Calicchio Trumpets: 6409 Willoughby Ave., Hollywood, Calif. 90038.
Callet: 633 W. 130th St., New York, N.Y. 10027 [trumpets].
Conn: 1000 Industrial Parkway, P.O. Box 727, Elkhart, Ind. 46515.
Couesnon: 37 Ave. d'Essomes, F-02400 Chateau Thierry, France.
Courtois: P. Gaudet & Cie, rue de Nancy, 75010, Paris, France.
DEG Music Products: Box 408, Lake Geneva, Wis. 53147.
Demusa: (the information agency for brass instruments manufactured in the German Democratic Republic) Leninstrasse 133, DDR-9652 Klingenthal, E. Germany.
Der Bläserspezialist: Grossherzog-Friedrich-Strasse 56, D-6600 Saarbrücken 3 W. Germany [trumpets].
De Prins: Lammekensstraat 60, 2200 Borgerhout, Belgium.
Egger: Turnerstrasse 32, CH 4058 Basel, Switzerland.
Engel: Koppstrasse 94, 1160 Vienna, Austria [Vienna horns].
Finke: D-4973 Vlotho-Exter, Postfach 2006, W. Germany [horns, natural trumpets, sackbuts].
Freebell: (see Der Bläserspezialist).
Ganter: Bayerwaldstrasse 51, D-8000 Munich 83, W. Germany [rotary valve trumpets, Vienna horns].
Getzen Co.: Elkhorn, Wis. 53121.
Glassl: Kohlstrasse 13, 6090 Rüsselsheim, W. Germany [trombones].
Gronitz: Brennerstrasse 12, 2000 Hamburg 1, W. Germany [tubas].

---

1. Most manufacturers produce a range of instruments. Where it has been thought helpful, a firm's specialty has been noted.

Hirsbrunner: 3454 Sumiswald, Switzerland; (dist.) Tuba World-Custom Music Co., 1414 S. Main St., Royal Oak, Mich. 48067 [tubas, euphoniums].

Holton: (see LeBlanc).

Hoyer: (information through Demusa, see above) [horns].

HBS: Norbert Böpple, D-7143 Vaihingen/Enz, Alter Postweg 27, W. Germany.

Kalison: Via Pelleg. Rossi 98, 1-20 161 Milan, Italy [horns, tubas].

King: United Musical Instruments USA, Inc. P.O. Box 787, Elkhart, Ind. 46515.

Knopf, August: (information through Demusa, see above) [horns].

Knopf, Herbert Fritz: (information through Demusa, see above) [horns].

Kromat: Bahnhofstrasse 11, D-2733 Wilstedt [rotary valve trumpets & flugel-horns].

Lätzsch: Schmidtstrasse 24, Bremen 28, W. Germany [trombones, sackbuts].

Lawson: Rt. 3, Box 41, Keadle Road, P.O. Box 38, Boonsboro, Md. 21713 [horns & leadpipes].

LeBlanc Corp.: 7019 30th Ave., Kenosha, Wis. 53141.

Lechner: Gaisberggasse 23, A5500 Bischofshofen, Austria [rotary valve trumpets, Vienna horns].

Lewis Orchestral Horns: 1770 W. Berteau Ave., Chicago, Ill. 60613.

Martin: (see LeBlanc).

Meinl, Wenzel: Seniweg 4, Postfach 710, 8192 Geretsried 2, W. Germany [tubas].

Meinl, Rudolf: Blumenstrasse 21, D-8531, Diespeck/Aisch, W. Germany; (dist.) Tuba World-Custom Music Co., 1414 S. Main St., Royal Oak, Mich. 48067 [tubas].

Meinl-Weston: [tubas] (see Getzen).

Melton: [tubas] (see Wenzel Meinl).

Miraphone: Graslitzer Musikinstrumenten-Erzeuger e.G., 8264 Waldkraiburg, W. Germany.

Mirafone Corp.: 25570 Rye Canyon Rd., Valencia, Calif. 01355 [tubas, euphoniums] (Mirafone and Miraphone [Germany] are the same firm).

Molter: Marktstrasse 13, 6751 Mackenbach/Pfz., W. Germany [trumpets].

Monette: 130 N. Franklin St., Chicago, Ill. 60606 [trumpets].

Monke: Körnerstrasse 48-50, Köln 30 (Ehrenfeld), W. Germany [rotary valve trumpets, sackbuts].

Mönnig: (information through Demusa, see above) [horns].

Olds: (dist. by PJL/A, see Ransalear).

Otto: D-8267 Neumarkt-St. Veit, W. Germany [horns].

Paxman: 116 Long Acre, London WC2E 9PA, England [horns].

Peter: (information through Demusa, see above) [rotary valve trumpets].

Ransalear Modified Trumpets: (dist.) PJL/A Music Products, 22N159 Pepper Rd., P.O. Box 242, Barrington, Ill. 60011.

Sanders: (dist.) Tuba World-Custom Music Co., 1414 S. Main St., Royal Oak, Mich. 48067 [tubas].

Scherzer: (information through Demusa, see above) [rotary valve trumpets].

Schilke: 529 S. Wabash Ave., Chicago, Ill. 60605 [trumpets].

Schmid: Kohlstattstrasse 8, D-8949 Kirchheim-Tiefenried, W. Germany [horns].

Selmer Co.: Box 310, Elkhart, Ind. 46515.

Selmer: 18, rue de la Fontaine-au-Roi, 75010 Paris, France.

Smith-Watkins: Richard Smith Ltd., 110 The Vale, London N14 6AY, England [trumpets].

Stomvi: Honiba, s.a., Bon Pastor, 19, Mislata, Valencia, Spain [trumpets].

Syhre: Cöthner Strasse 62A, Leipzig, DDR-7022, E. Germany [rotary valve trumpets, clarin horns, natural trumpets].

Thein: Stavenstrasse 7, 2800 Bremen, W. Germany [trumpets, trombones].

Voigt: (information through Demusa, see above) [trombones].

Warburton: (see below) [modular trumpets].

Wedgewood: (dist.) The Woodwind & The Brasswind, 50741 U.S. 33 North, South
    Bend, Ind. 46637 [piccolo trumpets].
Weltklang: (information through Demusa, see above)
Wunderlich: (information through Demusa, see above) [rotary valve trumpets].
Willson: 8890 Flums, Switzerland (see DEG Music Products) [euphoniums, tubas]
Yamaha: Nippon Gakki Co., 10-1, Nakazawa-cho, Hamamatsu, 433, Japan.
Yamaha (U.S.): 3050 Breton Rd. S.E., P.O. Box 7271, Grand Rapids, Mich. 49510

HISTORICAL INSTRUMENTS

Alexander: (see above) [natural horns].
Antique Sound Workshop: (retail) 1080 Beacon St., Brookline, Mass. 02146.
Ewald Meinl: Postfach 1342, D-8192 Geretsried 1, W. Germany [natural trumpets
    horns, sackbuts].
Finke: (see above) [natural trumpets, sackbuts].
Christopher Monk: Stock Farm House, Churt, Farnham, Surrey GU10 2LS En
    gland [cornetts, sackbuts, serpents].
Monke: (see above) [sackbuts].
Paxman: (see above) [natural horns].
Webb: (dist.) Scott Sorenson, Michael Leander, 1721 W. Burnsville Parkway, Suite
    304, Burnsville, Minn. 55337 [natural trumpets].

MOUTHPIECES

Atkinson: 447 S. Glenoaks Blvd., Burbank, Calif. 91502.
Bach: (see Selmer Co., above).
Custom: 114 Elmwood Ave., Buffalo, N.Y. 14223.
Elliott: 13619 Layhill Rd., Silver Spring, Md. 20906.
Endsley: 2253 Bellaire, Denver, Colo. 80207.
Giardinelli: 151 W. 46th St., New York, N.Y. 10036.
JBS: (see above).
Klier: D-8531 Diespeck, W. Germany.
Marcinkiewicz: 126 Graham Place, Burbank, Calif. 91502.
Mirafone: (see above).
Paxman: (see above).
Purviance: (see Reeves).
Reeves: 711 N. Ridgewood Pl., Hollywood, Calif. 90038.
Sanders: 952 124th Ave., Shelbyville, Mich. 49344.
Schilke: (see above).
Stork: P.O. Box 20558, Columbus Circle, New York, N.Y. 10023.
Tilz: Postfach 1745, 8530 Neustadt a.d. Aisch, W. Germany.
Tottle: 236 Harvard, Medford, Mass. 02155.
Tru-Vu: L-S Music Innovations, 1896 Lionel Groulx, Montréal, Québec, H3J 2P5
    Canada [transparent mouthpieces].
Warburton: P.O. Box 5279, Orlando, Fla. 32855.
Wick: (see Boosey & Hawkes, above).
Zottola: 32 Browndale Pl., Port Chester, N.Y. 10573.

BRASS MUSIC

There are over 420 publishers who offer music for brass, many of them specializing
in this area. A comprehensive list of publishers with their addresses may be found
in the *Brass Players' Guide* (1985–1986 edition, pp. 71–75) available from Rober

King Music Sales: 28 Main St., Bldg. 15, North Easton, Mass. 02356. In addition to the latter, the following firms can supply brass music of many publishers:

Ward Music Ltd.: 412 W. Hastings St., Vancouver, B.C. V6B 1L3.
Stanton's Sheet Music: 100 E. Main St., Columbus, Ohio 43215.
S. Eugene Bailey: 502 Division St., Northfield, Minn. 55057.
Purdy's Brass Connection: P.O. Box 18862, Raleigh, N.C. 27619 [brass band music and recordings].
Magnamusic-Baton: 10370 Page Industrial Blvd., Saint Louis, Mo. 63132.
Jerona Music: 81 Trinity Pl., Hackensack, N.J. 07601.
Broad River Press: P.O. Box 50329, Columbia, S.C. 29250.

PERIODICALS

Brass Bulletin: CH-1630 Bulle, Switzerland.
The British Bandsman: The Old House, 64 London End, Beaconsfield, Bucks. HP9 2JD England.
The Brass Band Bridge: J. Perry Watson, ed., Music Department, North Carolina State Univ., Box 7311 Raleigh, N.C. 27695-7311.
The Horn Call: Paul Mansur, ed., Southeastern Oklahoma State Univ., Durant, Okla. 74701.
The Instrumentalist: 200 Northfield Rd., Northfield, Ill. 60093.
International Trombone Association Journal: Vern Kagarice, ed., School of Music, North Texas State Univ., Denton, Tex. 76203.
International Trumpet Guild Journal: Bryan Goff, ed., School of Music, Florida State Univ., Tallahassee, Fla. 32306.
National Association of College Wind & Percussion Instructors Journal: Division of Fine Arts, Northeast Missouri State Univ., Kirksville, Mo. 63501.
T.U.B.A. Journal: Paul Ebbers, ed., School of Music, Florida State Univ., Tallahassee, Fla. 32306.
Windplayer: P.O. Box 234, Northridge, Calif. 91328.
Woodwind, Brass, & Percussion: 138 Front St., Deposit, N.Y. 13754.

APPENDIX D
Fingering/Position Charts

Trumpet/cornet

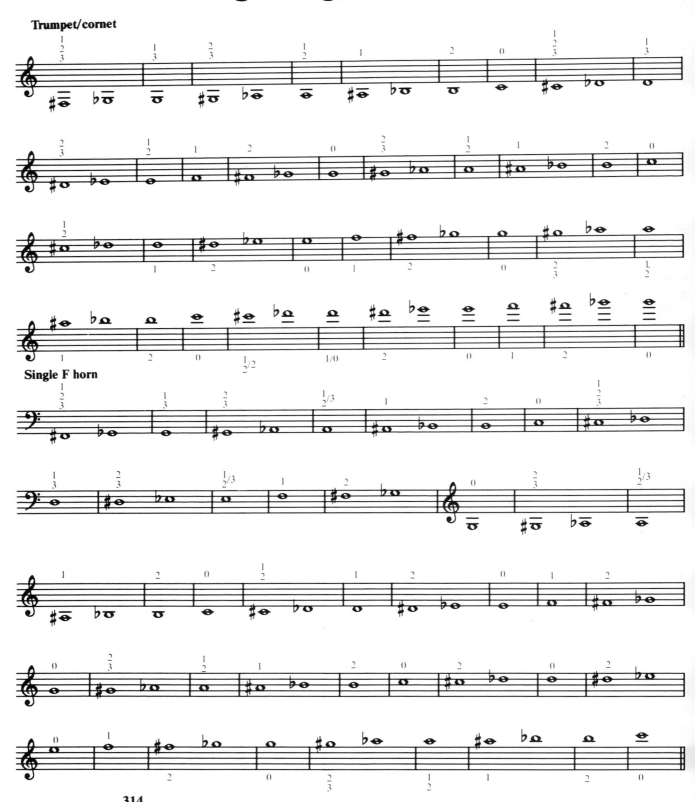

Single F horn

Single B♭ horn

F/B♭ double horn
(pedal tones on B♭ side)

Trombone with F attachment

B♭ pedal tones

Four-valve euphonium

Pedal tone

Four-valve BB♭ tuba

To facilitate intonation, valve slides of the fingerings circled should be pulled outward.

ex. ①
2 = pull 1st valve slide outward.
4

When a valve slide is to be pushed **inward**, an arrow is added to the circle.

ex. 1
3 = push 4th valve inward.
④↑

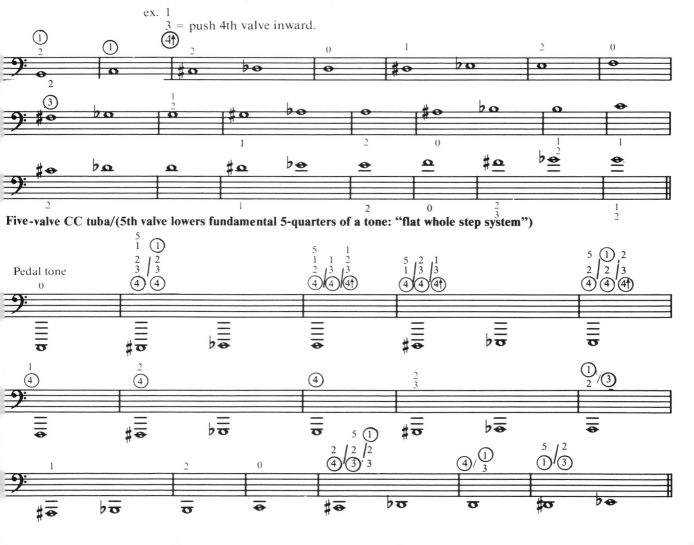

Five-valve CC tuba/(5th valve lowers fundamental 5-quarters of a tone: "flat whole step system")

Five-valve CC tuba (5th valve lowers fundamental two whole steps: ⅔ system)

For intonation adjustment, the 1st valve slide should be pulled outward approximately one inch.

Both systems

Four-valve EE♭ tuba
Pedal tone

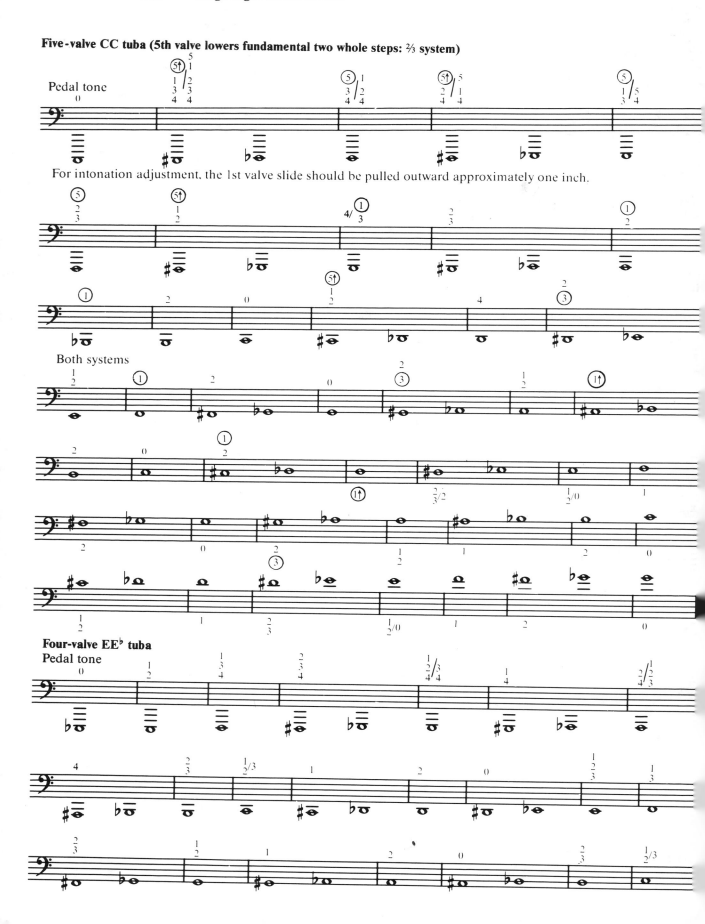

ive-valve F tuba /"⅔ system"

For intonation adjustment, the fifth valve slide should be pulled outward approximately 3 inches.

Five-valve F tuba (5th valve lowers fundamental 5-quarters of a tone)

Pedal tone

Harmonic Fingering Chart

Common fingerings are shown as whole notes.

Harmonic Fingering Chart

Common fingerings are shown as whole notes.

Harmonic Fingering Chart

Common fingerings are shown as whole notes.

Horn in B♭

Harmonic Fingering Chart

Common fingerings/positions are as shown as whole notes.

Trombone or 3-valve baritone

Harmonic Fingering Chart

Common fingerings are shown as whole notes.

Fundamental (8va lower)

Bibliography

BOOKS

ALTENBURG, JOHANN ERNST. *Trumpeters' and Kettledrummers' Art*. Trans. by Edward H. Tarr. Nashville: Brass Press, 1974.

ANDERSON, PAUL G. *Brass Solo and Study Material Music Guide*. Evanston, Ill.: Instrumentalist Co., 1976.

ARLING, HARRY J. *Trombone Chamber Music: An Annotated Bibliography*. Nashville, Tenn.: Brass Press, 1983.

BACH, VINCENT. *The Art of Trumpet Playing*. Elkhart, Ind.: Vincent Bach Corporation, 1969.

BACH, VINCENT. *Embouchure and Mouthpiece Manual*. Elkart, Ind.: Vincent Bach Corporation, 1956.

BAINES, ANTHONY. *Brass Instruments: Their History and Development*. London: Faber & Faber, 1976.

BAKER, DAVID. *Contemporary Techniques for the Trombone*. 2 vols. New York: Charles Colin, 1974.

BARBOUR, J. MURRAY. *Trumpets, Horns, and Music*. East Lansing, Mich.: Michigan State University Press, 1964.

BATE, PHILIP. *The Trumpet and Trombone:* An Outline of Their History, Development, and Construction. 2nd ed. London: Ernest Benn, 1978. New York: Norton, 1978.

BELL, WILLIAM. *Encyclopedia of Literature for the Tuba*. New York: Charles Colin, 1967.

BELLAMAH, JOSEPH L. *Brass Facts*. San Antonio, Tex.: Southern Music, 1961.

BENADE, ARTHUR H. *Fundamentals of Musical Acoustics*. New York: Oxford University Press, 1976.

BENDINELLI, CESARE. *The Entire Art of Trumpet Playing, 1614*. Nashville: Brass Press, 1975.

BEVAN, CLIFFORD. *The Tuba Family*. New York: Scribner's, 1978.

BOWMAN, BRIAN L. *Practical Hints on Playing the Baritone (Euphonium)*. Melville, N.Y.: Belwin-Mills, 1983.

BRASS ANTHOLOGY. Evanston, Ill.: Instrumentalist Co., 1984.

BROWN, MERRILL E. *Teaching the Successful High School Brass Section*. West Nyack, N.Y.: Parker, 1981.

BRÜCHLE, BERNHARD. *Horn Bibliographie*. 3 vols. Wilhelmshaven: Heinrichshofen's Verlag, 1970.

BRÜCHLE, BERNHARD, and JANETZKY, KURT. *Kulturgeschichte des Horns*. Tutzing: Hans Schneider, 1976.

BUSH, IRVING. *Artistic Trumpet Technique and Study*. Hollywood, Highland Music, 1962.

BUSHOUSE, DAVID. *Practical Hints on Playing the Horn*. Melville, N.Y.: Belwin-Mills, 1983.

CARSE, ADAM. *Musical Wind Instruments*. London: Macmillan, 1940. Reprint: New York: Da Capo Press, 1965.

COAR, BIRCHARD. *The French Horn*. DeKalb, Ill.: Coar, 1947.

COAR, BIRCHARD. *A Critical Study of the Nineteenth-Century Horn Virtuosi in France*. DeKalb, Ill.: Coar, 1952.

COUSINS, FARQUHARSON. *On Playing the Horn*. London: Samski Press (distributed by Paxman Musical Instruments), 1983.

CUMMINGS, BARTON. *The Contemporary Tuba.* New London, Conn.: Whaling Music, 198.

DALE, DELBERT A. *Trumpet Technique.* London: Oxford University Press, 1967.

DAHLQVIST, REINE. *The Keyed Trumpet and Its Greatest Virtuoso, Anton Weidinge* Nashville: Brass Press, 1975.

D'ATH, NORMAN W. *Cornet Playing.* London: Boosey & Hawkes, 1960.

DAVIDSON, LOUIS. *Trumpet Techniques.* Rochester: Wind Music, Inc., 1970.

DEMPSTER, STUART. *The Modern Trombone.* Berkeley, Calif.: University of California Pres 1979.

DEVOL, JOHN. *Brass Music for the Church.* Plainview, N.Y.: Harold Branch, 1974.

DRAPER, F. C. *Notes on the Besson System of Automatic Compensation of Valved Bra. Wind Instruments.* Edgware, England: Besson, 1953.

EICHBORN, HERMANN. *The Old Art of Clarino Playing on Trumpets.* Trans. by Bryan / Simms. Denver, Colo.: Tromba Publications, 1976.

ELIASON, ROBERT E. *Early American Brass Makers.* Nashville, Tenn.: Brass Press, 1981.

ENDSLEY, GERALD. *Comparative Mouthpiece Guide for Trumpet.* Denver, Colo.: Tromb Publications, 1980.

ENRICO, EUGENE. *The Orchestra at San Petronio in the Baroque Era.* Washington, D.C Smithsonian Institution Press, 1976.

EVERETT, THOMAS G. *Annotated Guide to Bass Trombone Literature.* Nashville, Tenn.: Bra: Press, 1978.

FANTINI, GIROLAMO. *Modo per imparare a sonare di Tromba: A Modern Edition of Girolam Fantini's Trumpet Method.* Boulder, Colo.: Empire Printing, 1977.

FARKAS, PHILIP. *A Photographic Study of 40 Virtuoso Horn Players' Embouchure* Rochester, N.Y.: Wind Music, 1970.

FARKAS, PHILIP. *The Art of Horn Playing.* Evanston, Ill.: Summy-Birchard, 1956.

FARKAS, PHILIP. *The Art of Brass Playing.* Rochester, N.Y.: Wind Music, 1962.

FARKAS, PHILIP. *The Art of Musicianship.* Bloomington, Ind.: Musical Publications, 1976

FINK, REGINALD H. *The Trombonist's Handbook.* Athens, Ohio: Accura Music, 1977.

FISCHER, HENRY GEORGE. *The Renaissance Sackbut and Its Use Today.* New York Metropolitan Museum of Art, 1984.

FITZPATRICK, HORACE. *The Horn and Horn-Playing and the Austro-Bohemian Traditio 1680–1830.* London: Oxford University Press, 1970.

FOSTER, ROBERT E. *Practical Hints on Playing the Trumpet/Cornet.* Melville, N.Y.: Belwin Mills, 1983.

FOX, FRED. *Essentials of Brass Playing.* Pittsburgh, Pa.: Volkwein, 1974.

GREGORY, ROBIN. *The Horn.* London: Faber and Faber, 1969.

GREGORY, ROBIN. *The Trombone.* New York: Faber and Faber, 1973.

GRIFFITHS, JOHN R. *The Low Brass Guide.* Hackensack, N.J.: Jerona Music, 1980.

HILL, DOUGLAS. *Extended Techniques for the Horn.* Hialeah, Fla.: Columbia Picture Publications, 1983.

HANSON, FAY. *Brass Playing.* New York: Carl Fischer, 1975.

HERNON, MICHAEL. *French Horn Discography.* New York: Greenwood Press, 1986.

JOHNSON, KEITH. *The Art of Trumpet Playing.* Ames, Iowa: Iowa State University Pres: 1981.

KAGARICE, VERN L. *Annotated Guide to Trombone Solos with Band and Orchestr* Lebanon, Ind.: Studio P/R, 1974.

KAGARICE, VERN L. *Solos for the Student Trombonist: An Annotated Bibliography.* Nashvill Tenn.: The Brass Press, 1979.

KLEINHAMMER, EDWARD. *The Art of Trombone Playing.* Evanston, Ill.: Summy-Birchar 1963.

KNAUB, DONALD. *Trombone Teaching Techniques.* 2nd ed. Athens, Ohio: Accura Musi 1977.

LAWRENCE, IAN. *Brass in Your School.* London: Oxford University Press, 1975.

LAWSON, WALTER A. *Development of New Mouthpipes for the French Horn.* Boonsboro, Md.: Lawson, n.d.

LITTLE, DONALD C. *Practical Hints on Playing the Tuba.* Melville, N.Y.: Belwin-Mills, 1984.

LOUDER, EARLE L. *Euphonium Music Guide.* Evanston, Ill.: Instrumentalist Co., 1978.

LOWREY, ALVIN. *Trumpet Discography.* Denver: National Trumpet Symposium, n.d.

MACDONALD, DONNA. *The Odyssey of the Philip Jones Brass Ensemble.* Moudon, Switzerland: Editions BIM, 1986.

MASON, J. KENT. *The Tuba Handbook.* Toronto: Sonante Publications, 1977.

MATHIE, GORDON. *The Trumpet Teacher's Guide.* Cincinatti, Ohio: Queen City Brass Publications, 1984.

MENDE, EMILIE. *Pictorial Family Tree of Brass Instruments in Europe Since the Early Middle Ages.* Moudon, Switzerland: Editions BIM, 1978.

MEREWETHER, RICHARD. *The Horn, the Horn . . .* London: Paxman Musical Instruments, 1979.

MORLEY-PEGGE, REGINALD. *The French Horn.* London: Ernest Benn, 1973.

MORRIS, R. WINSTON. *Tuba Music Guide.* Evanston, Ill.: Instrumentalist Co., 1973.

MUSIQUE POUR TROMPETTE. 2nd ed. Paris: Alphonse Leduc, n.d.

NAYLOR, TOM L. *The Trumpet and Trombone in Graphic Arts, 1500-1800.* Nashville, Tenn.: Brass Press, 1979.

PIZKA, HANS. *Hornisten-Lexikon/Dictionary for Hornists 1986.* Kirchheim b. München: Hans Pizka Edition, 1986.

PETTITT, STEPHEN. *Dennis Brain.* London: Robert Hale, 1976.

PORTER, MAURICE M. *The Embouchure.* London: Boosey & Hawkes, 1967.

SCHULLER, GUNTHER. *Horn Technique.* London: Oxford University Press, 1971.

RASMUSSEN, MARY. *A Teacher's Guide to the Literature for Brass Instruments.* Durham, N.H.: Brass Quarterly, 1968.

ROSE, W.H. *Studio Class Manual for Tuba and Euphonium.* Houston, Tex.: Iola Publications, 1980.

SEVERSON, PAUL, and MCDUNN, MARK. *Brass Wind Artistry.* Athens, Ohio: Accura Music, 1983.

SHERMAN, ROGER. *The Trumpeter's Handbook.* Athens, Ohio: Accura Music, 1979.

SKEI, ALLEN B. *Woodwind, Brass, and Percussion Instruments of the Orchestra: A Bibliographic Guide.* New York: Garland, 1985.

SMITHERS, DON. *The Music and History of the Baroque Trumpet Before 1721.* London: J.M. Dent, 1973.

SOLOS FOR THE STUDENT TROMBONIST. Nashville, Tenn.: The Brass Press, 1979.

STEWART, DEE. *Arnold Jacobs: The Legacy of a Master.* Northfield, Ill.: Instrumentalist Co., 1987.

TAYLOR, ARTHUR R. *Brass Bands.* London: Granada, 1979.

THEVET, LUCIEN. *Méthode Complète de Cor.* Paris: Alphonse Leduc, 1960.

TUCKWELL, BARRY. *Horn.* New York: Schirmer Books, 1983.

TUCKWELL, BARRY. *Playing the Horn.* London: Oxford University Press, 1978.

WATSON, J. PERRY. *The Care and Feeding of a Community British Brass Band.* Farmingdale, N.Y.: Boosey and Hawkes, n.d.

WATSON, J. PERRY. *Starting a British Brass Band.* Grand Rapids, Mich.: Yamaha International Corporation, 1984.

WEAST, ROBERT. *Keys to Natural Performance for Brass Players.* Des Moines, Iowa: Brass World, 1979.

WEBSTER, GERALD. *Piccolo Trumpet Method.* Nashville, Tenn.: Brass Press, 1980.

WICK, DENIS. *Trombone Technique.* London: Oxford University Press, 1975.

WIGNESS, C. ROBERT. *The Soloistic Use of the Trombone in Eighteenth Century Vienna.* Nashville, Tenn.: Brass Press, 1978.

WILKINS, WAYNE. *The Index of French Horn Music.* Magnolia, Ark.: Music Register, 1978.

WINTER, DENIS. *Euphonium Music Guide.* New London, Conn.: Whaling Music, 1983.

VAUGHAN WILLIAMS, RALPH. *The Making of Music.* Ithaca, N.Y.: Cornell University Pre 1955.

YANCICH, MILAN. *A Practical Guide to French Horn Playing.* Rochester, N.Y.: Wind Musi 1971.

ARTICLES

AGRELL, JEFFREY. "An Indexed Bibliography of Periodical Articles on the Horn." *The Ho Call,* VI, no. 2 (May 1976), pp. 51–54; VII, no. 1 (November 1976), pp. 45–51; V no. 2 (May 1977), 49–55.

ANDERSON, STEPHEN C. "The Alto Trombone, Then and Now." *The Instrumentali November, 1985, pp. 54–62.

BENADE, ARTHUR H. "The Physics of Brasses." *Scientific American,* July 1973, pp. 24–3

EVERETT, THOMAS G. "Solo Literature for the Bass Trombone." In *Brass Antholog Evanston, Ill.: Instrumentalist Co., 1976, pp. 587–590.

DROSTE, PAUL. "Begged, Borrowed, and Stolen Solo Euphonium Literature." *The Instr mentalist,* May 1981, pp. 30–32.

LOUDER, EARLE L. "Original Solo Literature and Study Books for Euphonium." *T Instrumentalist,* May 1981, pp. 29–30.

ROBERTS, B. LEE. "Some Comments on the Physics of the Horn and Right Hand Tech nique." *The Horn Call,* VL, no. 2 (May 1976), pp. 41–45.

SMITHERS, DON; WOGRAM, KLAUS; and BOWSHER, JOHN. "Playing the Baroque Trumpet *Scientific American,* April 1986, pp. 108–115.

TURRENTINE, EDGAR M. "The Physiological Aspect of Brasswind Performance Techniqu A Bibliographic Essay." *NACWPI Journal,* 26, no. 2 (November 1977), pp. 3–5.

WERDEN, DAVID R. "Euphonium Mouthpieces—A Teacher's Guide." *The Instrumentali May 1981, pp. 23–26.

YEO, DOUGLAS. "The Bass Trombone: Innovations on a Misunderstood Instrument." *Th Instrumentalist,* November 1985, pp. 22–28.

DISSERTATIONS

BAHR, EDWARD RICHARD. "A Discography of Classical Trombone/Euphonium Solo an Ensemble Music on Long-Playing Records Distributed in the United States." D.M.A thesis, University of Oklahoma, 1980. UM 80-16, 922.

BECK, FREDERICK ALLAN. "The Flugelhorn: Its History and Literature." D.M.A. thesi University of Rochester, 1979. UM 79-21, 124.

CARNOVALE, AUGUST N. "A Comprehensive Performance Project in Trumpet Literatur with an Essay on Published Music Composed Since ca. 1900 for Solo Trumpe Accompanied by Orchestra." D.M.A. thesis, University of Iowa, 1973. UM 74-16, 70

CHESEBRO, GAYLE M. "An Annotated List of Original Works for Horn Alone and for Hor with One Other Non-Keyboard Instrument." D.M.A. thesis, Indiana University, 1976

HYATT, JACK H. "The Soprano and Piccolo Trumpets: Their History, Literature, and Tutor." D.M.A. thesis, Boston University, 1974. UM 74-20, 473.

KEAYS, JAMES HARVEY. "An Investigation into the Origins of the Wagner Tuba." D.M.A thesis, University of Illinois, 1977. UM 78-4044.

RANDOLPH, DAVID MARK. "New Techniques in the Avant-Garde Repertoire for Sol Tuba." D.M.A. thesis, University of Rochester, 1978. UM 78-11, 493.

SCHUMACHER, STANLEY E. "An Analytical Study of Published Unaccompanied Solo Lit erature for Brass Instruments." Ph.D. dissertation, Ohio State University, 1976. UM 77-2497.

SENFF, THOMAS E. "An Annotated Bibliography of the Unaccompanied Solo Repertoire for Trombone." D.M.A. thesis, University of Illinois, 1976. UM 76-16, 919.

SMITH, NICHOLAS EDWARD. "The Horn Mute: An Accoustical and Historical Study." D.M.A. thesis, University of Rochester, 1980. UM 80-19, 070.

SMITH, DAVID. "Trombone Technique in the Early Seventeenth Century." D.M.A. thesis, Stanford University, 1981.

SORENSON, RICHARD A. "Tuba Pedagogy: A Study of Selected Method Books, 1840–1911." Ph.D. dissertation, University of Colorado, 1972. UM 73-1832.

TRUSHEIM, WILLIAM H. "Mental Imagery and Musical Performance: An Inquiry into Imagery Use by Eminent Orchestral Brass Players." Ed.D. dissertation, Rutgers University, 1987.

WHALEY, DAVID R. "The Microtonal Capability of the Horn." D.M.A. thesis, University of Illinois, 1975. UM 76-7010.

Index